BRAVEHEARTS OF
BHARAT

ADVANCE PRAISE FOR *BRAVEHEARTS OF BHARAT*

'How many names in this list of fifteen Bharat Bravehearts ring a bell? Contrary to perception, history is rarely objective. Such is the retelling of Bharat's history, and the lens used, that few of these names will be recognized. Vikram Sampath has done a great service by correcting a biased narrative that has coloured perceptions of Bharat's history.'—Bibek Debroy, eminent economist, author and translator

'The mainstream historiography of India is not the history of Indians at all but that of foreign invaders. It was imposed on us to deliberately inculcate a sense of inferiority. Vikram's book is a wonderful effort to revive the memory of those who fought, often successfully, to defend our civilization. Never forget that the privilege of being the world's oldest surviving civilization was bought in blood.'—Sanjeev Sanyal, economist and writer

'Celebrated author, Vikram Sampath has single-handedly upturned the narrative on many contested issues and personalities of Indian history. He now ventures into a largely uncharted territory, chronicling the contributions of fifteen "civilizational warriors", hailing from diverse regions and timespans, who find little space in our history books. Roughly, half the list comprises incredibly fearless women. The cut-off date of his study is the year 1857, developments thereafter falling under the rubric of the freedom struggle.

Vikram Sampath is aware of the need to skilfully navigate the path between jingoism and the professional narrative of a historian. At the same time, he takes cognisance of, and elevates, the multiple-layered Indian tradition of *itihasa* ("It thus happened").

Among the neglected dimensions of the Indian past was the dogged resistance to the Arab armies at the frontiers of al-Hind by three tiny Hindu kingdoms of Kabul, Zabul, and Sindh. The resistance surprised and shocked the Arabs, who had by then established a world empire greater than that of Rome at the pinnacle of its power. Records of resistance in other parts of the subcontinent are recorded in several early epigraphs, among them the Kavi plates from Bharuch (736 CE), the Navasari plates (739 CE), and an inscription from Hund, Attock district (second half of the eighth century CE).

There were incredible rulers like Lalitaditya Muktapida, who halted the Arab advance into Kashmir, and towards that end, entered into a tactical alliance with Yashovarman of Kanauj. Also largely forgotten are the Chola father and son, Rajaraja and Rajendra, empire builders and Shiva devotees, promoters of the Brihadisvara temple, the *Dakshin Meru* of the south.

Remembrance is also due to the nameless proud devotees of the Somnath shrine, who posed as guides and avenged their deity by deliberately misleading Mahmud Ghaznavi into an arid waterless stretch on his way back home. And Queen Naiki Devi, immortalized by Merutunga in his *Prabandhacintamani*, "taking her son in her lap, fought at a *ghat* named Gardararaghatta, and conquered the king of the Mlecchas. . ."

No less sterling were the contributions of Rudrama Devi of Warangal, trained in statecraft by her father; the daring Rani Abbakka Chowta of Ullal who took on the Portuguese; Chand Bibi of Ahmednagar, intrepid challenger of the mighty Mughals; Lachit Barphukan, Assam's man of destiny and hero of the battle of Saraighat; Kanoji Angre, steadfastly loyal to the Maratha kingdom; Banda Bahadur who valiantly embraced death rather than surrender to the Mughals; Martand Varma, who faced the European powers and dedicated his kingdom to Sri Padmanabhaswamy; Ahilya Bai Holkar, builder of the Kashi and Somnath temples; the great Krishna devotee, Rajarshi Jai Singh of Manipur; Velu Nachiyar of Shivaganga and her Dalit military commander in the turbulent conditions of the south; and Begum Hazrat Mahal who held the British forces at bay till her escape to Nepal.

These "civilizational warriors" have been rehabilitated and given their place under the sun, in yet another landmark work by Vikram Sampath.'—Meenakshi Jain, historian and senior fellow, Nehru Memorial Museum and Library

BRAVEHEARTS OF
BHARAT

VIGNETTES
FROM
INDIAN HISTORY

VIKRAM
SAMPATH

PENGUIN
VIKING
An imprint of Penguin Random House

VIKING

USA | Canada | UK | Ireland | Australia
New Zealand | India | South Africa | China | Singapore

Viking is part of the Penguin Random House group of companies
whose addresses can be found at global.penguinrandomhouse.com

Published by Penguin Random House India Pvt. Ltd
4th Floor, Capital Tower 1, MG Road,
Gurugram 122 002, Haryana, India

First published in Viking by Penguin Random House India 2022

Copyright © Vikram Sampath 2022
Illustrations' copyright © Amit Srivastava

All rights reserved

10 9 8 7

The views and opinions expressed in this book are the author's own and the
facts are as reported by him which have been verified to the extent possible,
and the publishers are not in any way liable for the same.

ISBN 9780670094684

Typeset in Adobe Caslon Pro by MAP Systems, Bengaluru, India
Printed at Thomson Press India Ltd, New Delhi

www.penguin.co.in

Contents

CONTENTS

For my parents—my pillars of strength and the perennial wind beneath my wings!

कोटि -कोटि कण्ठ कल-कल निनाद कराले
कोटि -कोटि भुजैर्धृत खरकरवाले,
अबला केन मा एत बले।
बहुबलधारिणीं नमामि तारिणीं
रिपुदलवारिणीं मातरम्।
वन्दे मातरम्।

Koti Koti Kantha Kal Kal Ninad Karale
Koti Koti Bhujaidhruta Kharakaravale
Abala Keno Ma Eto Bole
Bahubaladharineem Namami Tarineem
Ripudala Varineem Mataram
Vande Mataram|

Who hath said thou art weak in thy lands,
When the sword flesh out in the seventy million hands
And seventy million voices roar
Thy dreadful name from shore to shore?
With many strengths who art mighty and stored,
To thee I call Mother and Lord!
Thou who savest, arise and save!
To her I cry who ever her foe man drove
Back from plain and Sea
And shook herself free.

This stanza of Bankim Chandra Chatterjee's epic poem 'Vande Mataram' (Mother! I bow to Thee!) is translated by Sri Aurobindo. Written by Chatterjee in 1875, it is an ode to the Motherland in Bengali-Sanskrit and is included in his novel Anandmath [1882]).

Prologue

It was a warm summer evening in 2016 in the national capital when my friend Sanjeev Sanyal, eminent writer and economist, and I decided to meet after a long hiatus. In a meandering conversation, Sanjeev brought up something that hooked my attention. 'Have you ever noticed,' he asked, 'the manner in which Indian history is depicted as a long litany of failures? Every battle that we are taught about is one in which India or Indians have only lost. We are made to appear like a nation of losers. In these centuries of our existence, did we even put up some resistance or were we just cowering before every invader who came our way? If we did, then where are those stories, who are those heroic resisters?'

We did scratch our heads to think of a couple of names, but we also realized how precious little we knew about the few protagonists that we could list or how our education system had completely skipped these instances of victories and resistance. The conversation with Sanjeev stayed with me for long, even as I ruminated about the several other defects that traditional Indian historiography suffers from. History is after all the handmaiden of the victor. We had been handed down our understanding of our own past from our erstwhile colonial matters, which we had then further perfected with our own set of biases, political expediency and ideological tilts. As Nigerian author Chinua Achebe said in 'Chinua Achebe, The Art of Fiction No. 139'[1]

(1994): 'Until the lions have their historians, the history of the hunt shall always glorify the hunter.' This African proverb metaphorically describes how dominant groups inscribe power through historical narratives. The very foundation on which historical writing has been based is a legacy that promoted European and western ethnocentrism, in which the tales of the subjugated, be it in India, Asia, Africa or Latin America would hardly find a voice of their own. In India's case, we have sadly gone several steps ahead of even our colonizer in deriding our own past and identity, plagued with a constant sense of apologia about our history. While it is certainly not a historian's task to create a sense of pride (often bordering on the slippery slope of jingoism), the converse too holds that it is not her task to merely induce a sense of shame and guilt over perceived past excesses and omissions.

The other glaring loophole in the way popular Indian historiography exists, especially the one that is taught to our future generations in schools and colleges, is that it is heavily tilted towards Delhi. The popular historical narratives about 'regional history' terming the stories coming from different parts of India as being 'regional' alludes to there being a mainstream, central theme and everything that does not fall within that rubric is merely 'regional'. How does one determine what is 'central' and what is 'regional'? Do the Vijayanagara Empire or the mighty Karkotas of Kashmir or the Ahoms of Assam constitute 'regional' stories and the Delhi Sultanate the mainstream history of India and not of a limited region? Vast swathes of this land seem to have been completely ignored even as a child learns about the most obsolete and short-lived dynasties that ruled in and around Delhi—the Tughlaqs, or Lodhis or Khiljis, whose substantial and lasting contribution to this country, beyond a few pieces of architecture, could well be considered as largely minimal. It is not my argument to excise anyone from the historical narrative of the country as we cannot wish away our past; the coverage needs to be inclusive of all regions and commensurate with the importance and contribution of individual dynasties and rulers to the story of Bharat. It is a sad fact that a student of history would dutifully be able to reel out the succession lines of these dynasties, whereas she might not be able to do so readily with say the Rashtrakutas or the Maratha Empire that ruled over most of the subcontinent by the end of the eighteenth century. We come across mere fleeting references to the dynasties of the southern part of India like the Rashtrakutas, the Chalukyas, the Satavahanas, the mighty Cholas, the Pandyas, the prosperous Vijayanagara Empire, the Adil Shahis of the Deccan, the Wodeyars of Mysore or the rulers of Travancore, among others. The eastern belts of Odisha and Bengal—the Gajapati Empire of the Bhoi dynasty, the Palas, the Senas or the Nawabs of Bengal and Murshidabad, or their histories, seldom feature. Similarly, and sadly, the history of the north-east of India is a forgotten and therefore, a mostly ignored blackhole. Beyond perhaps naming the eight states and their capitals (which too I suspect a child might do with difficulty), our understanding of the people, the rulers and the pasts of the North East, from the Ahoms of Assam to the Tipras, the Mangang and Meitei rulers of Manipur or those of Nagaland make a shocking absence in our books, at the altar of Delhi-centrism. The Rajputs or even the Marathas from whom the British eventually captured India do not get a coverage commensurate to their strategic importance in the tale of our past. One could rightly argue, however, that the history of India is not merely a long litany of dynasties that have ruled various regions and across time spans but encompasses several aspects of social and cultural life and the voice of the subaltern. If such an argument holds, then we must altogether do away with the narration of kingly tales and confine ourselves to people's stories alone. But when we selectively portray in detail the deeds and exploits of certain dynasties confined to limited geographical expanses of the country, quite incommensurate to their importance in history, much to the detriment of several others from other regions, the argument of 'people's history' automatically falls flat. The stories of rulers and the ruled from all parts of this vast nation need to find a rightful place in a chronicle that goes by the name of the 'history of India.' History, after all is, as E.H. Carr has pointed out, 'a process of selection in terms of historical significance . . . Just as from an infinite ocean of facts the historian selects those which are significant for his purpose, so from the multiplicity of sequences of cause and effect he extracts those, and only those, which are historically significant; and the standard of historical significance is his ability to fit them into his pattern of rational explanation and interpretation.'[2]

Bharat, therefore, needs to snatch back the narrative of her history from Delhi, reclaim it and narrate the stories of large parts of the country that have largely remained untold and therefore unknown for a long time.

Alongside this negligence and amnesia, several women and their stories of valour and sacrifice continue to remain subsumed to the stories of their numerous male counterparts. In all aspects of Indian life, from royalty to knowledge production to bravery, the agency of the Indian woman has always been an exalted one but 'his-story' has foregrounded her voice. Hence, we know precious little about the Mahadevis of Odisha of the Bhaumakara dynasty, Rani Didda of Kashmir, Rani Durgavati, the Abbakka Ranis of Ullal, Rani Karnavati of Garhwal, Rani Mangammal of Madurai, Kittur Rani Chennamma, Chennamma of Keladi, Maratha queen Tarabai, Devi Ahilyabai Holkar or the Begums of Bhopal, among numerous others.

I am conscious of the fact that the counter to such a widespread and accepted narrative runs the acute risk of being 'revisionist' and excessively chauvinistic, hurtling down the slippery slope of jingoistic chest thumping. Everything about a golden past and the nostalgia associated with it tends to get exaggerated and eulogized. But the truth of history is always in the sober middle ground. The fact that we are still surviving as one of the most ancient civilizations of humanity, and that our cultures, traditions, languages and religions have survived clearly indicates that there must have been strong resistance we always offered or some battles we decisively won as well, and this must have come from every region of this vast nation.

Even as I kept thinking about that stray conversation with Sanjeev, there was an intense desire to bring to the fore some of these long-forgotten, neglected, unsung heroes and heroines of our past. The next task was to prepare this list, which was more akin to deciding who were to be omitted as the names kept increasing! Capping it at a number, say fifteen or twenty too was important and I chose the former. Fifteen different lives, from various parts of India and varied time spans, but united in the theme of courage, resistance and bravery against all odds that stood them apart. Notably, half the number selected is that of women. Briefly, accounts of the several dynasties that are seldom referred to in 'mainstream' history have also been weaved into the narrative. There are instances such as that of 'Rajarshi' Bhagyachandra of Manipur or Devi Ahilyabai Holkar of Indore who were not the conventional warriors who donned an armour and burst into the battlefield. But their inclusion was important as civilizational warriors whose contribution to keep the flame alive under adverse circumstances made them indispensable. Each of their stories is stand-alone and can be read by the reader as such. Any of them, in any order, skipping someone in the middle, would not hamper the narrative in any way. I also wanted to have an end date to this chain of stories and chose 1858 when the country formally passed under the British Crown with the proclamation of Queen Victoria. The resistance we put up after that is an altogether different theme that comes under the larger rubric of 'freedom struggle' necessitating an altogether different treatment. Hence the bravehearts in this collection largely pre-date British colonialism. I am sure my selection would raise disappointment among many enthusiastic readers who might have hoped to see one or the other of their favourite warriors of the past in this anthology. My only answer to those 'Why not X?' or 'What about Y?' is that this is not the final word on the subject, and I am sure numerous such anthologies on similar themes can always be put together by other historians too. I have tried to balance geographies, time spans and gender in my selection, which I sincerely hope will catch the interest of all my readers.

Like all other things, in historiography, too, there has been a very unique Indic way of historiography, exemplified by this *shloka*, often attributed to Kashmir's historian Kalhana in his seminal work, the *Rajatarangini*:

> *Dharmartha Kama Mokshanam Upadesha Samanvitam*
> *Kathayuktam Puravruttam Itihasa Tachakshmate.*

Puravruttam or narratives of the past that are in story form (*katha yuktam*) and impart *upadesha* or instruction in the four limbs of humanity's pursuits—*dharma* (righteousness), *artha* (material pursuits), *kama* (sensual pleasures) and *moksha* (liberation) is called *itihasa* (literally translating to 'It thus happened'). This is a very clear, cognitive and self-assured vision of what history and its role needs to be in society, which is an Indic alternative to the modern, Western empiricist historiography that is popular, but also one that has hardly been entertained or engaged with in any serious manner. I hope these fifteen stories also have their own didactic message for the readers about what they wish to take away from these glorious lives.

May this book inspire the flowering of the retelling of the tales of numerous other such unsung and forgotten heroes of the past.

VIKRAM SAMPATH   BENGALURU
                                                    July 2022

Notes

1   Interview by Jerome Brooks, 'Chinua Achebe, The Art of Fiction No. 139', *The Paris Review*. Available at https://www.theparisreview.org/interviews/1720/the-art-of-fiction-no-139-chinua-achebe.

2   E.H. Carr, *What is History?* Penguin Classics (Penguin Random House UK, 2018), p. 100.

Lalitaditya Muktapida
of Kashmir

Climbing up the tall steps that led to the inner sanctum of the colossal, grand, intricately carved and geometrically precise temple, he turned around to admire the beauty of his own creation. The snow-capped mountains in the background seemed to provide a perfect foil to the holy shrine. This temple, named after Martand or the Sun God of the Hindu pantheon, was built by his architects on silted ground (karewas) on the top of a plateau that overlooked the entire Kashmir valley. He looked admiringly at the wide premises—220 x 142 feet in dimension, which he had walked to reach the central sanctorum. His creation had aesthetically blended the best of Gandhara, Gupta and Chinese forms of architecture,[1] as also the ancient Greek and Roman peristyle,[2] to create a distinctive Kashmiri style of architecture. The water tank (*kund*) in the centre of the yard was glistening with the reflections of nearly eighty-four smaller shrines that dotted the entire perimeter of the courtyard. The walls of the antechamber had beautiful carvings of Hindu gods such as Shiva, Vishnu, and river Goddesses Ganga and Yamuna, among others. His face beamed with joy as he looked at this sheer spectacular expanse, brimming with his subjects who were showering encomiums on him and his recent spate of numerous successful conquests. This auspicious moment was definitely the crowning glory in the career of Kashmir's 'world-conqueror'[3] monarch, Lalitaditya Muktapida.

Its beauty though significantly devastated by a ruthless demolition in the fifteenth century ordered by the tyrannical Sultan Sikandar Butshikan of the Shah Miri dynasty[4] did not fail to catch the attention of several chroniclers. Centuries later, in 1909, British army officer and explorer Sir Francis Younghusband, who was famous for his travelogues through Central Asia and the Far East, was to eulogize these magnificent ruins thus:

> On a perfectly open and even plain, gently sloping away from a background of snowy mountains looking directly out on the entire length both of the Kashmir valley and of the snowy ranges, which bound it—so situated in fact as to be encircled, yet not overwhelmed by snowy mountains—stand the ruins of a temple second only to the Egyptian in massiveness and strength and to the Greek in elegance and grace. It is built of immense rectilinear blocks of limestone, betokening strength and durability . . . any overweighing sense of massiveness is relieved by the elegance of the surrounding colonnade of graceful Greek-like pillars . . . no one without an eye for natural beauty would have chosen that special site for the construction of a temple and no one with an inclination to the ephemeral and transient would have built it on so massive and enduring a scale . . . Of all the ruins in Kashmir the Martand ruins are both the most remarkable and the most characteristic. No temple was ever built on a finer site. It stands on an open plain, where it can be seen to full advantage. Behind it rises a range of snowy mountains. And away in the distance before it, first lies the smiling Kashmir valley, and then the whole length of the Pir Panjal range, their snowy summits mingling softly with the azure of the sky. It is one of the most heavenly spots on earth . . . the finest example of what is known as the Kashmirian [sic] style of architecture . . . the most sublime site occupied by any building in the world—finer far than the site of the Parthenon or of the Taj, or of St. Peters, or of the Escurial—we may take it as the representative, or rather the culmination of all the rest, and by it, we must judge the people of Kashmir at their best.[5]

The Lineage of Lalitaditya Muktapida

This master builder Lalitaditya was the fourth ruler of the Karkota dynasty of Kashmir. One of the most popular sources of the history of this period is the Sanskrit treatise *Rajatarangini*, literally meaning a 'River of Kings', by the scholar Kalhana, written a long time thereafter in the twelfth century. Exaggerated in its poetic flourish and sometimes contested by scholars for its historical and chronological accuracies, Kalhana's magnum opus is still the most referred-to text for any historian researching Kashmir. Kalhana's historical account depicts Kashmir to have been ruled by Hindu rulers and dynasties for over five millennia—again a claim that divides scholars deeply.

Kalhana paints a rather romantic advent to the Karkotas, who drew their descent from the mythical snake-king (Naga) Karkotaka of the Mahabharata epic.[6] This snake deity is still worshipped by several Kashmiri Hindus. The Karkotas peacefully transitioned from the Gonandiya dynasty whose last king Baladitya was heirless. Deeply troubled by the absence of a male heir, Baladitya consulted his royal astrologer who foretold that it would be his son-in-law who would succeed him. He got his daughter Anangalekha married to an ordinary but able officer of his administration, Durlabhavardhana, in the hope of forestalling destiny by her selecting an insignificant spouse. Quite fantastically, Kalhana draws Durlabhavardhana's ancestry to the Naga Karkotaka by describing his birth as the result of the union of a woman and a snake when 'she took her purifying bath'![7] He ascended the throne in 625 CE.

About five years after Durlabhavardhana's ascension, the Chinese Buddhist monk and scholar and traveller Hsuan-Tsang visited India and reached Kashmir in c. 631 CE. Durlabhavardhana's maternal uncle received the monk who was accorded a grand welcome and led to meet the king in a procession on a bedecked elephant. Tsang's account gives us a picture of Kashmir during this time and its political expanse and importance in contemporary geopolitics. He alludes to the expansion of Kashmir under Durlabhavardhana, as places like Taxila (which was part of the Kamboj kingdom or Dardistan in Kashmir's immediate neighbourhood), Simhapura, Orsa (today's Khyber Pakhtunkhwa in Pakistan, known as Hazara), Poonch and Rajpuri (today's Rajauri) had all become vassal states of Kashmir. Neighbouring kingdoms kept trying to attack Kashmir but never succeeded in their attempts, Hsuan-Tsang records. According to him, the Kashmiri people were eager learners, though 'cunning', and lived harmoniously among themselves despite following various faiths.[8] Kashmir was indeed cosmopolitan because despite being a Shaivite, the king was deeply tolerant of the Vaishnava and Buddhist faiths. Kashmir, in fact, became a pivotal force for Buddhism in the region and facilitated its spread to China, Tibet and Central Asia. In fact, it is believed that Tibetan Buddhism had its origins in Kashmir.[9] A peculiar feature of the Buddhism in Kashmir was the deep influence of Shaivism on it with the advent of deities like Avalokiteshwara and Manjushri (drawn from the Shiva-Shakti theology of Hinduism).[10]

The imperial Chinese court records of this time mention that between c. 627 CE and 649 CE, Kashmir's king 'Tu-lo-pa' (Durlabhavardhana) had established control over the route between China and Kabul, thereby enabling the Chinese ambassador to travel freely on this route.[11] This implies that though Durlabhavardhana did not rule over Kabul directly, he exerted political influence there because of possibly annexing surrounding regions within a few years of coming to power.

After Durlabhavardhana's death in c. 661 CE, his son Durlabhaka ascended the throne and assumed the name of Pratapaditya. In a glorious and peaceful fifty-year reign, he expanded the frontiers of Kashmir till Jalandhar in Punjab where coins with the seal 'Sri Pratap' were found. Kalhana mentions an interesting account of Pratapaditya's personal life. One of his dear friends was the wealthy merchant and moneylender Nona and the king was known to visit his house regularly. During one such visit he happened to see Nona's stunningly pretty wife Narendraprabha. The arrows of Cupid seemed to have hit both, though Pratapaditya was so besotted by her that he fell sick pining for Narendraprabha relentlessly. In the interest of their camaraderie and the ethics of kingship he, however, kept his obsession a secret from his friend. But when Nona heard of this, he voluntarily decided to give up his wife for the sake of their friendship. To this queen was then born three sons Chandrapida, Tarapida and Muktapida (also known as Vajraditya, Udayaditya and Lalitaditya respectively).[12]

Chandrapida, the eldest son, succeeded his father on the latter's death in 711 CE. He ruled for a mere eight years and eight months as his deceitful and capricious younger brother Tarapida allegedly got him killed through a sorcerer by employing black-magic spells and became king. Kalhana is ruthless in his admonishment of Tarapida as a barbarian 'who created terror by his glory, mangled with blood on account of the fratricide.'[13] A despotic reign born of such an unethical act ended similarly in a short while. Around the end of c. 724 CE, his own Brahmin officers conspired against Tarapida and employed similar black-magic sorcery to have him eliminated.[14] It was at this point of political flux within the kingdom that the youngest brother Muktapida was crowned king in c. 724 CE, assuming the name of Lalitaditya. Though completely silent about the new king's younger days, Kalhana gushes about his ascent to power:

> After that [after Tarapida] Shri Lalitaditya became the universal monarch, he who was far beyond the conception of Fate, which creates only rulers of limited territories. He bedecked the elephant-like Jambudwipa by the glory of his military exploits as someone should make his clothes fragrant with the fragrant powders[15] . . . For rivers, which have set out from their own region, the ocean is the limit, but nowhere is there a limit for those who are frankly aspiring to be conquerors.[16]

His reign was to mark the veritable golden era in the annals of Kashmir's history.

Geopolitics of Central Asia at Lalitaditya's ascension

The southern Hindukush region in the eighth century was occupied by three powerful kingdoms: Kapisha (present-day Kabul), Zabulistan (present-day Ghazni) and Kashmir of the Karkotas. Kapisha and Zabulistan were under Turk Shahi rulers who were Buddhists and descendants of the Turkish king Burhatakin. Some historians like P.N.K. Bamzai and C.V. Vaidya claim that the dynasties of Kabul and Zabulistan were Hindu by faith. The three kingdoms had asserted themselves after breaking away from the White Hunas (known also as Kidarites or Later Hephthalites) who held sway over Gandhara and Kashmir after the weakening of the Gupta Empire. Notably, all the three maintained close and congenial ties with the imperial power on their eastern frontier—China, which was under one of its most powerful and prosperous dynasties, the T'ang (618–907 CE). Regular delegations from their courts to and from China corroborate this fact. The three powers often collaborated with China in their efforts to prevent another pesky, expansionist power in the region—Tibet from penetrating deeper into the Hindukush–Pamir belt. At the foot of the towering peaks of the Himalayas, the ancient Tibetan people, the Bod, emerged victorious from their age-old intertribal rivalry and established a unified monarchy of the Yar-kung-spurgyal family.

Towards the west, a series of historical events led to a sudden rise of the Arabs. After the passing away of Prophet Muhammad, the founder of Islam, in 632 CE, four of his companions succeeded him as leaders of the Muslim community—Abu Bakr Abdullah ibn Uthman, Umar ibn al-Khatttab, Uthman ibn 'Affan and Ali ibn 'Abi Talib. They assumed the title of *Khalifa* or Caliph that literally meant the 'one who follows behind'. After consolidating the authority of the Islamic nerve centre of Medina over the various nomadic Arab tribes that had already been set into motion by the Prophet, the Caliphs undertook an expansion—both of the territory and of their faith. Umar (r. 634–44 CE), the second Caliph, diverted the martial power of the Arabs against the two prominent powers of the time—the Byzantine and the Sassanian Empires. Byzantine territories of Syria, Palestine and Egypt and the Sassanian territories of Persia and Iraq fell to Arab might that was propelled by the desire to conquer the lands of infidels, pagans and idolators as an ordained, holy work of God. This religious zeal unified them further to an extent that within a century of the passing away of the Prophet, the empire of the Caliphs had emerged as a global power that dominated Central Asia and North Africa, touching the shores of the Atlantic in the west and knocking at the very gates of India on the east. Syrians, Persians, Berbers, Turks and others were rapidly Islamized, and their languages and cultures Arabicized. Such was the glue of faith that a generation thereafter, even the Mongols who were responsible for the decline of the Caliphate, themselves adopted Islam.

Trade, especially that of silk, played an important role in the economic and consequently political life of the kingdoms, ensuing constant skirmishes with each other for supremacy over the commercial passages. The possession of Gilgit (Palur minor) and its neighbour Baltistan (Palur major, today's Skardu) was of great strategic importance to all the players. For Tibet, it allowed control over the main route from Kashkar (present-day Chitral in north-western Pakistan) through the Mintaka Pass to Kashmir and the Indus valley and made it possible for them to establish direct contact with the Turkic tribes of the Tarim area and the Arabs of Central Asia. The Sino–Tibetan rivalry, which lasted for over two centuries, brought several other powers in this region into the conflict that was driven by a motley combination of commercial interests. Control over these strategic locations kept oscillating between the different competitors. Political, trade, military and even matrimonial alliances were constantly stitched to keep one another at bay and gain greater control over the trade routes.

The Invasion of Sindh

The politico-religious force of the Arabs that had subjugated several countries and peoples across the world was to now make a violent interaction with a living faith that was possibly as old as human civilization itself—India. Historian Ram Gopal Misra states: 'The early successes of Islam were against religions that had lost their hold on the minds of the people. But in India, the Hindu way of life—symbolized by high moral values of tolerance, truthfulness, and justice—was very much the part and parcel of the vast multitude's mental and material being.'[17] Unable to face the persecution of the Arabs, a large group of Persians abandoned their homes towards the end of the seventh century CE to set sail to Gujarat 'near the site of the later colony of Sanjan.'[18] They were welcomed and sheltered by the king of Gujarat and they were to become the ethnic community of the Parsis, who are still a thriving group in contemporary India. This innate embracive and inclusive nature of the Hindu faith that allowed every strand of religious opinion, including atheism and agnosticism, as part of the fold made the Indian society that Islam encountered, one that was just, vibrant and adherent to its tenets. As Arab cartographer Muhammad al Idrisi noted:

> The Indians are naturally inclined to justice, and never depart from it in their actions. Their good faith, honesty, and fidelity to their engagements are well known, and they are so famous for these qualities that people flock to their country from every side; and hence the country is flourishing and their condition prosperous.[19]

Like the quote above, several of these chronicles of the invaders themselves, their historians and the early Arab travellers clearly reveal that quite unlike the popular myth about the decadence in the social and moral values of Indian society being the cause of her subjugation by foreign powers, it was these invasions that resulted in this decline.[20] But the inherent nature of the eternal moral values is what sustained Indian society for the next five centuries of Islamic rule and two centuries of British subjugation.[21]

A little over a decade before the ascendancy of Lalitaditya to the throne of Kashmir, calamity struck the province of Sindh. Ruled by a Brahmin family founded by Chacha Rai,[22] it had valorously repelled the repeated Arab onslaughts, mounted under the reign of several Umayyad Caliphs. Arab invasions of India, at Thane (636 CE), Bharuch (643 CE) and Debal in Sindh (643 CE) were all valiantly repulsed.[23] During the Debal expedition, the leader of the Arab army, al-Mughirah was defeated and killed by Chacha. So jolted were the Arabs by this crushing defeat that any successive plans made to the Caliph to attack India were always met with apprehension and never got a sanction. During the Caliphate of Mu'awiya ibn Abi Sufyan (r. 661–80 CE), the Arabs made as many as six determined efforts to conquer Kikan, a frontier post of Sindh but failed miserably each time.[24]

However, a good pretext for a final kill offered itself. Some ships that were conveying male and female Muslim pilgrims from Ceylon with valuable gifts of jewels and pearls from the king of Ceylon to Caliph Al-Walid I who ruled in Baghdad, by way of the Persian Gulf, were compelled by the adverse winds to go to Debal (about 60 km from today's Karachi), a seaport town of Sindh situated on the western bank of the Indus.[25] Hsuan-Tsang, too, had mentioned that the Indus delta was infested with robbers and sea pirates who often created hurdles in the sea trade routes. On coming to know about this ship carrying precious gifts, the pirates attacked it, plundered the wealth and took all passengers hostage. Raja Dahar, the son of Chacha, who was in power, pleaded his inability to the Arabs to overpower the pirates. 'That is the work of a band of robbers,' claimed Dahar, 'They do not even care for us.'[26]

One of the Caliph's most notable governors Al-Hajjaj ibn Yusuf induced him to declare a holy war (*jihad*) against Sindh to avenge this act. Budail was sent to attack Sindh, but his armies were routed and he too was killed by Dahar's son Jayasimha (Jaisiah).[27] The Arab Empire that had successfully vanquished so many super powers was being routed repeatedly in India and this shook the Caliph. He was indignant at Hajjaj for these misadventures, but the latter made it a prestige issue to win this expedition at any cost.

Accordingly, Hajjaj's son-in-law Mohammad-bin-Qasim was sent to conquer Sindh in 710 CE with 6,000 men from Sham (Syria) joining him, along with battering rams and catapults to assail fortified towns. In addition, were:

> . . . six thousand armed camel-riders, thoroughly equipped for military operations, with a baggage train of three thousand Bactrian camels . . . in Makran, Muhammad Kasim was joined by the Governor, Muhammad Harun, with other reinforcements; and five catapults (*manjaniks*), together with the necessary ammunition, were transported by sea to Debal. The number of men conveyed by the naval squadron may be estimated by the fact, that we find one catapult alone requiring no less than five hundred men to work it.[28]

Before reaching Sindh via the Bolan Pass, Qasim had to face stiff resistance from the Turk Shahi rulers and Kashmir's Chandrapida. Qasim, however, managed to reach Sindh and attack the Debal port. The town was surrounded by a large fort at the centre of which was a towering stupa of about 120 yards. The *Chachanama* that chronicles[29] the exploits of the Sindh royal family of Chacha and Dahar states that the stupa was surmounted by so large a flag that when the wind blew it used to fly all over the town and touched the turrets of the fort wall. The belief was that the stupa had a magical talisman in it and if it stood and the flag fluttered, Debal would never fall to any conqueror. An insider, however, turned treacherous and informed Qasim about this secret and hence the stupa and the flag became the first target of his battering artillery. Debal fell to the invaders on the ninth day of the conquest. The conquerors gave their first lessons of a bloody conquest to the Hindu and Buddhist population of Debal by massacring the entire male population of the town in a gory blood bath.[30] Women were taken as slaves and the town was pillaged. As historian Chintaman Vinayak Vaidya states: '700 beautiful females under the protection of Buddha who were of course made slaves.'[31] Debal was largely Buddhist, as was its governor whom the *Chachanama* names as Jahin Budh and he ran to take shelter under Dahar's son Jayasimha (Jaisiah).

Dahar had all along complacently presumed that the port would resist these attacks like it had done so successfully in the past. He even wrote to Qasim nonchalantly, with an air of bravado:

> Be it known to you that the fortified town of Debal, which you have taken is an insignificant town, where only traders and artisans reside . . . If I had sent against you Rai Jaisiah who is the most victorious of all the rulers on the face of the earth, and who can wreck vengeance on the strongest men of his age, or the King of Kashmir who is the mighty possessor of a crown; who sways the whole of Hind and even the country of Makran and Turan . . . if I had sent these heroes against you, you could not have done the slightest harm to them and no army would have dared to pass through the remotest limits of this country.[32]

But this invasion was different given the superior military might and weapons of destruction of the Arabs that were unknown to the Indian side. Qasim obviously had not come all the way to merely capture a small seaport. After its capture he advanced towards Brahmanabad, the summer capital of Sindh, defeating several chieftains enroute. Dahar decided to take on the enemy frontally and left his capital Alor and marched towards Rewar to halt Qasim's victorious march. However, about 500 Arabs who were in Dahar's army under one Allafi and who could have assisted in knowing the mind and strategy of the invaders deserted Dahar as they were reluctant to attack their co-religionists. Undeterred by this treachery, Dahar faced Qasim's forces along with Jayasimha. He bravely declared:

> My plan is to meet the Arabs in open battle, and fight with them with all possible vigour. If I overpower them, I shall crush them to death and my kingdom will then be put on a firm footing. But if I am killed honourably, the event will be recorded in the books of Arabia and Hind, and will be talked of by great men, and it will be said that such and such a king sacrificed his precious life for the sake of his country, in fighting with the enemy.[33]

When the two armies finally met in a dreadful conflict, for a while, it seemed that Sindhi forces had an upper hand in the battle. But again, the opponent's numerical strength, treachery of insiders and sheer bad luck had turned the game against Dahar. A burning arrow fired by an Arabian rear guard pierced his white elephant. The scared animal ran towards the river where the Arabian encampment had been established. Dahar single-handedly fought the Arab soldiers there till an arrow pierced his shoulder and another, which got buried in his throat, appeared out from the back of his neck. The last mighty Hindu king of Sindh had thus fallen, in 712 CE. His decapitated head was sent back as a gift to the Caliph.[34]

The capital of Sindh was pilloried to the last brick. Sixty thousand people including several women of princely families were taken as slaves. Dahar's wife Rani Bai decided to defend the fortress of Raor with about 15,000 warriors, but eventually gave up.[35] As documented by Chintaman Vinayak Vaidya, Qasim molested and forcefully married one of Dahar's wives Ladi,[36] while Rani Bai immolated herself along with several Rajput women after failing to protect the fortress—perhaps the first instance of *jauhar* in India where royal women gave up their lives to prevent themselves from falling into the hands of lustful and barbaric conquerors. Dahar's daughters Suryadevi and Parimaldevi were packed off to the Caliph's harem.

After giving some resistance even after Dahar's death, Jayasimha fled from Sindh and was given shelter in Kashmir.[37] This incensed Qasim, who attacked Kashmir, but he could only reach till the border of the kingdom at Jalandhar as he was given a stiff opposition by Chandrapida.[38] Qasim was forced to turn away and instead attack the smaller kingdom of Kangda in Himachal Pradesh.[39] Thus Chandrapida had managed to keep the borders of Kashmir safe against the Arab army that was equipped both with the latest weaponry and brutal savagery.

Qasim had planned to attack Kannauj too. But his envoy who had been sent to the court of Kannauj's ruler Rai Harchandar with an order to surrender was given a dressing down:

> This kingdom has remained in our possession for nearly 1,600 years; and during our rule no enemy has ever dared to set foot within our territories with offensive intentions or to stretch his hand to dispossess us of any part of our country. What fear we have of your absurd vapourings? It is improper and against the rules of etiquette to imprison an envoy or put him in chains; or else, for this nonsensical talk and absurd boast of yours, I would have made an example of you to serve as a warning to other enemies of kings. Now go back to your amir and tell him that we must meet once and measure each other's strength and prowess. Then, either we shall overpower you or be overpowered. When the strength and bravery of both sides is put to test on the field of battle, we shall decide whether to make peace or to carry on war.[40]

Even before Qasim could react, he had by then he received a stern message from the Caliph to return immediately. Dahar's daughter Suryadevi was somehow able to convince the Caliph that Qasim had already 'used her' and, therefore, she was not worthy of being a part of the Caliph's harem. An enraged Caliph issued orders to arrest Qasim and drag him to Baghdad stitched and packed in a leather box. Qasim meekly followed the orders but died in the route due to suffocation. Later, Suryadevi confessed to the Caliph that she lied to him only to avenge her father's death from Qasim. An enraged Caliph ordered his soldiers to bury her and her sister alive in the ground (or in a wall). Both sisters died but as true warriors they had avenged their father's death.[41] Thus ended the story of the royal house of Sindh in great tragedy. Sindh remained under the distant rule of the Caliphs with different governors stationed at Multan to administer the province and several subordinate governors in the minor towns of the Indus. The Arabs could not extend their conquests into the Indian mainland due to the stiff resistance they faced during each such misadventure and with the passage of time their influence remained shrunk to Multan and Mansurah. A major bulwark to their expansionist plans was Kashmir.

The Conquests of Lalitaditya

Lalitaditya was conscious of the Arab plans to avenge Kashmir and to conquer it, under the new governor of Sindh Junayd-al-Murri. Crossing the Punjab border, he took on Junayd's forces and defeated them through a deft deployment of his cavalry and returned to his capital triumphantly.[42] There are very sketchy details of this war, but the conclusion is that he managed to check Arab expansion in the region as Junayd never dared to attack Kashmir again. One reason for Lalitaditya's victory over the Arabs was that his army largely comprised cavalry and foot soldiers. Indian kings usually had more elephants in their armies while their opponents the Arabs used faster moving and agile horses and camels. But they seemed to have met their match in Lalitaditya.

After facing a defeat in Kashmir, Junayd shifted his focus. He subjugated Kangda, turned southwards towards Kutch and Rajasthan and took over Jodhpur and Jaisalmer, and Bharuch in Gujarat. However, his victory march was halted. A united and strong Hindu confederacy of Gurjara Pratihara king Nagabhata I in Ujjain, the Guhila ruler Bappa Rawal in Mewar, the Lat king Pulkeshiraja, Gurjara ruler Jayabhat IV and others dealt their death blows on Junayd who had now suffered three reverses in a row after what had seemed an invincible Arab conquest in Sindh, Multan, Balochistan and Gandhar. The Chalukyan king Vikramadaitya II who ruled from Badami, and his feudatory, the Rashtrakuta ruler Dantidurga, too lent support to Pulkeshiraja, thereby successfully stemming Arab incursion into Rajasthan–Gujarat regions in the 730s.

Junayd then decided to move menacingly towards Central India, towards Ujjain that was ruled by the king of Kannauj, Yashovarman.

But in a diplomatic checkmate against the Arabs, Lalitaditya and Yashovarman joined hands in a strategic alliance to repel and defeat them. Junayd was recalled by the Caliph and Tamim-al-utbi was made the new governor. The Arab trade centres in Sindh decayed, the momentum in trade decelerated and the emboldened vassal states stopped paying taxes. Arab power shrunk to merely the Debal port in just two decades after their victorious rampage over Sindh. Lalitaditya utilized this opportunity of a weakened power to chase Tamim away, right up to Zabulistan. Due to continued reverses, Tamim soon fled back to Baghdad but died on his way back, in 731CE. Arab soldiers were rather scared to go to India again. Al-Haqam was made the new governor, but he was not able to establish Arab supremacy. After the Arabs were defanged, it took nearly three centuries for invasions from the west, starting with the Turkish forces of Ghazni to even consider invading India and her frontiers. This speaks of the heroic resistance that was put up by the Indian powers against an expansionist, marauding global hegemony.

After driving back the Arabs around 730–31 CE, Lalitaditya turned his attention towards consolidating Kashmir's influence over Kabul, Gandhar, Zabulistan and Tokharistan. Though these were hitherto friendly states they had been increasingly weakened due to the frequent skirmishes with the Arabs. They had defied the Arab conquerors for about two centuries and for another 175-odd years, were to guard the north-western frontiers of India against Turkish attacks. In the recent past, in c. 700 CE these Turk Shahi kingdoms under one of their brave kings Ranbal[43] had forced Hajjaj into complete submission and became a hero across Central Asia. However, these powerful frontier states had slowly weakened. Additionally, these kingdoms were of strategic importance for Kashmir since five crucial trade routes passing through the Gilgit split into different directions from Tokharistan. It was hence important for Lalitaditya to reduce Arab ascendancy on these routes and also safeguard them against the prying attacks from Tibet. Between 725 CE and 730 CE, Lalitaditya kept a close watch on the Tibet border to prevent any incursions. He crushed the rebellion of the Darads of Gilgit and revolts influenced by Tibet in tribal kingdoms of the Chitral region. Lalitaditya seemed to have installed loyalists or retained the incumbents in states such as Kabul, Zabulistan and Tokharistan as quasi-independent feudatories. For instance, in 729 CE the exiled ruler of Tokharistan, Qutluy Ton Tardu, had sent a delegation to China for help against the Arabs but got no response from the imperial court. Lalitaditya stepped up, defeated the Arabs in his ongoing campaign, freed Tokharistan and the trade routes passing through it and installed Qutluy as king. Though a semi-independent state, Tokharistan under Qutluy was hence bound to accept Lalitaditya's supremacy. Stein corroborates that 'it is by no means improbable that some among them [the Shahi rulers] should have acknowledged the suzerainty of a powerful ruler in the possession of Kashmir and the adjacent hill districts.'[44]

It was perhaps during this Tokharistan campaign that Lalitaditya met Chankuna, a skilled army general whose military skills impressed him. He took Chankuna on to his side to employ modern and also Turkish and Chinese-style army formations in the Kashmir army. Kalhana talks of him too as someone from Tukkhar (Tokharistan) who built a Chankuna Vihara in Kashmir.[45] Chinese traveller Ou-K'ong who visited Kashmir during 759–63 CE also says that Chankuna had an important position in Lalitaditya's court and calls him 'Jiangjun' (Chinese word for Army general).

While Lalitaditya was away in the conquest of Tokharistan, Tibet began to eye central and eastern India—Madhya Desha, Magadh (present Bihar) and Vanga (today's Bengal). As the local power in that region, Yashovarman of Kannauj had to defend the borders against Tibetan onslaughts. In 731 CE, he even sent a delegation to China under his minister Simhagupta (named as Sengpo Ta in Chinese records) seeking help from an imminent threat to his dominions from Tibet. China was then grappling with immense internal turmoil and rebellions and was averse to engaging in any external conflicts. With no help forthcoming from China, Yashovarman took on Tibet independently. After his conquests to subjugate the Turkish states, Lalitaditya, too, jumped into this attack on Tibet from a different direction as that of Yashovarman. The combined attacks of both these kings ensured that the five trade routes were completely freed from Tibetan control, around 733 CE. Kalhana alludes to this defeat of the Tibetans (called by him as Bhauttas): 'The anxiety [felt] by the Bhauttas could not be seen on their faces, which are white in their original state, as the anger of the monkeys [cannot be seen] on their faces, reddish-brown by nature.'[46] For about four to five years thereafter Tibet remained largely subdued in its attacks on the trade routes and the credit for that goes to the resistance posed by the Indian kings Lalitaditya and Yashovarman.

That Lalitaditya's successes left an indelible imprint on the minds of Kashmiris is illustrated in the account of eleventh-century Iranian scholar and polymath Al-Biruni. In his *Qitab-Al-Hind* he records that Kashmiris celebrated a festival every year to commemorate the victory of Raja Muttai (Lalitaditya) over the Turks.[47] That such a festival was witnessed and recorded four centuries after Lalitaditya implies that his victorious exploits must have been so grand as to have still been a part of public memory. Scholar P.N.K. Bamzai, however, attributes this festival that was celebrated by Kashmiris on the second day of the Hindu month of Chaitra to Lalitaditya's victory over Tibet.[48]

For maintaining a lasting dominance over the Gilgit and the trade routes, Lalitaditya sent an emissary to the T'ang court in 733 CE seeking an alliance in stationing a permanent joint military base:

> After having [established this] kingdom, [I have] submitted to the Heavenly Qaghan ... and received [orders] to position and dispatch [my forces]. [My] kingdom has three kinds of troops, elephant [-mounted], cavalry, and foot soldiers. The Tibetans on the five great routes distressed this vassal and the king of Middle India. [The Tibetans] blocked [us from] entering and exiting [through these routes]. [Therefore, we] fought, and at once emerged victorious. Now, if the Heavenly Qagan's army arrives at Palur, even if it [numbers] two hundred thousand, [I] can assist with the supply of provisions. In [my] kingdom, there is a dragon pond [called] Mahapadma (present-day Wular lake). I am willing to let the [troops] of the Heavenly Qagan encamp there.[49]

In the past too, the T'ang dynasty had sent a delegation to the Karkota court in 722 CE expressing their gratitude to Tarapida (called by them as 'Ti-an-mu') for providing food supplies and military assistance to the Chinese army that had established its base in Gilglit.[50] The Chinese control over Gilgit during this period is further corroborated in the account of Korean monk Hyech'o who visited Kashmir around 723–24 CE.[51] But this time around, in 733 CE, China was in no position to respond to this generous offer of Lalitaditya as the T'ang Emperor Xuanzong was busy quelling the rebellion of his general Gan Lah Shan, an officer of Turkish descent. Civil wars and dissensions were tearing the T'ang Empire apart and as a consequence the Chinese emperor had to eventually flee his capital.[52]

The successful campaigns against the Arabs, Turks and Tibetans brought for Kashmir immense prestige and wealth from war spoils. It was at this juncture in his reign that Lalitaditya seems to have conceived the idea of leaving his legacy behind on the footprints of time by becoming a master builder of iconic monuments and cities. He established a new capital city named Parihaspur (City of Joy, today's Paraspore, which is about 22 km from Srinagar and part of Baramulla district). A massive palace for himself and the construction of four grand temples, other than the Martand Sun temple was commissioned at Parihaspur. These were the Parihaskeshav, Muktakeshav, Govardhan Dev and Mahavaraha temples. Kalhana states that the idol of Parihaskeshav was made of 3,600 kg of silver, while the Muktakeshav idol was made of 84,000 tolas (about 840 kg) of gold. A fifty-four-arm's length tall Garuda pillar was also erected. Inspired by the gigantic sculptures of the Buddha at Bamiyan in Tokharistan, Lalitaditya had a chaitya established in his capital with a giant Buddha statue that was made of 62,000 kg of copper and seemed to 'reach the sky'.[53] German art historian Hermann Goetz opines that the Afghanistan influence could be deeply seen in the architecture styles of Kashmir under Lalitaditya.[54]

Lalitaditya's 'Digvijaya'

After a brief hiatus from the battlefield, Lalitaditya seems to have set out on what Kalhana describes as his 'digvijaya'. It was a campaign in ancient India that a king (or a scholar) undertook in all the proverbial four directions against their political opponents (or intellectual, for a scholar) and after a victory in which he was acclaimed as a 'Chakravarti'. Quite ironically, the first target of this campaign was his hitherto ally in his expeditions against the Arabs and Turks—Yashovarman of Kannauj. Some scholars opine that Yashovarman's own successful *digivijaya* expeditions conquering Gaud (Bengal), Magadh (Bihar), Thanesar (Haryana) and parts of Maru Desh (Rajasthan)[55] made Lalitaditya both jealous as well as insecure. Yashovarman had the king of Gaud, Dharma, killed and from among his court the talented poet Vakpati was captured and imprisoned. In captivity, Vakpati wrote a eulogy to Yashovarman in Prakrit titled *Gaudavaho* or the 'Killing of the Gaud king', where he painted an exaggerated picture of the valour of his new master, possibly to escape the pain of captivity. This work paints a picture of an ambitious and expansionist Yashovarman, bolstered by the victory against the Tibetans.

The last straw in this thawed friendship between the two hitherto allies was a long-drawn encampment by Yashovarman in Kurukshetra, which was quite near the border of Lalitaditya's domains. It is quite possible that Lalitaditya declared war when Yashovarman tried to extend his boundaries at Jalandhar up to the Yamuna.[56] Stein determines the possible year of his launching an attack on Kannuaj to sometime after 736 CE.[57] (He possibly left Kashmir for Kannauj in 738 CE). On his way to the Antarved or the Doab region between the Ganga and Yamuna, where Kannauj was located, Lalitaditya vanquished smaller kingdoms such as Kangda, Kumaun, Lohara (Poonch), Garwhal (the then Strirajya or matriarchal 'queendom', which is perhaps Suvarnagotri and could have comprised Kumaun and Garwhal) and brought them all under the suzerainty of Kashmir. About this victorious conquest till Kannuaj, Kalhana states:

> When he [Lalitaditya] launched his *digvijaya* he used to abandon his anger on seeing the opposite kings standing in the battlefield with their hands folded in respect; when the thunderous noise of the war drums rent the air people ran away leaving their homes and estates behind. Such towns looked like women having had an abortion. Like the sun revolving around the earth constantly that victorious king spent

most of his days in travelling, when he collected the obeisance money
in the East, the cloth of prestige over his head had lent glory to the
Antarved region.[58]

When the armies of the two equally competent and valorous warrior
kings met, it was naturally a long-drawn skirmish that left the armies
and soldiers exhausted.[59] There are very few details of this war but
what we do know is that Lalitaditya eventually emerged victorious.
As Kalhana states: 'At Gadhipura where Vayudeva (wind God) had
made the virgins humpbacked, in that very place, he (Lalitaditya) bent
the backs of many great warriors. Like the bright sun that evaporates
rivers in a moment he dried up the river-like army of the mountain-
like Yashovarman. The ruler of Kanyakubja was intelligent. He bowed
before the great Lalitaditya.'[60] Yashovarman sent a draft peace treaty
to his friend turned foe. Rather inadvertently (or knowingly) in the
treaty he preceded his own name before that of Lalitaditya. This
supposed lapse and breach of protocol by the vanquished towards a
victor was spotted by Lalitaditya's alert minister Mitrasharma who
brought it to the notice of his monarch who was enraged.[61] The treaty
was shredded, and Kashmir's forces remounted a virulent attack that
resulted in a complete rout for Yashovarman, who was made a vassal
of Lalitaditya. He remained a feudatory of Kashmir till his death in c.
753 CE. All the territories that were part of Kannauj now came under
the control of Kashmir. To stamp his suzerainty over these places,
which included the latest conquests of Yashovarman in Magadh,
Gaud and Vanga, Lalitaditya marched along to all these kingdoms,
parading his new vassal to instill a sense of fear in the feudatories
there and to let them know who their new master was. Without a war
with any of these kingdoms, all of them came under the control of
Kashmir, which now extended 'from the northern banks of Yamuna
to river Kalika (possibly around Gwalior), the Kanyakubja (Kannauj)
country became the courtyard of his house for Lalitaditya',[62] potentially
making it the largest empire of contemporary India. Lalitaditya took
back all the renowned poets and scholars—Vakpati, Bhavabhuti,
Kamalayudh and Atrigupta from Kannauj to his court. Of these,
Atrigupta, was an ancestor of the most celebrated icon of Kashmir

Shaivism Abhinavagupta. In the Indic imagination of the building of an empire, not only were massive structures, palaces and temples important, but the emergence of an intellectual and philosophical centre for excellence and learning was also paramount.

After this conquest, Kalhana makes Lalitaditya set off on a triumphant conquest across the length and breadth of India, which seems extremely mythical and legendary. As Stein cautions, 'The absence of all historical details, as well as the strict geographical order of the countries named, shows that we have in this account merely a conventional elaboration of the popular belief, which attributed to Lalitaditya the customary 'Digvijaya' of an Indian hero.'[63] From Bengal he moved towards Kalinga (Odisha) and brought it under his sway. Kalinga was under the Shailodbhava dynasty during this time and the meltdown of their kingdom is obscure. In either case Kashmir's control over this region, if at all, seems to have been short-lived as the Bhaumakara dynasty became a prominent power in Kalinga towards the end of the eight century.

From Kalinga, we see the victory march of Lalitaditya moving southwards to the Karnata land (a reference to the Rashtrakuta dominions, possibly Karnataka) where Kalhana mentions a certain Queen Ratta sending him an emissary seeking help. Contextualizing the dominant queens of the south during this time, Ratta perhaps is an allusion to the Rashtrakuta Queen Bhavanaga. She was a princess of the dynasty of the Chalukyas from Gujarat and was abducted and married by Indra I of the lineage of the Rashtrakutas of Manyakheta. After Indra's death, Bhavanaga was the regent queen of the minor, Dantidurga (735–56 CE).[64] With her brother-in-law Krishna casting threats on the throne, she is supposed to have sought Lalitaditya's help as he was right there in the vicinity in Kalinga. Along with his vassals Jivitagupta of Gaud and Yashovarman, Lalitaditya is said to have come to her aid against her detractors. However, no Rashtrakuta inscription mentions either a visit or a war fought in their domains by a Kashmir monarch.

Kalhana then takes us through Lalitaditya's victorious march through the Tamil country, crossing over the seas and reaching Sri Lanka as well.

On his way back to Kashmir he is supposed to have launched another victorious avalanche over the Konkan, Dwarka, Ujjain, Kathiawar, Malwa and Marwar, shaking the tottering power of the Maitrakas of Vallabhi (in Gujarat) and the Mauryas of Chittorgarh (in Rajasthan).[65] He also talks of Lalitaditya's annexation of Pragjyotishapura, the capital of the ancient Kamarup kingdom of Assam. Most scholars, including Stein who has translated the *Rajatarangini*, have discounted this as a fantastic tale and being highly unlikely. While Vakpati's eulogy to his victorious master is understandable, one wonders why Kalhana who was writing about Lalitaditya 400 years after his reign needed to employ such hyperbole, other than the need to reinforce the supremacy of his Kashmir kingdom in the pan-Indian context. He also exaggerates the treatment that Lalitaditya meted out to the vanquished: 'That victorious king made the defeated kings wear certain emblems showing their status as defeated kings, which they continue to wear even today. To the Turks, he made them shave only half their heads, which they continue to do even today. To prove the lower status as animal of the southerners, he made them leave one end of their loin cloths long enough to touch the ground behind them.'[66]

A few mentions of victories seem plausible, however, such as the conquest of the Lat principality (Gujarat) and its ruler Kayya becoming a vassal. Kayya's construction in Kashmir of a Kayyeshwar Shiva temple and a vihara called Kayyavihara where a Buddhist monk Sarvadnyamitra lived corroborates this theory that he must have been brought under the Karkota umbrella and then encouraged to contribute to the construction activities in the empire.

Despite all the exaggeration of Kalhana, undoubtedly at the end of a long war campaign, when Lalitaditya returned to his capital in c. 744 CE, he had built one of the largest contemporary empires of India and stamped the dominance of Kashmir in the subcontinent.

After a period of lull in the Gilgit–Baltistan region for four to five years after their defeat to the combined forces of Lalitaditya and Yashovarman, Tibet began to flex its muscles yet again. In 737–38 CE, the Tibetan army under its minister Bel Kyesang Dongstab tried to regain control over the important trade routes of the region. But

Lalitaditya forced him to retreat after inflicting a crushing defeat. Almost a decade later, in 747 CE, when the Tibetan aggression made a menacing reappearance, China sent its military commander Kao Hsien-chih to ally with Lalitaditya in order to repel Tibet.[67] Lalitaditya got a strategic bridge over the Sei River that used to send in reinforcements to the Palur region for the Tibetan army destroyed, thereby choking them eventually. The combined forces won yet another decisive victory over Tibet in a war where Kashmir provided military and civil assistance along with food supplies to the Chinese army. The trade routes to Khurasan and Gandhara were thus secured. In a region where control normally oscillated between the powers, it was Lalitaditya's efforts, with and without the Chinese, that kept the Palur free from Tibet for a long period from 731 to 747 CE.

Though Tibet was subdued, its ally, the Jieshi kingdom in the Kashkar–Chitral mountain region strategically placed between Kashmir and Gilgit kept mounting low-intensity attacks. A concern about this was raised by Tokharistan too when it sent a delegation to the Chinese court in 749 CE, drawing attention to the nuisance from Jieshi.[68] It also recommended that China renew its successful alliance with Kashmir that had stood the test of time and wars and to win over the king of Kashmir through costly gifts. These recommendations were promptly acted upon by the T'ang court. In 750 CE, Lalitaditya's forces, along with the Chinese army under Kao Hsien-chih, sacked Jieshi. Its ruler Botemo was deposed, and his elder brother Suojiya put in his place as a vassal. Kalhana perhaps alludes to Botemo when he talks about a certain ruler named 'Mummuni' whom Lalitaditya decisively vanquished in a third attempt. Historian R.C. Majumdar contends that Mummuni was perhaps the Arab governor whom Lalitaditya had defeated early in his career. Thus, there are various allusions about who this man Mummuni really was.

Lalitaditya: The Benevolent Builder

Each time he won significant battles, Lalitaditya established new towns and constructed temples in the classic mould of an empire builder. After the capital city of Parihaspur, to commemorate his foreign victories he established Sunischitpur and Darpitapur towns.[69] There are no traces of these towns in contemporary Kashmir. Close to the capital, he established Phalapura near the confluence of the Jhelum and Sindhu (a village somewhere in Shadipur today), as also Parontsa (a town now called Poonch). Lalitapura (today's Letapur) and Lokpunya (modern Lokbhavan on the Anantnag–Verinag road) were other towns that are credited to this monarch. His three wives too undertook several construction and charity works. Kamalavati was his favourite spouse whom he perhaps married prior to his coronation as the king of Kashmir. Chakramardika was the middle queen while Ishandevi the youngest, who was a possibly a Turkish princess whom he took during the Tokharistan–Kabul–Gandhara campaign. Chakramardika founded a town called Chakrapur that had nearly 7,000 homes. A grand marketplace called Kamalahaat came up in Parihaspur with an idol of Kamalakeshav installed there. Ishandevi had a huge water reservoir constructed in Parihaspur.

In the town of Hushkpur (today's Ushkur), Lalitaditya installed the idol of Shrimuhkswami and built a stone temple of Jyeshteshwar, donating several villages for their upkeep. At Lokpunya a Vishnu temple was established, while in Strirajya, a marvellous Narahari temple was built. The Narahari idol was fitted with magnets above and below it and due to this it was kept suspended in mid-air. That the Turks were his vassals even towards the end of his reign is bolstered by Ou-k'ong's records. It seems that Lalitaditya made his vassal states contribute to the architectural beauty of Kashmir by building structures there, just as he had done with Kayya of the Lat principality. Similarly, Ou-k'ong's mentions two viharas in Kashmir that were built by Yeli Tegin (possibly a Turkish prince of Kabul) and Quatun (a Turkish queen). He also notes that royal guests from Tokharistan regularly visited Kashmir.[70]

Rope machines and water wheels were installed on the Jhelum to pump water to villages that were on elevated ranges and thereby water starved. Kalhana mentions such water systems being installed in a Chakrapur (Tsakdar in today's Anantnag) on the banks of the

Jhelum.[71] Several dams were built over rivers to harness water and a network of roads linked the Kashmir Valley with the outside world. Given the constant flooding in the Jhelum due to silting, Lalitaditya had this cleared and constructed canals to supply water to distant locations. Swamps were reclaimed and bunds built in low-lying areas to make them fit for farming.

As an astute administrator, he constituted a cabinet of sorts of five top-ranking officials (called *Karmasthanas*) who collectively formed what was known as '*Panch Mahashabda*'. These five positions were named: *Mahapratiharpida* (High Chamberlain), *Mahasandhivigrahika* (ChiefMinister), *Mahashvashala* (Minister of Horses), *Mahabhandagra* (Treasurer) and *Mahasadhnabhaga* (Chief Executive Officer).

Despite heaping encomiums on Lalitaditya, Kalhana also brings to the fore several of the monarch's shortcomings. One of them was his alcoholism under the sway of which he often took brash decisions that he later repented for. So much so that he even ordered his ministers once 'that the orders he issued when intoxicated should never be followed'.[72]

Another act of moral decadence that Kalhana mentions is Lalitaditya reneging on a promise he made in the presence of the idol of Parihaskeshav to the Gaud king of protecting him.[73] However, the Gaud king was killed in stealth by a spy named Teekshna in Trigami when the former came to Kashmir. The soldiers of the deceitfully murdered Gaud king decided to avenge this foul act. Under the pretext of visiting the temple of Goddess Sharada, they entered Kashmir and besieged the temple of Parihaskeshav, the god who had let their master down. The priests of that temple shut all the doors to protect the idol. The soldiers however mistakenly or wantonly then attacked the Ramaswamy temple and destroyed the idol completely. As Kalhana mentions: 'They shred it into fine particles and scattered the powder in all directions. At that time, the soldiers of Srinagar attacked them and killed them at different places. Drenched in blood, those dark-skinned soldiers of the Gaud king looked like the boulders of the Anjan mountain daubed in red liquid mineral.'[74] It was a rare and tragic case of the soldiers and adherents of one principality destroying a sacred space of a Hindu co-religionist for political purposes. The idol that was so destroyed had a fantastic story behind it. The king, on his daily horse rides to the forest, noticed a few women who sang and danced at the same spot each day. When questioned, they mentioned that they were devadasis from the town of Shuravardhan and had been instructed by their mother to dance at that very location daily. On excavating the spot, two ancient, dilapidated temples with idols of Lord Rama and his brother Lakshmana were found to everyone's bafflement. Lalityaditya then consecrated the Rama idol in a stone temple in Parihaspur that was known as the Ramaswamy temple, and his queen Chakramardika had the Lakshmana idol installed in another shrine. It was this idol of hoary legends that got caught in the political crossfire and tragically destroyed.[75]

The Final Far-North Campaign to 'Uttarapatha'

The year 751 CE ushered doom for China. The Arabs under the command of Ziyad b. Salih joined hands with the Karluks and other Turkic peoples to mount a combined attack on the T'ang dynasty that was already beset with internal turmoil. They easily defeated the Chinese forces that were under the military governor Kao Hsien-chih near the Talas River, paving the way for the later Islamization of the whole area. The Battle of Talas fuelled the internal rebellion that had been brewing for long in China, culminating in the outbreak of the An Lushan rebellion (755–63 CE) in China and the consequent withdrawal of the Chinese armies from the western regions. This left the Arabs in a strong position to extend their influence over a large part of Central Asia. However, chronicled evidence of both Chinese and Tibetan sources reveal that the Tibetans temporarily checked any further advance of the Arab power.[76] Even as China was reeling under the impact of the rebellion, the new Tibetan king Trisong Detsun attacked the Chinese capital Chang'an with an army of 2,00,000 soldiers, defeating the defenders and forcing Emperor Daizong to flee from his capital to Shancheng. The rout in the war with the Arabs, the bloody An Lushan rebellion and the Tibetan attack brought the tottering T'ang Empire to its very knees. China had to withdraw its forces from several regions in and around its vast empire to redirect them towards the numerous internal skirmishes and external attacks. They had vacated from the Taklamakan and Gobi deserts and the Tarim in view of these developments. The Taklamakan, a cold desert, had very little water and was considered hazardous to cross for the merchant caravans that passed through the Silk Route, which passed through the Tarim Valley. To quench their thirst, they would stop by at streams of the river Tarim, in places known as the Oasis States.

Possibly given the confusion in China, Lalitaditya was seized by a strong urge to bring these vast areas, too, under his suzerainty and set out on what Kalhana terms as the Uttarapatha campaign.[77] Goetz concludes that in his final years, Lalitaditya conquered this Tarim Valley and also the city states in the Taklamakan and Gobi deserts and attacked Kuchha and Turfan around 755–56 CE.[78] History remains silent on the extent of this mysterious campaign or the victories that Lalitaditya earned. However, it is quite probable that he did traverse the Taklamakan Desert and carried Kashmir's flag to hitherto unchartered territories.[79]

When his ministers back in Kashmir did not hear from him in a long time, they sent messengers to trace him and send their inquiries about his well-being. Lalitaditya was apparently agitated by this move and is said to have told them: 'What sort of attachment is this on your part that you want me to return having come to this country? I am achieving victories on newer regions here. What greater work is waiting for me back home? The river having left its origin shall ultimately merge in the ocean. How to decide the limit or time for the journey of a king, who has likewise left his kingdom for victory? Therefore, O! Ministers! I tell you some basic principles to manage the kingdom in my absence. Please run the state according to them without any hindrance or blemish.'[80]

These principles that had the imagery of the legendary Ashokan edicts became the maxims of state policy for Kashmir and illustrated 'the principles of political wisdom, which influenced Kashmir administration in Kalhana's own time and for long after.'[81] Lalitaditya is supposed to have cautioned his administrators thus:

> Like the urban people, if these bucolic people (Damars) get good clothes, good food, ornaments, beautiful women, good houses and good horses or if the king arrogantly ignores the security of his forts, if the royal servants start being injudicious in their actions, if soldiers are recruited from only one region, if the *kayasthas* [government officials, clerks, accountants, not the caste] come together through marriages and if the king adopts a *kayastha* mentality, be sure that the misfortune of the citizens is around the corner.[82]

He also instructed them that in the eventuality of his non-return, his eldest son from Kamaladevi, Kuvalayapida should be crowned king and if found wanting, he should be dismissed. He had a special word for his favourite grandson Jayapida (son of Lalitaditya's son Vajraditya, from Chakramardika) to emulate his grandfather and carry forward the legacy. In a tragic and mysterious turn of events, Lalitaditya never returned from this far-north campaign. A monarch whose life and achievements were coloured by fantastic legends had his death, too, shrouded in equal myth and obscurity.

Various theories abound of how he met his end. According to one legend that Kalhana mentions, the Kashmir battalion was struck with severe water shortage in the midst of their expedition within the Taklamakan Desert. An emissary of a rival king appeared as an imposter trying to guide them to a water source and misled them to their eventual nemesis. On his disappearance and death, Kalhana states with poetic flourish:

> Some say the king died because of the enormous snowfall in the Aryajak (or Aryanaka) country. Some even say he submitted himself to fire when faced with an imminent, inevitable danger to preserve his eternal prestige. Some others say, in the Uttarapatha that is beyond the human reach but easily reachable for the divine beings, that king went into the earth along with his army. Just like the story of his astonishing achievements is told, the various wondrous stories about his death are also narrated. When the sun sets, some say it drowned in the sea, some say it entered the fire and some say he [the sun] went to another

country. Likewise, many marvelous stories are related to the death of the great men.[83]

Just as he abruptly evanesced from the scene of Kashmir's history after such an iconic and illustrious reign, Lalitaditya, hailed as the 'Alexander of India' and the second Samudragupta, slowly disappeared from popular consciousness and historiography of India. The Karkota dynasty could not produce another emperor as glorious and brave as Lalitaditya and it collapsed under the weight of its own contradictions a century later, by 855 CE. Like the gigantic edifices he established have defied time and survived till date as magnificent ruins, the stories of Lalitaditya's chivalry, his victories and his charitable works have survived, too, in local folklore and public memory. Lalitaditya Muktapida thus created a permanent niche for himself not only in the history of India, but that of Central and South Asia, positing the primacy of Kashmir as a political, spiritual, intellectual and cultural focal point that was integral to the subcontinent.

Notes

1   Andre Wink, *Al-Hind, The Making of the Indo-Islamic World: Early Medieval India and the Expansion of Islam, 7th–11th Centuries* (BRILL, 2002), pp. 250–51.
2   Peristyle, a feature of Greek and Roman architecture, is a continuous porch formed by a row of columns surrounding the perimeter of either a building or a courtyard.
3   Repeatedly referred to as such through his '*digvijaya*' or world conquest according to twelfth-century Kashmir scholar Kalhana whose Sanskrit text *Rajatarangini* (The River of Kings) is one of the extant chronicles of Kashmir and its Hindu rulers.
4   Walter Slaje, ed., *Kingship in Kashmir (A.D. 1148–1459): From the Pen of Jonaraja, Court Pandit to Sultan Zayn al-'Abidin* (Germany: Studia Indologica Universitatis Halensis, 2014), p. 171.
5   Sir Francis Younghusband, *Kashmir* (London: Adam & Charles Black, 1911), pp. 114–15, 135–36.

6   The *Nilamata Purana* also mentions the Naga Karkotaka in the beginning of the list of Kashmir Nagas along with Nila, Vasuki and Takshaka.

7   Kalhana. *Kalhana's Rajatarangini: A Chronicle of the Kings of Kashmir*, Book 3, trans. Marc Aurel Stein. (London: Archibald Constable & Co. Ltd., 1900), verses 490–91, p. 115.

8   Hsuan-Tsang, *Si-Yu-Ki: Buddhist Records of the Western World*, trans. Samuel Beal (London: Trubner & Co., 1884), p. 148.

9   P.N.K. Bamzai, *Cultural and Political History of Kashmir*, Vol. 1 (Srinagar: Gulshan Books, 1994), p. 83.

10 Ibid., pp. 87–88.

11 M.L. Kapur, *Kingdom of Kashmir* (Srinagar: Gulshan Books, 2005), p. 50.

12 Kalhana, *Kalhana's Rajatarangini: A Chronicle of the Kings of Kashmir*, Book 4 (Hereinafter referred to as RT4), trans. M.A. Stein (London: Archibald Constable & Co. Ltd., 1900), verse 43, p. 123.

13 RT4, verse 119, p. 130.

14 RT4, verse 124, p. 130.

15 RT4, verses 126–27, pp. 130–31.

16 Ibid., verse 343, p. 154.

17 Ram Gopal Misra, *Indian Resistance to Early Muslim Invaders up to 1206 A.D.* (Bengaluru: Sahitya Sindhu Prakashana, 2020), p. 37.

18 M.S. Commissariat, *A History of Gujarat*, Vol.1 (Bombay: Longman, Green & Co., 1938), p. LI.

19 H.M. Elliot and John Dowson, *The History of India as Told by Its Own Historians: The Muhammadan Period*. Vol.1 (London: Trubner and Co., 1867), p. 88.

20 Ram Gopal Misra, *Indian Resistance to Early Muslim Invaders up to 1206 A.D.* (Bengaluru: Sahitya Sindhu Prakashana, 2020), p. 37.

21 Ibid.

22 Chacha Rai supplanted the last ruler of the Rai dynasty, Rai Sahasi II.

23 *The Origins of the Islamic State*, pt. 2, trans. Francis Murgotten Clark from the *Kitab Futah al-Buldan* by al Baladhuri (New York: Columbia University, 1924), p. 209.

24 Ram Gopal Misra, *Indian Resistance to Early Muslim Invaders up to 1206 A.D.* (Bengaluru: Sahitya Sindhu Prakashana, 2020), p. 43.

25 H.M. Elliot and John Dowson, *The History of India as told by its Own Historians: The Muhammadan Period*, Vol. 1 (London: Trubner and Co., 1867), p. 118.

26 *The Chachanamah: An Ancient History of Sind*, trans. Mirza Kalichbeg Fre-
    dunbeg from the Persian original *Tarikh al-Hind wa al-Sind* (Karachi:
    Commissioners Press, 1900), p. 71.

27 Ibid. pp. 71–72.

28 H.M. Elliot and John Dowson, *The History of India as told by its Own Histo-
    rians: The Muhammadan Period*, Vol.1, (London: Trubner and Co., 1867), p.
    120.

29 *The Chachanamah: An Ancient History of Sind*, trans. Mirza Kalichbeg Fre-
    dunbeg from the Persian original *Tarikh al-Hind wa al-Sind* (Karachi:
    Commissioners Press, 1900).

30 Chintaman Vinayak Vaidya, *History of Mediaeval Hindu India: Being a His-
    tory of India from 600 to 1200 A.D.* (Poona: The Oriental Book-Supplying
    Agency, 1921), p. 171.

31 Ibid.

32 *Chachanama*, p. 87.

33 Ibid., p. 123.

34 Ibid.

35 Elliot and Dowson, *The History of India*, p, 171–72.

36 Vinayak Vaidya, *History of Mediaeval Hindu India*, p. 179.

37 *A Gazetteer of the Province of Sindh* (Sindh: G. Bells & Sons, 1874), p. 25.

38 Andre Wink, *Al-Hind: The Making of the Indo-Islamic World: Early Medieval
    India and the Expansion of Islam, 7th–11th Centuries* (BRILL, 2002).

39 Rama Shankar Tripathi, *History of Kanauj: To the Moslem Conquest* (Motilal
    Banarsidass, 1989), p. 218.

40 *Chachanamah*, p. 193.

41 This is one version as stated in *The Chachnamah*, pp.142–44. However,
    al-Baladhuri states (as is translated by Elliot and Dowson, pp. 437–38) that
    the new Caliph Sulayman ibn 'Abd al-Malik bore grudges against Hajjaj and
    his relatives, and to take revenge he ordered Qasim back, had him impris-
    oned, tortured and murdered.

42 Mohibbul Hasan, *Kashmir under the Sultans* (New Delhi: Aakar books,
    1959), p. 30.

43 Not much details are known of him, or if this was the name of a dynasty.
    Arab records, like Al-Bahaduri's account, mention him variously as Ranbal,
    Rantal, Rantbil, Ratbal, Zambil, Zantil etc. Historian Ram Gopal Misra

contends in his book that this could be a corruption of the word 'Ratna Pala' or 'Rana Bala' (strong in battle), p. 66, fn. 12.

44 RT 4, p. 89.

45 Ibid., verse 211, p. 143.

46 Ibid., verse 168, p. 137.

47 Andrew Wink. *Al-Hind: The Making of the Indo Islamic World, Volume 2, 11ᵗʰ -13ᵗʰ Centuries,* (New York: Brill, 1997), pp. 73-74.

48 Bamzai, *Cultural and Political History of Kashmir,* p. 141; RT 4, 168.

49 Tansen Sen, 'Kashmir, Tang Dynasty, and Muktapida Lalitaditya's Ascendancy over the southern Hindukush Region', *Journal of South Asian History,* Vol. 38, no. 2 (2004), pp. 145–46.

50 Ibid., p. 143.

51 Ibid., p. 152.

52 Bamzai, *Cultural and Political History of Kashmir,* p. 141

53 RT 4, verses 193–203, pp. 141–42.

54 For more, please see Hermann Goetz, *Studies in the History and Art of Kashmir and the Indian Himalaya* (Wiesbaden: Otto Harrassowitz, 1969).

55 Shyam Manohar Mishra, *Yas'ovarman of Kanauj: A Study of Political, Social and Cultural Life of Northern India during the Reign of Yas'ovarman* (New Delhi: Abhinav Publication, 1977), p. 92.

56 RT 4, p. 90.

57 Ibid., p. 89.

58 Ibid., verses 128–32, p. 131.

59 Ibid., p. 4.

60 Ibid., verses 133–36, p. 132.

61 Ibid., verses 136–40, pp. 132–33.

62 Ibid., verse 145, p. 134.

63 Ibid., p. 90.

64 The Rashtrakutas of Manyakheta (near Gulbarga) were vassals of the Chalukyas of Badami. Dantidurga (735–56) refused ascendancy of Chalukyan King Kirtivarman II from Badami and founded the Rashtrakuta dynasty. He eventually defeated the Chalukyas in 753 and became a major power in the south.

65 Bamzai, *Cultural and Political History of Kashmir,* p. 140.

66 RT 4, verses 178–80, pp. 188–89.

67 René Grousset, *The Rise and Splendour of the Chinese Empire* (Berkeley: University of California Press,1962), p. 160.

68 Tansen Sen, 'Kashmir, Tang Dynasty', p. 147.

69 Bamzai, *Cultural and Political History of Kashmir*, p. 142.

70 Tansen Sen, 'Kashmir, Tang Dynasty', pp. 147–48.

71 RT 4, verse 191, pp. 140-41.

72 Ibid., verses 309–21, pp. 151–52.

73 Ibid., verse 323, p. 152.

74 Ibid., verses 322–29, pp. 152–53.

75 Ibid., verses 265–76, pp. 147–48.

76 Mu Shun-ying and Wang Yao, 'The Western Regions under the Tang Empire and the Kingdom of Tibet', in *History of Civilizations of Central Asia*, Vol. 3, ed. B.A. Litvinsky et al. (Paris: UNESCO Publishing, 1996).

77 RT 4, verses 337–38, p. 153.

78 Goetz, *Studies in the History and Art of Kashmir*, p. 20.

79 Sanjay Sonawani, *Emperor of Kashmir: Lalitaditya the Great* (Pune: Chinar Publishers India, 2019), p. 218.

80 RT 4, verses 340–44, pp. 153–54.

81 Ibid., p. 93.

82 Ibid., verses 349–52, p. 154.

83 Ibid., verses 367–71, pp. 155–56.

Rajaraja Chola and Rajendra Chola

R ajendra Chola's naval fleet shocked the countries of South East Asia
with its heroic raid in 1025 CE of fourteen flourishing port cities
on the Malay Peninsula and in Sumatra, called then as Suwarnadwipa
or the island of gold. The Chola navy had a combination of merchant
vessels, which were possibly assembled to carry the troops on their long
voyage to South East Asian shores. Merchant coastal vessels called
sangara[1] were built with single logs of wood bound together tightly
with ropes, to carry large amounts of cargo. Another category, the
colandia, which were possibly used in this expedition, was the larger
ocean-going vessel, capable of distant voyages. This conquest of South
East Asia was a culmination of a four-decade strenuous effort on the
part of the Cholas—the illustrious Rajendra and earlier his chivalrous
father Rajaraja to establish Chola supremacy, particularly in the sea-
trade routes. From Sri Lanka to Maldives and later Indian coasts in
Odisha and Bengal, the Cholas successfully sealed their authority over
the seas with this conquest of Srivijaya in Sumatra.

The Majestic Cholas

The Cholas made their presence felt in the annals of Indian history
for more than a millennium, as one of the longest ruling dynasties of
the world. The earliest mention of the Cholas in historical records
occurs in the inscription of Mauryan Emperor Ashoka[2] (BCE 273–
36). They make an impactful appearance during the classical age of
Tamizh cultural and literary renaissance, the Sangam era, which came
to an end by c. 300 CE.[3] Little is known of the history of the Cholas

from 300 CE till the ninth century when Vijayalaya, the first ruler of the imperial Cholas, burst on the scene. He established his power in the area around Uraiyur, captured Thanjavur from the Muttaraiyar chieftains and extended his kingdom along the lower Kaveri. He accepted the overlordship of the Pallavas, who were thereafter weakened and overthrown.

The Cholas were one of the triumvirates, the *Moovendhar* ('Three Crowned Kings') of the *Tamizhakam* or Tamizh country. In modern geographical parlance, this was the region covering today's Tamil Nadu, Kerala, Puducherry, Lakshadweep and southern parts of Karnataka and Andhra Pradesh. These three rival dynasties were the Cholas, the Pandyas and the Cheras. The Cholas eventually vanquished the others, and their empire came into existence only around mid-ninth century, despite their hoary origins. The heralding of a golden era of the Cholas began with the accession to the throne of Rajakesari Arumolivarman, popularly known as Rajaraja the Great (985–1014 CE).

This period coincidentally saw the simultaneous emergence of three powerful dynasties in the world—the Fatimids in Egypt (969 CE), the Song in China (960 CE) and the Cholas (985 CE). With the decline of the Abbasids of Baghdad and the emergence of the Fatimids as the alternative dominating power of the Muslim world, there was a shift in Muslim trading activities from the Persian Gulf to the Red Sea.[4] This shift also led to an increase in the importance of the Malabar Coast that lay right in the hinterland of the emerging Chola power. This was because while the earlier trade with India from the Persian Gulf followed the coastal line to the great harbours of Gujarat, the new routes from the Red Sea and Aden enabled ships to easily cross the Arabian Sea, directly to southern India's Malabar Coast. The famous Geniza records of Jewish traders of Cairo/Al-Fustat and Aden with the Malabar Coast document these new developments.[5] After the collapse of the T'ang dynasty in China and a reunification that followed, the Song emerged as a paramount Asian player. Along with the Fatimids and the Cholas, they heralded a new era in the maritime history of Asia.

Rajaraja Chola and the Foundations of the Empire (r. 985–1014 CE)

The swift rise of the Cholas under the father–son duo was spectacular. After a long apprenticeship as heir apparent or *yuvaraja*, Rajaraja, the son of Parantaka II Sundara Chola and Vanavan Mahadevi ascended the throne in 985 CE. His thirty-year rule marked the era of grandeur and glory for the dynasty in its crucial, formative phase of the Chola Empire. From his dynastic core in the Kaveri Delta region, Rajaraja wasted no time in undertaking a blitzkrieg against several neighbouring kingdoms of southern India. Constant skirmishes with the other two major powers, the Pandyas and Cheras (in today's Kerala), who often joined hands against the growing Chola hegemony, were the order of the day. With his young son Rajendra leading the army as its commander, Rajaraja managed to significantly subjugate his rivals, even capturing the Pandya capital of Madura. Rajaraja then turned his attention to the island of Lanka (Ceylon) that was under the Singala ruler Mahinda V. Rajendra invaded Lanka and a harried Mahinda fled to take refuge in the inaccessible hills in the south-east of Lanka called Rohana. The copperplates of Tiruvalangadu, which are a major source of Chola history, have a glowing and dramatic account of Rajaraja's invasion and conquest of Lanka:

> Rama built, with the aid of the monkeys, a causeway across the sea and then slew with great difficulty the king of Lanka by means of sharp-edged arrows. But Rama was excelled by this (king) whose powerful army crossed the ocean by ships and burnt up the king of Lanka.[6]

With the Chola invasion, Anuradhapura—the traditional capital of Lanka for nearly a millennium—was destroyed and a new Chola capital of Polannaruwa was established. It was a military outpost earlier but given its central location and relative ease to control turbulences emanating from Rohana, Rajaraja chose this as the seat of his new-founded power in the island kingdom. Being an ardent devotee of Shiva, Rajaraja got a temple to his favourite deity constructed in the new capital. Built of granite and limestone, the temple is among the few well-preserved ancient Hindu monuments in modern Sri Lanka. Inscriptions talk of another shrine, the Rajarajeswara temple being built in Mahatittha (Mantota in today's Northern Province of Sri Lanka) by a Chola officer Tali Kumaran. The town was also renamed Rajarajapura after its new ruler and it richly endowed the temple.

With vast swathes of land now under the suzerainty of an expanding empire, Rajaraja then managed easy success over the Gangas and their feudatories the Nolambas around 1000 CE. This brought the end of the Western Ganga dynasty that had been ruling over parts of modern South Karnataka since 350 CE. They had accepted the overlordship of the powerful Rashtrakutas who took them under their shield. With the gradual dissipation of the Rashtrakuta power that began to yield to the Western Chalukyas, the Gangas became sitting ducks for Chola expansionist designs. Today's districts of Tumkur, Chitradurga, Bangalore, Kolar and Bellary in Karnataka and parts of Salem and North Arcot in Tamil Nadu thus passed into Chola hands. The Ganga conquest brought Rajaraja directly in conflict with the Western Chalukyan Empire that had replaced the Rashtrakutas at Manyakheta. They offered a stiff resistance to Chola expansion. Inscriptions talk of a Chola rout against Western Chalukya ruler Tailapa II in 992 CE and a capture of 150 elephants from the former.[7] But Tailapa's untimely death did not augur well for the Western Chalukyas who were also being hemmed in from the north by the Paramaras of Malwa. Epigraphic evidence speaks of a convincing avenging of the earlier defeat by Rajaraja who vanquished Tailapa's son Satyashraya in c. 1007 CE. Though briefly overwhelmed by the strength and rapidity of the Chola onslaught, Satyashraya soon recovered and kept challenging the Chola might. The occupation of the town of Vengi became 'a bone of contention' between the two dynasties 'and for the next 135 years, with few intervals, it was to become the theatre of their hostilities.'[8] But the Eastern Chalukyas were easily subordinated by the Cholas and through marital alliances and political subjugation, they maintained a comfortable alliance.

The last of Rajaraja's conquests was that of Maldives—the 'old islands of the sea numbering twelve-thousand.'[9] Unfortunately no details are extant of this naval conquest. But both the Lankan and the Maldives conquest, exemplify the power of the navy that Rajaraja had organized, which Rajendra was to later use effectively in his Far East expedition.

In the final years of his rule, Rajaraja began to become increasingly dependent on his son Rajendra who had proved his mettle and military prowess on numerous occasions. In 1012 CE,[10] when he was around twenty-five years old, Rajendra was made heir apparent. Two years later, when his father breathed his last, Rajendra succeeded to the throne of the Chola Empire in 1014 CE.

The Big Temple

Apart from his military conquests, Rajaraja was a great builder. One of the most enduring specimens and finest achievements of Chola art and architectural grandeur is the breathtaking Brihadeswara or the Big Temple in Thanjavur that was completed in 1010 CE. The gigantic structure continues to enchant historians, archaeologists, architects, epigraphists and visitors alike to this day. Despite the fact that there is no granite found anywhere in the vicinity of the temple for at least 50 mi, the temple is built of 130,000 tons of granite—many of which are huge giant pieces that would be quite impossible for human beings to move. We have little information on the colossal labour involved in transporting these huge blocks of granite over great distances or the technical problems in raising them to those positions. This was most probably done by several elephants that were employed for the purpose. It is quite a feat to have such intricate carvings, too, on granite that is otherwise such a hard rock. The skilled artisans perhaps used an ingenious method of ancient engineering to cut the rocks. They made small holes in the granite and then placed wooden plugs inside the holes. When it rained, the water expanded the plugs and caused the rock to soften and break. Also, there is no binding material for the different blocks and only interlocking stone—something never found in tall buildings today. The gate guardian of Lord Shiva, the Nandi bull, that is seated at the entrance is a huge 25 ton monolith carved out of a single piece of stone and measures 12 ft in height, 19 ft in length and 18 ft in width. Myths abounded that it was continuing to grow, threatening to break the pavilion within which it was seated. So, locals put a nail into the back and that is supposed to have miraculously stopped the growth. But these are just some of the numerous myths that make up the mystique of this fascinating shrine.

The main temple complex has a rectangular court that is 750 ft by 250 ft and is divided into two by a partition wall, which carries a low tower of beautiful design. The inner court is twice as long as the outer one. The chief shrine, the *garbhagriha* or sanctum sanctorum, is in the inner court and atop it rises a *vimana* or tower that rises to 216 ft from the square base of 100 ft. The intricate, chiselled carvings and decorative motifs on the vimana make it a sight to behold. There are elaborate paintings, too, on the walls, and the brightness and vibrancy of the colours come from the natural dyes that were used to paint them. Villages from all parts of the empire were required to supply men and material according to a fixed schedule for the various requirements of the temple.

Upon its completion, the temple in the capital city became an epicentre of political, cultural, social and religious activities and had close business relations too with the rest of the dominion. The temple is also a rich source of documentation of the Chola period, especially Rajaraja's reign with more than eighty-five inscriptions. They begin with a *prashasti* or verse where breaking from the normal practice of tracing one's lineage, Rajaraja speaks of his own greatness. The inscriptions point to a Chola country that had a large army with several divisions of the elephant corps (*anaiyatkal*), cavalry (*kudirai chevagar*) and infantry (*kaaltpadai*), which in turn was divided into subunits. The army was deployed across the Chola territory and were stationed in *kadagams,* that is garrisons or cantonments. The temple had more than fifty singers who sang verses in praise of the deity and at least 400 dancers, musicians and artists whose names, addresses and emoluments, too, are meticulously carved on the temple wall inscriptions.

The entire complex is supposed to have taken twelve years to be completed and stands as a sentinel of Chola magnificence and the vision of Rajaraja Chola to this day.

Rajendra Chola (r. 1012–1044 CE)

Parakesarivarman Rajendra Choladeva I inherited an extensive empire from his father. This covered the entire modern Tamil Nadu and Andhra, parts of Karnataka and Kerala and the islands of Lanka and Maldives. Rajaraja had left behind a meticulously organized administrative set-up, an efficient bureaucracy and a powerful army with a strong naval force that also protected the overseas trade of the empire with the islands of South East Asia and China. Like his father's reign, the story of Rajendra's thirty-three-year rule is a story of unending conquests that he undertook to build on and consolidate the position that was bequeathed to him. Again, quite like his father, he too left behind stone inscriptions and copperplates at Tiruvalangadu and Karandai (Thanjavur) that have been the most reliable and important sources for the reconstruction of his reign and its military and naval exploits. Within a few years of his ascension, he appointed his son Rajadhiraja Rajakesari, who was not his eldest son, as *yuvaraja* to assist him in administration and war.

Skirmishes with the Western Chalukyas continued unabated. But within three years of his coming to power, Rajendra had crossed the Tungabhadra River, carrying the war directly into the heart of the Chalukya domain, attacking their very capital and annexing Banavasi. Around 1017–18 CE the conquest of Lanka was complete, with the entire island becoming a Chola province. The several Hindu stone temples in Chola style and dedicated to Shiva and Vishnu that have been found in and around Polannaruwa testify to this annexation.

Several years later, Kassapa, the son of the deposed Lankan king Mahinda V, who had been secretly raised by the Sinhalese owing to the fear of the Cholas, emerged as a major centre of resistance. He even managed to liberate Rohana and ruled as a regional satrap under the name of Vikramabahu I for twelve years from 1029 to 1041 CE.

In 1018 CE Rajendra attacked the Chera kingdom in Kerala and seized it. The Tiruvalangadu plates talk of the Pandyan king abandoning his home in fright and fleeing for refuge to the Malaya Mountain, the abode of Agastya.[11] War soon resumed with the eternal rival, the Western Chalukyas, under Jayasimha II. There were two theatres of war between the Cholas and the Western Chalukyas. On the western front Manyakheta (Malkhed in Karnataka's Kalaburgi) and Kalyani (Basavakalyan in Karnataka), with the Tungabhadra River forming the natural frontier between the two powers became a scene of war. On the eastern front the skirmishes centred around Vengi (fertile delta region between the Krishna and Godavari rivers), the possession of which was coveted by both powers. Southern India was exhausted with the constant turf wars between these two powers, with the balance frequently shifting in favour of one or the other.

Rajendra's *Digvijaya* Campaign

In this conquest against Rajendra, Jayasimha II was supported by the kings of Kalinga and Odda (Odisha) and hence they too became objects of Chola attack. These rulers had also tried to fish in troubled waters by exploiting a succession dispute in the Eastern Chalukyan kingdom that was ruled by Rajendra's maternal nephew Rajaraja Narendra. Rajendra undertook a *digvijaya* expedition with his general Araiyan Rajarajan to chastise these errant allies of his rival, marching all the way to northern and eastern India and touching the sacred Ganga River. His nephew was safely ensconced on the throne and vowed to teach a befitting lesson to the trouble mongers.

The climax of this expedition that was launched in 1019 CE from Sakkarakottam (possibly Chitrakoot in modern Madhya Pradesh) was the subjugation of Indraratha, the ruler of the Somavamsi dynasty of Kalinga,[12] and Mahipala I, the Pala king of Bengal. A Kannadiga chief who accompanied Araiyan Rajarajan on this campaign is said to have settled down in Bengal and later founded the Sena dynasty.[13] Chola armies also subordinated several small satraps in the region—Dharmapala of Dandabhukti belonging to the Kamboja–Pala dynasty[14] in Bengal, Ranasura (the ruler of Ladha) and Govindachandra of the Chandra dynasty in eastern Bengal.[15] The Paramaras and Kalachuris assisted the Cholas in this campaign that lasted for about two years.

As a symbol of his subjugation of these parts of the country, Rajendra brought back the water of the sacred Ganga to his kingdom. As the Tiruvalangadu plate states: 'The light of the Solar race (Rajendra), mocking Bhagiratha who by the force of his austerities caused the descent of the Ganga, set out to sanctify his own land with the waters of that stream brought (thither) by the strength of his arm.'[16] With this conquest, by 1023 CE the expanse of the Chola Empire across the breadth of India and offshore can be imagined. They had eliminated all possible rivals on the eastern coast of the subcontinent, captured Kerala with its many important ports of Malabar and occupied Maldives and Sri Lanka. This put them in a pole position as a leading player in the maritime trade of Asia as they held sway over several of the major trading ports.

To commemorate this feat of the conquest of the northern kingdoms, Rajendra decided to shift the capital city from Thanjavur to a new one that he built about 80 km away—Gangaikonda Cholapuram or the city of the Chola king who brought the water of the Ganga. This was to be the capital of the Chola Empire from 1025 CE for about 250 years thereafter. Here, Rajendra built a temple that looked much like his father's historic feat of the Brihadeswara shrine. This was called Gangaikonda Choleeswaram. While it is no match for the sheer size and brilliance of its predecessor, its stone and sculpture work has been done in an exquisite style and amazing detail. Rajendra also constructed a vast lake in the city, which was 16 mi long and 3 mi wide—still considered to be one of India's largest man-made lakes.

Chola Offshore Trade and the Stakeholders

By early eleventh century, Chinese markets and ports had emerged as one of the most lucrative centres for international commerce. Traders from across Asia sought Chinese commodities such as porcelain and silk. After a brief hiatus caused by the political instability and internal rebellion in China, things settled down in Guangzhou and trade flourished under the Song dynasty. On its part, the Song court actively promoted maritime trade and 'lobbied seafaring merchants to bring tribute to China by giving them several incentives'.[17] Revamping the traditional tribute system, the Song court not only procured 'foreign commodities without payment, but also derived substantial revenue by levying taxes on items sold in Chinese markets by the tribute carriers'.[18] This turned the system into a major source of income for the Chinese government. It also proved beneficial to foreign merchants who received preferential tax rates for appearing as tribute carriers, in addition to receiving gifts and honorific titles from the Song court that bolstered their maritime trade reputation and credentials. From the Arabs to the Cholas and the South East Asian kingdoms, the pull of the Chinese market was immense for everyone and hence they all vied for a share in the pie, leading to intense competition and rivalry amongst the main players. The recognition from Song court, the gifts and the handsome profits from tax rebates spurred this rivalry continuously, as also brought an unprecedented level of settlement of foreign merchants and royal missions to China.

The Malay world of today's Malaysia and Indonesia was divided between Srivijaya in the west and the kingdom of Mataram in Java.[19] In the early tenth century the capital of the Mataram kingdom was shifted from near Yogyakarta in south-central Java to north-eastern Java, near Surabaya. This was done possibly to gain better 'access to the spice trade routes from the Moluccas, which passed along the northern coast of Java'.[20] Right from the late seventh century, Srivijaya controlled the regions to the west of the Archipelago and its important trade routes. The ocean state of Srivijaya was supposedly a 'confederation of harbours and their respective hinterlands rather than being a large, centralized agrarian state',[21] but it was widely known in the entire region for its legendary prosperity. Srivijaya was also renowned for its military might, as also its infamous piracy-like activities.

Given the prominence of the Cholas in the maritime trade of the region, the South East Asian powers, including Srivijaya, maintained a healthy communication with them. The famous larger Leyden grant

(Chola plates preserved in the Museum of Leyden in Holland) of 1005 CE records Rajaraja donating the revenue of an entire village for the maintenance of the Buddhist shrine Chudamani Vihara, which was constructed by the Shailendra king of Srivijaya Sri Maravijayottunga Varman in the name of his father at Nagapattinam, the major port of the Chola empire.[22] The Srivijayan king had also informed the Chinese emperor of his intention to construct a Buddhist shrine in China to pray for the latter's long life. This seemed like a strategy of the South East Asian rulers to use spiritual diplomacy as a means to assuage all the great powers of the region and keep them all in good humour. Rajendra continued these diplomatic ties that his father had cultivated. In 1015 CE he confirmed the continuation of his father's donation to the Nagapattinam Vihara. That same year and again in 1018 CE, 'he also received large gifts of China gold (*China-kanakam*) from Srivijaya for a Hindu temple in the Chola harbour'.[23]

Angkor also entered into diplomatic ties with the Cholas. Shortly after 1012 CE, Suryavarman I (r. c.1006–50 CE) of the Khmer Empire under whom Angkor became the dominating power in the Gulf of Siam, opened his channels of communication with the Chola Empire through a curious gift that he sent across to Thanjavur. To protect his own royalty (*atma-lakshmi*) he presented the Chola emperor a war chariot with which he had defeated his own enemies.[24] One hypothesis is that Suryavarman I was seeking Rajendra Chola's help against the Tambralinga kingdom in the Malay Peninsula that was under the influence of Srivjaya.[25] Also, Angkor had perhaps 'entered troubled waters with its penetration into Srivijaya's sphere of influence in the northern Malay Peninsula'[26] and hence needed Chola support. For centuries Srivijaya had controlled the southern part of the Malay Peninsula up to Ligor and Chaiya and briefly even the Isthmus of Kra.

On learning about Suryavarman's emissary to the Chola court, the Tambralinga kingdom rushed to the Srivijaya king Sangrama Vijayottunga Varman[27] requesting his aid, thus bringing Srivijaya in direct conflict with the Cholas. Hence it was a constant jostling and one-upmanship among all the stakeholders to protect one's trade rights and routes. Possibly to protect their Angkor ally, a small Chola naval expedition reached Kadaram, Srivijaya's major outpost on the Malay Peninsula in 1017 CE. This perhaps was less of a raid and more of a Chola military and naval show of strength to Srivijaya, both in favour of their ally in Angkor and also to reassert their supremacy in the maritime trade route. The sending of an envoy and gifts of China gold in 1018 CE from Srivijaya was perhaps undertaken to ameliorate Rajendra's suspicions against their kingdom and keep him in good books so as to not upset the applecart.

In turn the Cholas, too, had active contacts with the islands of the Archipelago, as also with China's lucrative markets that were coveted by all the stakeholders. The annals of the Song dynasty record that the first mission to China from Chu-lien (Chola) reached that country in 1015 CE and state that the king of that country was Lo-ts'a-Lo-ts'a (Rajaraja).[28] The Chola mission had a stopover at Srivijaya for several months before they reached China. Though Rajaraja had died by the time the mission actually reached the Song court, the delegation conveyed his message to the Chinese emperor: 'My age, the stretch of the seas which separate us, and the great difficulties on the route to traverse, do not permit me to go, in order to carry myself the tribute that I wish to offer you . . . [This will therefore be done by] my envoys, to the number of 52, arriving at the foot of your throne. I have ordered them to offer you a robe and cap decorated with pearls, pearls of different sizes weighing about 21,000 liang, sixty pieces of ivory and 60 pounds of incense.'[29] In 1020 CE, five years after their first embassy reached China, the Cholas again sent a mission to the Song court.[30]

The Chola mission's success caused alarm in Srivijaya which had cultivated China and her markets for long. They had been the earliest to respond to the tribute system of the Song court. Large quantities of black pepper, rosewater, gharu wood, aromatics and medicine,[31] poured in as tribute from Srivijaya to China where they were in high demand. They had been sending envoys regularly to China in 1016, 1017 and 1018 CE. After the first Chola presence on Srivijaya in 1017 CE, curiously the latter stopped sending any emissaries to China for almost a decade from 1018 to 1028 CE. Srivijaya made it their diplomatic goal, all through the eleventh and twelfth centuries, to overstate their own importance in the region and misrepresent and discredit the Cholas in the Song court by terming the latter as their subjugated subordinates and vassals. The Chinese records make mention of the Cholas in this manner as being subservient to Srivijaya, which was far from the truth and was obviously fuelled by the Srivijayan misrepresentation.[32] When this information reached Rajendra's ears it only accentuated a further deterioration of ties with Srivijaya that had already come under strain for a long time now. In the long haul, in Srivijaya on its way to the Chinese court in 1015 CE, the Chola envoys had possibly done an excellent spying and intelligence gathering of the island kingdom, in preparation for a potential and inevitable conflict. Given all the suspicions, political alliances and clash of trade interests, an outbreak between the Cholas and Srivijaya was an inevitability that was merely waiting to occur. And occur it did in 1025 CE.

The Conquest of Srivijaya

A Tamizh *prashasti* gives a detailed account of what Rajendra actually did in this conquest of Srivijaya that he undertook in 1025 CE:

> [Who] having dispatched many ships in the midst of the rolling sea and having caught Sangrama Vijayottunga Varman, the king of Kadaram, together with the elephants in his glorious army, [took] the large heap of treasures which [that king] had rightfully accumulated; [captured] with noise the [arch called] Vidyadharatorana at the "war gate" of his extensive city; Sri Vijaya with the "jeweled wicked gate" adorned with great splendor and the "gate of large jewels;" Pannai with water in its bathing ghats; the ancient Malaiyur with the strong mountain for its rampart; Mayirudingam, surrounded by the deep sea [as] by a moat; Ilangashoka [i.e. Lankashoka] undaunted [in] fierce battles; Mapappalam having abundant [deep] water as defence; Mevilimbangam having fine walls as defence; Valaippanduru having Vilappanduru [?]; Talaittakolam praised by great men [versed in]) the sciences; Madamalingam, firm in great and fierce battles; Ilamuridesam, whose fierce strength rose in war; Manakkavaram in whose extensive flower gardens honey was collecting; and Kadaram, of fierce strength, which was protected by the deep sea.[33]

Historian Nilakanta Sastri tries to decode these places, and the chronology of their occurrence in the inscription gives us an indication of the sequence of the battle.[34] Nakkavaram was the Tamizh name of the Nicobar Islands and Papphala was a port in Ramanna, the Talaing territory of Burma. Pannai is identified with Pani/Panei on the east coast of Sumatra. Ancient Malaiyur was a principality 'at the southern end of the Malay Peninsula, and precisely on the northern shore of the Old Singapore Strait where one encounters the Malayu river'.[35] Mayirudingam that has the deep sea for a moat is among the dependencies of Srivijaya. Ilangaashokam identified as Ling-ya-sseu-kia was to the south of the state of Kedah in the Malay Peninsula. Mapappalam could be a place in the Tailang region of Lower Burma. Talaittakolam is localized in the modern Takuapa district, south of the Isthmus of Kra and identified by its chief town, also called Takuapa, and is on the West Coast of the Malay Peninsula. Madamalingam (Temiling or Tembeling) is at the mouth of the Kwantan River in Pahang on the East Coast of the Malay Peninsula. Ilamuridesam is the country in the northern part of the island of Sumatra.

The inscription makes it clear that it was a widespread conquest spread across the peninsula and aimed at Srivijaya and its several dependencies in the region. Kadaram port, too, was at the time a Srivijaya dependency and the first place that the Tamils touched in their passage into that kingdom. The Chola armada sailed directly to the west coast of Sumatra. The port of Barus in north Sumatra belonged to Tamizh trading guilds and helped the fleet to replenish and recharge before they continued to sail southward into the Strait of Sunda. The Srivijaya navy guarding the Malaccan Straits were caught completely unaware by this sudden and swift attack. Their capital city of Palembang was attacked and plundered by the Cholas. The armada seems to have taken advantage of the monsoons to keep moving from one port to another swiftly. These fast-moving, sudden attacks gave the opponent no opportunity to prepare or regroup, resulting in a complete rout of Srivijaya. After the successful raid Rajendra married Onang Kiu, the daughter of Sangrama Vijayottunga, and forced Srivijaya to make peace with the Javanese kingdom of Kahuripan. The Shailendra dynasty of Srivijaya collapsed after the raids. The hegemonic hold of Srivijaya over the maritime trade was weakened, though it did not result in a permanent Cholan occupation as that does not seem to have been Rajendra's intention.

This great naval expedition and conquest of more than a dozen harbour ports of Srivijaya and the Malay Peninsula was a unique event in the otherwise peaceful and culturally fruitful relationship that India shared with her South East Asian neighbours. Curiously enough, the Cholas seemed reluctant to convert this spectacular military and naval success into a more permanent political dominion, by, for instance, establishment of a fortified settlement of Tamizh merchants in the Straits of Malacca. South Indian merchant guilds named Ayyavole (Ainnaruvar) and Manigramam were already playing an important and active role in the maritime power politics, as mentioned earlier.[36] Their permanent establishment there could have cemented Chola supremacy for times to come, though this invasion clearly furthered the expansion and prestige of the guilds in the Malay Peninsula and Sumatra.

Though the naval raid stunned the wits out of Srivijaya, they slowly tried to regain their dominant position in the western Malay world with its important straits. A third offensive (after 1017 CE and the big naval raid of 1025 CE) was conducted on Srivijaya in the 1070s by Rajendra's successors Virarajendra and Kulottunga I to quell an internal rebellion. It was eventually under Emperor Kulottunga I (r. 1070–1122 CE) that Chola overlordship was established over the Srivijayan province of Kedah in the Malay Peninsula. An inscription of a Taoist temple in Guangzhou, dated c. 1079 CE declares Kulottunga, King of Chulien (Chola), to be the supreme chief of the Land of San-fo-tsi (Srivijaya).[37] According to Tan Yeok Seong, the editor of the inscription, Kulottunga ruled both the Chola and Srivijaya kingdoms.[38] In the small Leyden grant dated 1090 CE, the king of Kadaram is mentioned as a vassal of Kulottunga.[39]

Scholars have marvelled and hypothesized about the precision with which the Chola fleet managed to attack Srivijaya and have attempted to investigate the contributive factors for this. Their ships 'were not fitted with a rudder and magnetic compass and they had to do either coasting or parallel/great circle sailings'.[40] The Cholas had mastered the science of studying the winds and currents in the Bay of Bengal, South East Asian waters and even China, along with a thorough knowledge of astronomy, celestial objects and stars. It is said that the seafarers had knowledge of at least fifty-six stars seen in the lower latitudes of the northern hemisphere.[41]

Historian Radha Kumud Mookerji writes that Chola ports were marked by lighthouses built of brick and mortar that were kept alight at night to guide ships to ports.[42] Given the seasonal currents, the most appropriate time for the expedition to Sumatra from the Coromandel Coast might have been in December. Scholar B. Arunachalam opines that the voyage would have commenced after the sighting of Mrigasiram, Ardra and Ottaraivelli stars in the southern horizon and the Kootu star on the port bow of Ardra.[43] As scholars Vijay Sakhuja and Sangeeta Sakhuja postulate: 'Importantly the voyage had to be started before the Ardra Darshan i.e., Poornima (full moon) when Ardra is sighted at dawn for the last time. In case the voyage was delayed beyond mid-January, then the guiding star would be Sravan (Alpha Aquila).'[44] In their view the passage to west Sumatra would have been covered in about twelve to fifteen days. On reaching the Sumatra coast, the ships would have then coasted along the archipelago, through the Sunda Strait, into the Strait of Malacca.[45] The Chola mariners used a variety of instruments and objects for navigation—*Ra-p-palagai* (for sighting stars), *Tappu Palagai* (for speed measurements), human hand (for measurement of attitude of stars), flat bronze plates (for measurement of depth of water) and pigeons for sighting land.[46]

There were far-reaching cultural impacts too on South East Asia of both the Tamizh maritime trade and the invasion and conquest of Srivijaya. A South Indian cultural base had already been established with the Pallava influence on the region, which only got further cemented with the Chola conquests. Quite like the divine identification of the Cholan emperor, the Cambodian and Javanese monarchy, too, thought of themselves as Vishnu and Shiva or their representatives. The Thai kings considered themselves as incarnations of Indra. In

Champa, Shiva imagery and iconography became omnipresent. Cham sculptures in Vietnam were representations of the Hindu pantheon.[47] Just as Cholan temples were showcases of art, culture, painting, music and dance, we find similar echoes in peninsular Siam in the stone sculptures on Pranarai Hill at Takupa. Battle scenes from the Ramayana against a plain white background are popular in Bali, traceable to Chola temple hangings. Burmese *kalagas* or hangings have elaborate Jataka tales of Buddhist mythology. The influence of Hindu iconography and use of motifs of Garuda and Naga, as also *apsaras, kinnaras, gandhravas* on textiles is notable in many countries of South East Asia. This legacy of the fabric trade of the Cholas survived long after their empire itself declined. The Ramayana and Mahabharata epics became (and continue to remain) the subjects of royal ballets, classical theatre performances and village rituals. Royal ceremonies in Thailand and Cambodia still follow Hindu ritual procedures. Thus, a civilizational impact that India and the Cholas left on this region has lasted almost a millennium now.

The Last Years

After the *digvijaya* campaigns across the seas and within the subcontinent, Rajendra seems to have allowed his sons to take on most of the military campaigns. Rebellions that broke out in the Pandya and Kerala kingdoms were dealt with by his heir apparent, the *Yuvaraja* Rajadhiraja. One of the *prashastis* talks about these campaigns:

> Among the three allied kings of the South [Pandyas] [he] cut off on a battlefield the beautiful head of Manabharanam [which was adorned with] large jewels [and] was inseparable from the golden crown; seized in battle Vira-Keralan, whose ankle-rings were wide, and was pleased to get him trampled by his furious elephant Attivarana; and drove to the ancient Mullaiyur, Sundara Pandyan of endless great fame, who lost in a hot battle the royal white parasol, the branches [of hairs] of the white yak, and the throne, and who ran away, ---his crown dropping down, [his] hair disheveled and [his] feet tired. [He] sent the undaunted king of Venadu to the country of heaven and destroyed in anger the Senior

[chief] of Iraamakudam. While the strong Villavan [Chera], in his terror, hid himself in the jungle, [the Chola] put on a [fresh garland of] Vanji flower, and forthwith destroyed the ships at Kandalursalai on the never-decreasing ocean.[48]

Similar bloody wars continued in Lanka as also with the perennial archrival, the Western Chalukyas under Ahavamalla. The consolidation and expansion of the Chola Empire had been completely cemented under Rajendra's reign. His sons Rajadhiraja, Rajendra II and Virarajendra followed him in succession. In 1044 CE, this brave monarch breathed his last.

The legacy of this great ruler and naval commander was perpetuated by the independent government of India, when in 1972 the Government of India named a new Merchant Navy Training Ship as T.S. Rajendra and sought to train 250 cadets at a time. It was the perfect tribute to a man who led India's first concerted and powerful naval attack and brought under his sway vast tracts of territory across the shores.

Notes

1   K.A. Nilakanta Sastri, *The Colas* (Madras: University of Madras, 1955), pp. 85–86.

2   *Corpus Inscriptionum Indicarum*, Vol. 1, p. 2ff. and plate.

3   M. Rajamanikkam, *Tamilmoli Ilakkiya Varalaru* (Madras, 1963), p. 44.

4   J. Abu-Lughod, *Before European Hegemony: The World System A.D. 1250–1350* (New York: Oxford University Press, 1989), p. 226.

5   S.D. Goitein, 'From the Mediterranean to India: Documents on the Trade to India, South Arabia and East Africa from the Eleventh and Twelfth Centuries', *Speculum* 29 (1954), pp. 181–97. For more also see Hermann Kulke, 'The Naval Expeditions of the Cholas in the Context of Asian History' in *Nagapattinam to Suvarnadwipa: Reflections on the Chola Naval Expeditions to Southeast Asia*, ed. Hermann Kulke, K. Kesavapany and Vijay Sakhuja (Singapore: ISEAS Publishing, 2009), pp. 1–19.

6   Nilakanta Sastri, *The Colas*, p. 172.

7   R. Shama Sastry, ed., *South Indian Inscriptions*, Vol. 9, Pt. 1, No. 77. (Madras: Manager of Publications, 1939), pp. 47–49.

8   Nilakanta Sastri, *The Colas*, p. 182.

9   Ibid., p. 183.

10 E. Hultzsch, ed., *Epigraphia Indica*, Vol. 8 (Calcutta: Office of the Superintendent of Government Printing, India, 1905–06), pp. 261–62.

11 Nilakanta Sastri, *The Colas*, p. 207.

12 Ibid., p. 208.

13 Ibid., p. 210.

14 Sailendra Nath Sen, *Ancient Indian History and Civilization* (New Delhi: New Age International Publishers, 1999), p. 281.

15 J. Allan, Sir T. Wolseley Haig and H.H. Dodwell, eds., *The Cambridge Shorter History of India* (Cambridge: Cambridge University Press, 1934), p. 145.

16 Nilakanta Sastri, *The Colas*, p. 206.

17 Tansen Sen, 'The Military Campaigns of Rajendra Chola and the Chola–Srivijaya–China Triangle', in *Nagapattinam to Suvarnadwipa: Reflections on the Chola Naval Expeditions to Southeast Asia,* ed. Hermann Kulke, K. Kesavapany and Vijay Sakhuja (Singapore: ISEAS Publishing, 2009), p. 63.

18 Ibid. pp. 63–64

19 Hermann Kulke, 'The Naval Expeditions of the Cholas in the Context of Asian History' in *Nagapattinam to Suvarnadwipa: Reflections on the Chola Naval Expeditions to Southeast Asia,* ed. Hermann Kulke, K. Kesavapany and Vijay Sakhuja (Singapore: ISEAS Publishing, 2009), p. 4.

20 Ibid.

21 Ibid. Also, for more details on the region, please see O.W. Wolters, *Early Indonesian Commerce: A Study of the Origins of Srivijaya* (Ithaca and London: Cornell University Press, 1967).

22 Sten Konow, ed., *Epigraphica Indica*, Vol. XXII (Bombay: British India Press, 1913–14), p. 257.

23 Kenneth.R. Hall, 'International Trade and Foreign Diplomacy in Early Medieval South India', *Journal of the Economic and Social History of the Orient* 21.1 (January 1978), pp. 75–98. Also, Hermann Kulke, 'The Naval Expeditions of the Cholas in the Context of Asian History' in *Nagapattinam to Suvarnadwipa: Reflections on the Chola Naval Expeditions to Southeast Asia,* ed. Hermann Kulke, K. Kesavapany and Vijay Sakhuja (Singapore: ISEAS Publishing, 2009), p. 6.

24 Nilakanta Sastri, *The Colas*, p. 220.

25 Kenneth R. Hall, 'Khmer Commercial Development and Foreign Contacts under Suryavarman I' *Journal of the Economic and Social History of the Orient* 18 (3), October 1975, pp. 318–36.

26 Hermann Kulke, 'The Naval Expeditions of the Cholas in the Context of Asian History' in *Nagapattinam to Suvarnadwipa: Reflections on the Chola Naval Expeditions to Southeast Asia,* ed. Hermann Kulke, K. Kesavapany and Vijay Sakhuja (Singapore: ISEAS Publishing, 2009), p. 7.

27 R.C. Majumdar, 'The Overseas Expeditions of King Rajendra Cola', *Artibus Asiae* 24 (3/4), pp. 338–42.

28 Nilakanta Sastri, *The Colas,* p. 219.

29 Tansen Sen, 'Maritime Contacts between China and the Cola Kingdom of South India: 850–1279', in *Mariners, Merchants and Oceans: Studies in Maritime History,* ed. K.S. Mathew (New Delhi: Manohar, 1995), pp. 25–42.

30 N. Karashima, 'Relations between South India and China in Chola Times' in *Professor K.A. Nilakanta Sastri Felicitation Volume* (Madras: Prof. K.A. Nilakanta Sastri Felicitation Committee, 1971), p. 69f.

31 Tansen Sen, 'The Military Campaigns of Rajendra Chola and the Chola–Srivijaya–China Triangle', in *Nagapattinam to Suvarnadwipa: Reflections on the Chola Naval Expeditions to Southeast Asia,* ed. Hermann Kulke, K. Kesavapany and Vijay Sakhuja (Singapore: ISEAS Publishing, 2009), p. 66.

32 Ibid., pp. 68–69.

33 Nilakanta Sastri, *The Colas,* pp. 211–13.

34 Ibid., pp. 213–18.

35 Ibid., p. 215.

36 M. Abraham, *Two Medieval Merchant Guilds of South India* (New Delhi: Manohar, 1988).

37 Tansen Sen, 'The Military Campaigns of Rajendra Chola', p. 71.

38 Ibid.

39 Benjamin Lewis Rice, *Mysore Gazetteer,* Vol. 2, Pt. 2, (Bangalore: Government Press, 1930), p. 1030.

40 Vijay Sakhuja and Sangeeta Sakhuja, 'Rajendra Chola's Naval Expedition to Southeast Asia and the Chola–Srivijaya–China Triangle' in *Nagapattinam to Suvarnadwipa,* ed. Hermann Kulke et al., p. 81.

41 ibid.

42 Radha Kumud Mookerji, *Indian Shipping: A History of the Sea-Borne Trade and Maritime Activity of the Indians from the Earliest Times* (Bombay: Longmans, Green & Co., 1912), p. 137.

43 B. Aruṇachalam, *Chola Navigation Package* (Mumbai: Maritime History Society, 2004), pp. 81–82.

44 Vijay Sakhuja and Sangeeta Sakhuja, 'Rajendra Chola's Naval Expedition', p. 83.

45 Ibid.

46 Ibid., p. 84.

47 Hema Devare, 'Cultural Implications of the Chola Maritime Fabric Trade with Southeast Asia', in *Nagapattinam to Suvarnadwipa*, ed. Hermann Kulke et al., pp. 178–92.

48 K.V. Subrahmanya Aiyer, *South Indian Inscriptions*, Vol. LII (Madras: Government Press, 1937), p. 56.

Rani Naiki Devi
of Gujarat

Walking down the seven layers of stairs of the intricately carved, eleventh-century monument, known popularly as Rani ki Vav or the Queen's Step Well, is like taking a time machine through the very womb of history, utterly spellbound. Measuring 64 m in length and 27 m in depth, this marvellous subterranean water storage structure is built entirely of sandstone in Maru–Gurjara style. One is mesmerized by the sheer number of complex carvings—more than 500 principal sculptures and over a thousand minor ones—of gods, goddesses and mythical beings on the many pillared pavilions and terraces that lead one down to the reservoir. Jain scholar Merutunga who composed a poetic chronicle on the kings of Gujarat titled *Prabandha Chintamani* in 1304, records that this step well was built by a queen named Rani Udayamati of the Solanki or Chaulukya dynasty (942–1244 CE) of Gujarat. While generally it was kings who made monuments in memory of their favourite spouses, here was a queen who built this unique monument as a tribute to her husband, the Chaulukya king Bhimadeva I (1024–1066 CE).

The *vav* is located in the town of Patan in the Western Indian state of Gujarat—a town that was built by Vanraj Singh of the Chavda (or Chapotkata) dynasty in 746 CE. The older name of the town was Anahilvad Patan or Anahilapatan. Historian Tertius Chandler estimates that by 1000 CE Anhilwara was the tenth largest in the world, with a population of about 100,000.[1] In a generally arid, water-starved region, this inverted temple structure of the *vav* underscores the sanctity and importance of this indispensable natural resource. Even as the sands of time literally drowned the well that got submerged in silt, archaeological excavations in 1958 revealed a marble statue that had the name of 'Maharajni Shri Udayamati' inscribed on it, corroborating Merutunga's account. There was to be yet another queen in this lineage of the Chaulukyas of Gujarat who was to record an important milestone in the annals of Indian history.

The Chaulukyas (Solankis) of Gujarat

There were three other Chalukya families in India—the earliest one from Badami (in Karnataka's Bagalkot), the eastern branch from Vengi (in the Godavari and Krishna districts of Andhra) and a western branch from Kalyani (Western Deccan, Basavaklyan in Karnataka's Bidar). The Gujarat branch was distinctly named as 'Chaulukya' and quite like the other eponymous dynasties, claimed mythical descent. Bardic tales mention a huge sacrificial fire that was conducted at Mount Abu by the sage Vasishtha and 'from the fire fountain a figure issued forth, but he had not a warrior's mien. The Brahmins placed him as guardian of the gate, and thence his name "Pratihadwara" [the Pratihara dynasty]. A second issued forth and being formed in the palm (*chaloo*) of the hand was named "Chalooka" [the Chalukyas]. The third was "Paramar", and the fourth "Chauhan" [also called Chahamana]'.[2] These were the several prominent Hindu Rajput dynasties of northern and western India, all claiming a common fire ancestry or *agnikula*. This legend is also incorporated in the epic poem *Prithiviraj Raso* on the life of the twelfth-century monarch Prithiviraj Chauhan, by his court poet Chand Bardai.

The dynasty of the Solankis or the Chaulukyas of Gujarat was established by Mularaja I at Anahilapatan in 942 CE, succeeding the Chapotkata clan. There are several sources for the history of this set of rulers who ushered in a glorious period for Gujarat in the over three centuries of their rule. Other than Merutunga's work, there are Someshwara's *Kirti Kaumudi* and *Surathotsava*, Arisimha's *Sukrita Sankirtana*, the thirteenth-century Persian work of Minhaj-i-Siraj named *Tabaqat-i-Nasiri* and epigraphic evidence of numerous *prashastis* or inscriptions of praise. These together help us piece together the history, chronology and important events during the reign of this dynasty.

The Invasion from Ghazni

It was during Rani Udayamati's husband Bhimadev's reign that an unprecedented calamity befell Gujarat. A few decades after the emergence of the Solankis in Anahilapatan, a new power had arisen in the city of Ghazna in Zabulistan (today's eastern Afghanistan). Nasir ad-Daula Sabuktigin, a Turkish slave officer of the Samani dynasty of Khurasan had broken away and formed his own dynasty, of the Ghaznavids (977–1186 CE). Between Sabuktigin and his son Mahmud (famously known as Sultan Mahmud of Ghazni), expansionism both for political and theological purposes became the norm of Turkish conquests. They left an enduring and extensive empire in the Islamic world, after the fragmentation of the Abbasid Caliphate.

Mahmud is said to have taken a pledge to undertake a holy war (*jihad*) against India every year.[3] There are varied accounts of anything between twelve to seventeen expeditions that he undertook against India. Right from 1001 CE, Mahmud launched several attacks on various parts of India, looting treasures, perpetrating wanton destruction of temples and forcibly converting people to Islam. From Kabul to Kashmir, Punjab to Kannauj and Gwalior, northern and western India was constantly exposed to his frequent barbaric attacks. The Turkish raids were given a befitting reply several times by the Shahi ruler of Kapisha (Kabul), Jayapala. He, in fact, conducted raids against the territory of Ghazni around 986–87 CE.[4] In this battle Mahmud was reduced to great despair and peace was brokered with Jayapala. When the menace of Turkish raids continued even after the peace accord, Ferishta states that Jayapala formed a confederation of the Tomaras, Chahamanas and Chandelas to crush the rising power of Ghazni.[5] Eventually Jayapala was subdued by the forces of Ghazni and in the sheer embarrassment of his defeat Jayapala committed self-immolation. But Mahmud's skirmishes with the Shahis continued even after, with Jayapala's son and successor Anandapala. Like his father, Anandapala, too, created a coalition of the ruling powers of the time to repel the Turks in 1008 CE. As Ferishta states:

> Anundpal, hearing of his [Mahmud's] intentions [to attack him], sent ambassadors on all sides, inviting the assistance of the other princes of Hindoostan, who now considered the expulsion of Mohammedans from India as a sacred duty. Accordingly the Rajas of Oojein [Ujjain], Gualiar [Gwalior], Kalunjur [Kalinjar], Kunowj [Kanauj], Dehly [Delhi] and Ajmeer [Ajmer] entered into a confederacy, and collecting their forces advanced towards Punjab with the greatest army that had yet taken the field. The Indians and Mahomedans arrived in sight of each other on a plain on the confines of Pishawur [Peshawar], where they remained encamped for forty days without coming into action. The troops of the idolators daily increased in number. The Hindoo females, on this occasion, sold their jewels, and melted down their gold ornaments (which they sent from distant parts), to furnish resources for the war; and the Gukkurs [Khokars] and other warlike tribes joining the army, surrounded the Mahomedans, who were obliged to entrench their camp.[6]

In this Battle of Waihind (1008 CE) that followed, 'a dreadful carnage ensued, and 5000 Mahomedans in a few minutes were slain'.[7] Mahmud was forced to withdraw 'from the thick of the fight, that he might stop the battle for that day'.[8] But the tide of war changed in Mahmud's favour with Anandapala's elephant getting hit and beating a hasty retreat. The resistance from the Shahis continued even under Anandapala's son Trilochanapala and his son, 'Nidar' (fearless) Bhima who mounted several strategic attacks on Mahmud often. They were both killed while mounting these valiant checks on the invaders in 1021 CE and 1026 CE, respectively. It was hence not as is made out to be that Mahmud got away with a free pass to ravage India, but stiff resistance was posed during each of his annual misadventures.

In 1018 CE Mahmud attacked the holy town of Mathura, the land of Lord Krishna, considered one of the richest in the northern belt, after the abject surrender of the Gurjara Pratihara ruler Rajyapala. Just to give an idea of the amount of loot that Mahmud managed to ship back to Ghazni during each of his plunders of India, this is the account of his campaign in Mathura by Ferishta:

> It is said that the Sultan found in Muttra [Mathura] five great idols of pure gold, with eyes of rubies, each of which eyes was worth fifty thousand dinars. Upon another idol, he found a sapphire, weighing four hundred miskal; and the image being melted down, produced ninety eight thousand three hundred miskal of pure gold. Besides these, there were above a hundred idols of silver, which loaded a hundred camels with bullion. The Sultan having tarried here twenty days, in which time the city suffered greatly from fire, besides what it suffered from the hand of ravage and desolation, he marched against the other fortified places in these districts . . .[9]

Mahmud Ghazni's desecration of the holy town of Mathura invited indignation from a host of rulers of north India, including the Chandela king Vidyadhara, the Shahis Trilochanapala and Nidar Bhima and others. They formed another confederacy to avenge Mahmud's misadventure and forced a retreat of the invader in 1019 CE. As historian Sita Ram Goel rues: 'Hindus could have destroyed him [Mahmud] had they pursued him in his retreat . . . Hindus had lost [that vision]. Pursuit of a retreating enemy was contrary to the Rajput code of honour.'[10] It was thus the application of moral codes of ethical military conduct with an opponent who neither believed nor honoured such protocols that cost the Indian forces heavily during various critical milestones of history. Mahmud thus lived on to inflict more misery on the country.

But it was not merely a loot of treasures from India to build his empire back in Ghazni, but also a propagation of his faith that spurred Mahmud to return with a menacing regularity. A catalogue of his attempts to 'spread [the faith] over almost the whole face of the earth',[11] was routinely sent to the Caliph to be read with joy to the people of Baghdad. Mahmud was told once about the famous and rich temple of the *jyotirlinga* of Somnath in Gujarat. Ferishta explains:

> These infidels believe that souls, after death, went before Sumnat [Somnath], who transferred them into other bodies or animals,

according to their merits in their former state. The Sultan was also informed that the priests of this God, gave out, that the sins of the people of Delhi and Kinnoge [Kanauj] had incensed him so much, that he abandoned them to the vengeance of the Mussulmen, otherwise that in the twinkling of an eye, he [the God Somnath] could have blasted the whole army of Mahmood [sic]. The Sultan, no ways intimidated by this report, was determined to put the power of the God to a trial, by personally treating him ill. He therefore marched from Ghizni with a numerous army . . .[12]

From Multan, which he vanquished, he marched to Somnath in 1025 CE, via Anahilapatan that fell on his path to the temple town. Bhimadeva was taken by surprise as he had not expected this invasion of Mahmud and hence retreated to Kutch to reorganize himself. The defenceless capital (referred to by the Muslim chroniclers, numerously as Nahrwara, Narwalla, Naharwalah) was ravaged by the plunderer. But his eyes were set on Somnath to which he marched without delay. He was not expecting to see over 50,000 armed Hindus trying to defend their faith against this onslaught, even as they were 'prostrating themselves in tears before the Idol, prayed for assistance'.[13] The struggle to defend Somnath went on for three long days and Bhima and another Indian prince whom Ferishta calls as Dabishleem sent reinforcements to those who were defending their temple and their faith. But after three days of successfully holding back the invader, a dance of death followed with most of the defenders being killed by the marauders. Nearly all of the 50,000 men were mercilessly butchered.[14] Mahmud then rushed to the sanctum to find the stone idol of Somnath, 'five yards in height, two of which were sunk in the ground'.[15] The Brahmin priests tried their best to save their God by making a last-ditch attempt with Mahmud, bribing him with some crores in gold if he left the place without destroying the deity. The Sultan haughtily replied that accepting this offer would make him a seller of idols and that he would rather be known by the more honourable title of a breaker of idols. The idol was mercilessly uprooted from its foundation, broken into small pieces, some part of it being sent back to Ghazni on camels to be thereafter laid on the footsteps of the mosque, while the rest was sent to the Mecca and Medina. The enormous wealth of diamonds, rubies and pearls that were discovered below the idol astonished Mahmud as these far surpassed the bribe that the priests were offering him. He 'found in this temple, a greater quantity of jewels and gold, than, it is thought, any royal treasury, ever contained before'.[16] All of this was loaded back to his capital.[17]

While several chroniclers have berated Bhimadeva for his cowardly retreat in the wake of the marching forces of Ghazni, his army was now planning an attack on the retreating forces of the Sultan. Bhimadeva had refused to engage with the invader on the plains of Gujarat, of course with the temple of Somnath having had to face the consequences, but he chose to attack at a place that was disadvantageous to the opponent. By now, the invading soldiers were already exhausted due to the long campaign. Mahmud too had achieved more than what he expected in war booty and had no more zeal for another battle. As the Persian historian Gardizi mentions in the *Zayn-al-Akhbar:* 'Mahmud now returned. For Param Dev [referring to Bhimadeva],[18] the Badshah of the Hindus, stood in his way disputing his path. Mahmud therefore decided to leave the right road back to Ghazni from fear, lest this great victory of his should turn into defeat. He left by way of Mansura towards Multan. His soldiers suffered many hardships partly on account of water and partly on account of the Jats of Sindh and on other grounds. Many of the soldiers of Islam lost their lives on the way. At last Multan was sighted and Mahmud marched on to Ghazni.'[19]

To avenge the destruction of their sacred shrine, some Hindus even posed as guides to lead Mahmud's armies astray in the arid desert of Kutch before they somehow managed their way back to Ghazni. As Minhaj-i-Siraj mentions:

On his demand for guides, a Hindu came forward and promised to lead the way. When the army of Islam had for sometime [three days] marched behind him, and it became time to call a halt, people went in search of water, but it was nowhere found. The Sultan summoned the guide to his presence and asked him where water was procurable. He replied, "I have devoted my life for the sake of my deity Somnat, and have brought thee and thy army into this desert, where no water is, in order that all may perish." The Sultan ordered the guide to be killed, and the army to encamp.[20]

Bhimadeva then returned to Anahilapatan and commenced work on its restoration, the city having borne the onslaught of the Sultan. Later, his son Karnadeva (1064-1092 CE.) and celebrated grandson Siddharaja (1092–1142 CE.) led the Solanki dynasty to considerable prosperity. Karnadeva established the town of Karnavati (today's Ahmedabad).

The Princess from Goa

According to Merutunga, one of the future kings of this dynasty, Ajayapala (1173–76 CE) was stabbed to death by one Vayajaladeva, a Pratihara.[21] His minor son Mularaja II (1176–79 CE) was then placed on the throne. Ajaypala's wife Rani Naiki Devi became the regent and took over the actual reins of administration. History blanks out about any concrete details regarding Naiki Devi. Merutunga, however, mentions that she was the daughter of one Paramardin.[22] Paramardin is identified as the ruler of the Goa branch of the Kadambas, Permadi Varjadeva (c. 1147–97 CE), popularly known as Shivachitta, son of the chivalrous ruler of that clan, Jayakeshi II. Under Jayakeshi II, the kingdom was at its zenith. The Kadambas of Goa were a sub-branch of the earlier Kadambas of Banavasi.[23] These were fourteen kings who ruled Goa from the capital Chandrapur for about 350 years starting from the eleventh century, creating for Goa a distinctive political identity for the first time. Under Jayakeshi II, for the first time, gold coins stamped with their lion crest were minted, indicating the autonomy and prosperity of the clan. Permadi's queen (and possibly Naiki Devi's mother) Kamaladevi got the magnificent Kamala Narayana temple built, and this stands till date in the small village of Degaon, near Belagavi in Karnataka as a symbol of Goa's Hindu architectural style. Historian Asoke Kumar Mazumdar, however, also surmises that Naiki Devi might have been the daughter of a Chandela king Paramardi on the basis of a Chandela inscription dating Vikram Samvat 1261 (1329 CE) that 'the donnee's father died at Kakadadaha [possibly Gadaraghatta] while fighting the Turushkas'.[24] In either case, it seems that Permadi Varjadeva had his daughter trained in sword fighting, cavalry, military strategy, diplomacy and all other subjects of statecraft right from a very young age. Details of how she got married to the Chaulukya Solanki king Ajayapala are unknown. The couple had two sons, Mularaja II and Bhimadeva II.

Even as she was grappling with the personal loss of the sudden death of her husband, as well as taking on the mantle of the administration of the kingdom, a new challenge beckoned Naiki Devi. There was trouble brewing in distant Ghazni and sadly the destinies of Naiki Devi and several rulers in India were getting intertwined to the tumultuous rumblings there. The Ghaznavid Empire of Mahmud received a huge jolt when, towards the middle of the twelfth century, a clan of Afghans under their Suri chiefs revolted. These rebels were better known in history as Ghurids or Ghoris—derived from the name of their native place, Ghor, a mountainous tract that lies between Herat and Bamiyan (in today's Afghanistan). The first Ghori rebel of prominence Ala ud-din Hussain plundered and burnt the city of Ghazni in 1150 CE, earning him the deadly sobriquet of *Jahan Soz* or the World Burner. Even as he embarked on widespread expansionist military campaigns after forcing a petrified Ghaznavid Sultan to flee from the capital, he put his brother Mu'izz ud din Muhammad bin Saam in charge of the eastern conquests in the Indian subcontinent. This man is known to history as Muhammad Ghori, the founder of Islamic rule in India. Starting 1175 CE, he commenced his attacks on India with the capture of Multan and Uch that he converted into bases to mount future attacks. Instead of moving towards Lahore, he was advised to target South Rajputana and Gujarat. He was possibly advised to capture Gujarat, which was presumed to be a low-hanging fruit for the Ghorids, being weak and unable to offer much resistance at this point of time as it was under the reign of a woman and a young boy. He was to soon learn otherwise.

The Battle of Kasahrada (1178 CE)

Naiki Devi remained undaunted about the possibility of an invasion of her kingdom by the marauding forces of Ghor. She decided to throw herself completely into strategizing a well-conceived opposition to the invading hordes. She also opened diplomatic channels seeking support from neighbouring kingdoms for help including to the court of the chivalrous Prithviraj Chauhan who held sway over large parts of what is today's Delhi, Haryana, Rajasthan and even parts of Punjab, Uttar Pradesh and Madhya Pradesh. However, unfortunately for reasons best known to them, none of these provinces, including that of Chauhan, seemed to share the foresight of Naiki Devi in forging a united alliance against the recurring menace. It was left for her to merely garner the support of the vassal states of the Chaulukyas, the clans of the Naddula Chahamanas, the Jalor Chahamanas and the Arbuda Paramaras. Naiki Devi realized that in terms of size and strength this ragtag confederacy was no match to Ghori's superior army. She had to plan out a strategy that would help her even the odds that were stacked against Anahilapatan in this unequal battle.

Quite like her ancestor Bhimadeva I, who had drawn the forces of Sultan Mahmud of Ghazni to a battleground of his choice where the enemy was disadvantaged, Naiki Devi planned the conquest against the Ghorid army in the rugged terrains of Gadaraghatta. This was an area at the foothills of Mount Abu, near the village of Kasahrada (in today's Sirohi district). This masterstroke was to prove advantageous to the Gujarat armies since the narrow hill passes and the terrain were completely unfamiliar to the invaders. When the armies of Muhammad Ghori finally made their way towards Kasahrada, the Queen made a frontal attack on them, with her young son accompanying her on her lap. The Battle of Kasahrada of 1178 CE that followed was unique when an outnumbered army with its troops of war elephants managed to crush the force that had just vanquished the mighty Sultanate of Ghazni and thereafter the Sultans of Multan. It seems the weather, too, supported the forces of Naiki Devi as unseasonal monsoons put the Ghori army under further disadvantage from the position that they were camped in. Merutunga elucidates this rather poetically when he says: 'Queen Naiki, the daughter of Paramardin, fought at a ghat called Gadaraghatta and conquered the king of the Mlechchhas by the aid of a mass of rain clouds that came out of season attracted by her virtue.'[25]

The unexpected massive rout that befell his army shattered Muhammad Ghori's pride—more so since this defeat was wrought on him by a woman whom he had vastly underestimated. He fled from the battlefield with a handful of bodyguards to save his life. Such was the rude jolt he received from this battle that he never again turned towards Gujarat to conquer it and instead eyed the more vulnerable Punjab, making his entry through the Khyber Pass the following year. The wound of Gujarat remained with Ghori for long and it was later left to his slave Qutub-ud-din Aibak to avenge his master's humiliation, decades later in 1195–97. But thanks to the bravery and strategic assault of the fierce Queen of Patan, Gujarat remained invincible for Muhammad Ghori personally. Had this conquest been won by Ghori the whole of southern Rajputana and Gujarat would have gone under his control and the history of India might have taken a different course.

Naiki Devi's epic victory finds echoes in the works of several local chroniclers. Someshwara's works mention how the army of 'Bala' (infant) Mularaja had defeated the lord of *Turushkas* (Turkish people) and crushed the *mlechchha* (foreign) army.[26] Another poet, Udayaprabha Suri, states rather exaggeratedly about what seemed like a casual child's play. In his *Sukrita Kirti Kallolini*, he mentions that his mother gave Mularaja an army to play with and out of curiosity with that army he casually defeated *Hammira* (Sanskrit form of Emir) and his Turushka army, which (in order to protect themselves from the intolerable heat of the prowess of Mularaja) was dressed in robes that covered the soldiers from the head to foot.[27] Arisimha, too, notes the victory of Mularaja's forces over the Muslims.[28] A Chakukyan inscription from the reign of Bhima II (Mularaja II's brother and successor) states that even a woman could defeat the *Hammira* during the reign of Bala Mularaja.[29] The inscriptions of his successors, too, describe Mularaja II as: '*Paraabhoota durjaya Garjanakaadhiraja*' ('Garjanaka' according to Indologist scholar Bühler is a Sanskrit word to represent Ghazni and is intended to give the latter an etymological meaning, viz. the roarer[30]).[31]

Interestingly, the Muslim chroniclers, too, have unabashedly mentioned the rout that the Ghorid forces faced unexpectedly in Gujarat. The return to Ghazni seemed to have been extremely tortuous for Ghori's forces, as these accounts seem to suggest. Minhaj-i-Siraj states that in the Islamic year 574 AH (1178 CE) Mu'izz ud-Din 'marched an army towards Nahrwala by way of Uchchha and Multan. The Rae of Nahrwala . . . was young in years, but had numerous forces and many elephants, and when the battle took place, the army of Islam was defeated and put to rout, and the Sultan-i-Ghazi [Mu'izz ud-Din] returned again without accomplishing his designs'.[32] Nizam ud-Din records that 'the ruler of the country [Gujarat] gave him battle, and after a severe struggle the Sultan was defeated, and after much trouble, he returned to Ghazni and rested there for a short time'.[33] The sixteenth-century chronicler Badauni writes: 'Then in the year 574 A.H. proceeding by way of Multan he [Ghori] brought an army against Gujarat and suffered defeats at the hands of . . . the ruler of that country, and with great difficulty reached Ghazni and obtained relief.'[34] In his chronicle, Ferishta writes: 'In the year 574 he again marched to Oocha and Multan and from thence continued his route through the sandy desert to Guzerat. The prince (a lineal descendant from Brahma Dew of Guzerat, who opposed Mahmodd Ghiznvey) advanced with an army to resist the Mahomedans and defeated them with great slaughter. They suffered many hardships in their retreat before they reached Ghizny.'[35] It was evident that this was a defeat that the Turks were to remember sourly for a long time.

However, despite her stewardship in such a decisive moment in the annals of her kingdom, Naiki Devi is not credited much by any of the chroniclers, including the Gujarati poets (barring Merutunga). It is her infant son who is praised effusively for this rout of the Turkish forces that he so casually and playfully undertook! Far from acknowledging the sagacity and chivalry of the queen, even a mention of her name is not made in these accounts. And when made, it is done with utter condescension as the Chalukyan inscription does, stating that 'even a woman' could defeat the invading forces.[36] The thrust here is not on the bravery of the queen, but on the alleged impotence of the invading army that could not even stand steadfast in front of 'even a woman'. Hence, it is no surprise that barring this brief mention of her role in a momentous battle, the historiography of India blanks out any future mention of Naiki Devi. Mularaja died a year after this victory and was succeeded by his brother Bhimadeva II (1179–1242), the last ruler of the Chaulukyas, before the dynasty branched out under the Vaghelas. What role Naiki Devi played during this reign or was she alive when the subsequent invasions of Gujarat occurred under Aibak in 1195–97 remains shrouded in mystery.

Yet, just like no accounts are maintained on the life of the masterful architect of the Rani ki Vav, Queen Udayamati, the remnants of the contribution and brave resistance of queens like her and Naiki Devi will continue to leave an indelible stamp on the annals of Indian history.

Notes

1   Tertius Chandler, *Four Thousand Years of Urban Growth: An Historical Census* (New York: St. David's University Press, 1987).

2   Asoke Kumar Mazumdar, *Chaulukyas of Gujarat* (Bombay: Bharatiya Vidya Bhawan, 1956), p. 7.

3   H.M. Elliot and John Dowson, *The History of India as Told by its Own Historians: The Muhammadan Period*, Vol. 2 (London: Trubner and Co., 1869), p. 24 (citing the *Tarik-i-Yamini* of al-'Utbi).

4   Muhammad Nazim, *The Life and Times of Sultan Mahmud of Ghazna* (Cambridge: Cambridge University Press, 1931), p. 29.

5   Mahomed Kasim Ferishta, *Tarik-i-Firishta*; trans. Alexander Dow, *The History of Hindostan: From the Earliest Account of Time to the Death of Akbar*, Vol. 1 (London: T. Becket and P.A. De. Hondt, 1768), p. 18.

6   Ibid., p. 46.

7   Ibid., p. 47.

8   Elliot and Dowson, *The History of India*, Vol. 2, p. 447, citing the *Tarik-i-Firishta*.

9   Alexander Dow, *The History of Hindostan: From the Earliest Account of Time to the Death of Akbar*, Vol. 1 (London: T. Becket and P.A. De. Hondt, 1768), p. 73. This is a translation from the Persian *Tarik-i-Firishta* by Mahomed Kasim Ferishta.

10 Sita Ram Goel, *Heroic Hindu Resistance to Muslim Invaders* (New Delhi: Voice of India, 1984), p. 23.

11 Firishta, *History of Hindostan*, p. 75.

12 Ibid., pp. 80–81.

13 Ibid., p. 82.

14 Elliot and Dowson, *The History of India*, Vol. 4, p. 182.

15 Firishta, *History of Hindostan*, Vol. 1, pp. 86.

16 Ibid.

17 The entire episode at Somnath is drawn from Firishta's *History of Hindostan*, Vol. 1.

18 Some historians assume that this reference is to the great Paramar ruler Bhoja (r.1011–1055), though most others concur that it was the Chaulukyan king Bhima I.

19 Al Gardizi, *Zayn ul Akhbar*, Vol. IX, trans. (into English) R. Sarma, pp. 941–42.

20 Elliot and Dowson, *The History of India*, Vol. 2, pp. 474–75, citing the *Tabakat-i-Nasiri* of Minhaj-i-Siraj.

21 Merutunga, *Prabhanda Chintamani*, ed. Jinavijaya Muni, trans. (into English) C.H. Tawney (Calcutta: The Asiatic Society, 1901, p. 97 (in Kumarapaladi Prabandh).

22 Ibid; G.M. Moraes, *The Kadamba Kula: A History of Ancient and Mediaeval Karnataka* (Bombay: B.X. Furtado and Sons, 1931), 198 ff

23 The Kadambas of Banavasi ruled from the fourth century CE to the end of the sixth century CE. In the first half of the tenth century, a number of Kadamba branches came into existence—Goa Kadamba, Hanugal Kadamba, Chandavar Kadamba, Nolambavadi Kadamba, Rattihalli Kadamba, Bellary Kadamba, etc. The Kadambas of Goa ruled for over 350 years and later lost their power to the Yadavas of Devagiri.

24 Asoke Kumar Mazumdar, *Chaulukyas of Gujarat* (Bombay: Bharatiya Vidya Bhawan, 1956), p. 131.

25 Merutunga. *Prabhanda Chintamani*, p. 97
    The verses are as follows:

Balamularajena Rajyam kritam. Asya Maatra Naika devya paramaardi bhupati suthayotsange
Shishum sutham nripam nidhaaya GaaDaraaghaTTa naamani ghaaTe
SangrAmam kurvatya Mleccha raja tatsatavaadakaalagata
Jalada paTala sahayyena vijigye.

26 Someshwara. *Kirti Kaumudi*, ed. A.V. Kathvate (Bombay, 1882), verses 57–58:
    '*Chaapalaadiva Baalena Ringta SamaraangaNe,*
    Turushkaadi patheryena viprakeerna varuthini.
    Yachinna mleccha kankaala sthala muchhairvilokayan
    Pituhu praaleyashailasya, na smaratyarbudaachalaha'

27 Udayaprabha Suri, *Sukrita Kirti Kallolini*, ed. C.D. Dalal (Baroda, 1920; Mazumdar, *Chaulukyas of Gujarat*, p. 457.
    '*Yasmai dandam akhanda harsha kritaye Hammira bhoomeeruha*
    Prasveda Prabhavam Samarpitavati maatera kautoohalaat
    Santaapam yat prataapasya Turushkair- Asahishnubhih
    Aapada Mastvam chakre dhruvam vaasovagunthanam'

28 Arisimha, *Sukrita Sankirtana*, ed. Chaturvijaya Muni (Bhavnagar: Sri Jaina Atmanandasabha, 1917), verses 46–47, states:
    '*Tadangajo Diggaja dantha shayya vishranta keertihi kila Moolarajaha,*
    Tarushka sheershaaNi Shishurjayashri Lataa phalaaneeva Lasanna gruhNaat.
    Yasmin Sadochhaihi Shirasi Prateechi maheebhruti Sphaara balaamburaashau.
    Astham Samasthaari yashaha shashanka Prataapa chanDa Dhyuti ManDa-laabhyaam'

29 Mazumdar, *Chaulukyas of Gujarat*, p. 131.

30 Ibid., p. 133.

31 Ibid., p. 131, Also termed as '*Mlechcha Tamo nichaya-chchhanna- mahee val-aya Pradyotana vaalaarka*'

32 Minhaj ud-Din bin Siraj ud-Din, *Tabaqat-i-Nasiri*, trans. Major H.G. Raverty (Calcutta: Asiatic Society of Bengal, 1880), pp. 451–52.

33 Nizam-ud-Din Ahmad, *Tabaqat-i-Akbari*, trans. (into English) B. De, Vol. 1, Pt. I (Calcutta: The Royal Asiatic Society of Bengal, 1913), p. 36.

34 Abdul Qadir al-Badauni, *Muntakhwab-ut-Tawarikh* Vol. 1, trans. (into English) Lt. Col. G.S. Ranking (Calcutta: Asiatic Society, 1913) p. 66.

35 Firishta, *The History of Hindostan*, p. 150.

36 Mazumdar, *Chaulukyas of Gujarat*, p. 131.

Rani Rudrama Devi
of Warangal

Marco Polo, son of Niccolo Polo, was a merchant from Venice who travelled through Asia along the Silk Road between 1271 and 1295 CE. He assiduously documented the marvels of the East that he encountered during his extensive travels. During his sojourn through India, he crossed the southern provinces and stopped by at a kingdom he called 'Mutfili'[1]. About the sovereign who ruled here, he wrote:

> It belongs to a Queen, a woman of great wisdom. [When we were there], her husband had been dead forty years. Him she had loved tenderly, bearing him the softest affection and so, when he died, she solemnly declared that she would take no other husband, now that he whom she had loved more than herself, was dead. And so it was, that she never married again. But I assure you that during all those forty years she has ruled her kingdom most justly and equably, nor could her husband have done so better than she. And truly she is more beloved by her subjects than any Queen or King has ever been.[2]

Marco Polo had got the name of the kingdom wrong as also the relationship of the queen with the ruler who was deceased. 'Mutfili' was the Kakatiya kingdom of Andhra, and the queen he was referring to was the valorous Rudrama Devi, who had succeeded her father (not husband, as Marco Polo suggested) Ganapatideva, who had died in 1269 CE. She is, however, the only independent female ruler mentioned by Marco Polo in his journeys across the world.

The Kakatiyas of Orugallu

The Kakatiyas were feudatories of the mighty Rashtrakutas of the Deccan and later kept shifting their allegiances between the Eastern Chalukyas first and then the Western (Kalyani) Chalukyas. Beta Raju I, an early chieftain of the clan, established their seat of power in Kakatipuram—named so after the tutelary deity Goddess Kakati, and their dynasty came to be known as the Kakatiyas. From 1000 to 1158 CE, they conquered several areas in the Andhra region, thereby bringing almost the whole of today's Telangana under their sovereignty. The Kakatiyas first feature in historical records around mid-eleventh century as a minor family that was entrenched in the town of Hanumakonda in Warangal district. They had accepted the overlordship of the Western Chalukyas and even began issuing their inscriptions in the language of their masters, Kannada. They even participated in military campaigns of powerful Chalukyan kings such as Someshwara I (r. 1042–1068 CE) and Vikramaditya VI (1076–1126 CE), outside Andhra. The fierce competition between the imperial Cholas and the Western Chalukyas of Kalyani to dominate the coastal Andhra region drove their backing contenders to the Eastern Chalukya throne. The Kakatiyas, too, were drawn into all these skirmishes.

However, around the mid-twelfth century, both the Kalyani Chalukyas and the imperial Chola empires declined, leaving a political vacuum in vast swathes of southern India. Kakatiya Rudradeva (r. 1158–1195 CE) seized the opportunity and declared independence of the Kakatiya dynasty in 1163 CE. Hitherto feudatories of the erstwhile empires of the south, too, burst into prominence along with the Kakatiyas and they were equally balanced in terms of power. These included the Yadavas or Seunas of Devagiri holding sway in southern Maharashtra and northern Karnataka, the Hoysalas in the Mysore region with their capital at Dwarasamudram and the Pandyas ruling over today's Tamil Nadu and parts of Kerala. Soon after declaring his sovereignty, Rudradeva got the splendid thousand-pillared temple constructed in the Kakatiya capital of Hanumakonda, as an assertion of independent supremacy. Another important marker of this independence was linguistic assertion. The Kakatiyas broke away from issuing inscriptions in Kannada, the language of their hitherto masters, and instead Telugu became the dominant epigraphic language. This gave birth to a Telugu linguistic region as the dynasty began to grow in stature and autonomy. A new capital, too, was created, barely four miles away from Hanumakonda at Orugallu or Warangal. The name 'Orugallu' means a single stone, referring to a large granite boulder in the new fort.[3] While the Hanumakonda fort was located among hilly outcrops that both defended it and limited its growth, Warangal was on a relatively flat expanse of land with plenty of room to expand and grow.

In 1199 CE the third monarch of the independent Kakatiya dynasty, Ganapatideva, ascended the throne. Over the course of six decades that he ruled, till 1262 CE, the Kakatiyas emerged as a major dominant force of the Deccan—from a subregional power to a paramount force of Andhra. To project a new royal lineage that was commensurate with the emergent power, Ganapatideva also assumed the title of '*Maharajadhiraja*' or King of Kings, in comparison to his ancestors who called themselves '*Mahamandaleshwara*' or Great Tributary Lords. As historian Cynthia Talbot mentions: 'The epithets (*birudas*) associated with the Kakatiya rulers provide a convenient entry point into medieval Andhra constructions of the king. These *birudas* were not just bardic pleasantries meant to flatter a patron but were often physical objects in the form of an anklet or insignia—what we might consider a medal of honor—as well as titles announced in public appearances and enumerated in inscriptions. *Birudas* could not be adopted freely but had to be inherited from a predecessor, bestowed by an overlord, seized from an enemy, or justified by some deed. A list of *birudas* was a synopsis of a lineage's achievements, in effect, a summary of a person's claim to fame. The Kakatiya *birudas* are largely martial.'[4] Under Ganapatideva, we witness the beginnings of a new style of kingship for the Kakatiya dynasty that emulated the royal grandeur of the erstwhile southern empires of the Cholas and Chalukyas.

The Girl Who Was Crowned Maharaja

Ganapatideva had no sons but had two daughters, Ganapama Devi and Rudrama Devi from his queen Somaladevi. The former was married to Betadeva of the Kota dynasty, a feudatory of the Kakatiyas. She ruled with her husband for a decade from 1241 CE. Upon his death, Ganapama Devi ruled independently from 1251 to 1264 CE as a loyal satrap of her father. The younger daughter was groomed by her father to succeed him to the lion throne of the Kakatiyas. Folklore has it that Ganapatideva hid the gender of his second child and instead proclaimed her to be a male, till of course she came of age. This was necessitated by the evil eyes that were being cast on the throne by several men in the collateral line, in the absence of a male heir to Ganapatideva. When he realized that he was not going to have a male issue, Ganapatideva came up with something ingenuous and unprecedented. First of all, he groomed little Rudrama as a boy and as a valorous soldier who was trained in all aspects of warfare under Guru Sivadevayya. She was kept away from public glare and trained privately to become a superior warrior. The emotional impact on the little girl of having to don a false gender identity could be well envisaged. When it was no longer tenable to hold on to the charade, Ganapatideva invoked an ancient ritual of *Putrika Yagna* whereby a sonless monarch's daughter or his daughter's son is appointed as his own son and heir apparent.

Rudrama's official depictions always showed her in male attire, and she was always referred to her in the masculine as Rudradeva or as Maharaja. She even attended all public meetings dressed as a man and was often seen riding her horse in a warrior style. In around 1235 or 1240 CE, she was married to Virabhadra (son of Indushekhara of Nidadavolu), a Chalukyan prince who was a member of a minor branch of the Eastern Chalukyas, based in Vengi. These broad timelines come to light in the inscriptions of Malkapur (1261 CE) and Palakeedu (1269 CE). There are no records of Virabhadra occupying any prominent position either in public administration or in the army and he died young. The couple had three daughters—Mummadamma,

Ruyamma and Rudrama, all of whom were married to local noblemen. Towards the end of her reign, Rudrama overlooked her daughters and appointed Mummadamma's son Prataparudra as her successor.

Ganapatideva was extremely fond of his younger daughter and made her a co-ruler in 1259 CE, even when he was alive. He stepped aside in 1262 CE letting her assume independent charge, even as he guided her in the affairs of the state. She, however, ascended the throne only after he died in 1269 CE.

The ascent of a woman to the throne was detested by several male members of the family and the nobility, who became a constant thorn in Rudrama's flesh all through her reign. The eighteenth-century work *Pratapacharitra* by Ekambranatha talks of her stepbrothers Hariharadeva and Murarideva constantly creating obstacles for her. Rudrama defeated them with the help of her loyal nayakas (chieftains) Gona Ganna Reddy and Recherla Prasaditya, whom she had cultivated.

External Aggression

Towards the end of Ganapatideva's reign, skirmishes with the Pandyas led to loss of territories in southern Andhra for the Kakatiyas. Coupled with this loss of authority, the ascent of a woman to the throne seemed to have emboldened the other kingdoms in the neighbourhood as they saw this as an opportune moment to capture Warangal. She faced a series of attacks from the Yadavas of Devagiri, the Gangas from Kalinga and the Pandyas from the south. In the early years of her reign, the Yadava king Mahadeva invaded the Kakatiya domains and reached the very gates of Warangal. The *Pratapacharitra* mentions that after fifteen long days of incessant battle, Rudrama succeeded in chasing away the Yadava army back to Devagiri, killing 3,00,000 invading soldiers and even forced them to pay a large indemnity of a crore in money and horses.[5] To hide the loss of face that this defeat caused them, the Yadava records of court poet Hemadri, in his *Vrata Khanda*, talk of how their king magnanimously and voluntarily stepped back, taking pity on a woman and wished to spare her life![6] If such was the magnanimity, there was no reason to attack her in the very first place.

Yadava coins that were discovered later in archaeological finds buried deep inside the Andhra territories, and inscriptions where local rulers pledged allegiance to Rudrama—found in Bidar that was deep inside the Yadava territory—testify the Kakatiya claim of a complete rout of the invaders. After this victory, Rudrama took the title of 'Raya Gaja Kesari' or the lion to the elephant-like enemy kings. She also built a *rangamandapa* or pavilion in the Swayambhu temple in Warangal to commemorate this massive victory. In the motif there, she is shown as a warrior mounted on a lion with a sword and shield in her hands and an elephant trunk holds a lotus to her in abject submission. She also got coins and measures issued after this, carrying the same title of Raya Gaja Kesari.

In 1262 CE, it was the turn of the Ganga king of Kalinga Narasimha I (whose family had adopted the tile of Gajapati after the famed elephants of Odisha) to avenge an earlier defeat he had suffered at the hands of Ganapatideva. He marched into the Godavari Delta area and occupied Vengi. It took Rudrama Devi fifteen long years to recapture this territory. In 1278 CE, her commanders Poti Nayak and Proli Nayak fought against Vira Bhanudeva I, son and successor of Narasimha I, and inflicted a convincing defeat on him. They thereafter assumed titles of 'Thangasimha' (A lion to the strutting elephant, i.e., the Gajapati), and 'Oddiya raya manamardana' (the destroyer of the pride of Oddiyaraya or Odiya ruler). This re-established Kakatiya power in the coastal Andhra region.

The toughest challenge that Rudrama faced came from the south. In the first two or three years of her joint rule with her father, the kingdom was thrown into utter confusion and disarray due to the invasion of Jatavarma Sundara Pandya I. The Kakatiyas were disastrously defeated in the battle of Muttukur, near Nellore. They lost the principality of Nellore despite being able to turn the tide of the invasion, and it was after this that Ganapatideva decided to retire. Rudrama's loyal feudatories, the Kayastha Chief Jannigadeva and his brother Tripurarideva, later partially reoccupied some of this territory from the Pandyas[7] though the rest of the territory was permanently lost for the Kakatiyas.

Nayankaramu System and the Political Economy

Plagued by internal rebellions of traditional and hereditary families, Rudrama Devi introduced a novel concept of recruiting non-aristocratic warriors from different castes, as officers, chieftains and landowners. Older feudal families were gradually replaced, and land grants were now given to new meritocratic officers. This practice was carried on by her grandson and successor Prataparudra as well. Rudrama Devi also created a class of *angarakshakas* or designated soldiers who were part of the queen's entourage and who then became a class of warrior lords. The fort was provided with seventy-five bastions, which were properly organized with the security of each bastion being delegated to a nayaka in the ruler's service. In lieu of salary, the ruler assigned villages to the nayakas and also for maintaining an army. Similar responsibilities were assigned to subordinate chieftains known as *samanthas*. The ruler kept a check on the strength and stability of the subordinates and thereby also got an assessment of the collective military might of the kingdom.

The earliest references to this come from 1269 CE.[8] Several officials and bodyguards of the Rani made grants to temples in the same grandiose manner that the king might have, ruling as they were as feudatories in different parts of the kingdom. An inscription of the time reads as follows:

> While Rudrama-Mahadevi, the pattoddhati (?) of Ganapatideva was ruling at Orugallu and her servant Gandapendara Jannigadevaraja was governing the country from Panungallu to Marjavada, Karanam Namaya consecrated the image of Gopinatha at Pallinadu and made grants of land and assigned certain taxes for its worship [going on, then, to list about 110 such rituals in the temple.][9]

This tenurial right over territory known as *'nayankaramu'* got further adopted, strengthened and refined in the region under the Vijayanagara emperors who were the inheritors of several of these medieval dynasties of the Deccan. About twenty men are named in inscriptions in connection with *nayankaramu* tenure, most of whom were warriors bearing a variety of status titles in addition to nayaka. As historian Cynthia Talbot notes:

With rare exceptions, nayankaramu was a prerogative of officers rather than of nobles . . . nayankaramu holders controlled a small territory, that much is clear. What rights they possessed within the delegated territory is harder to determine. But they did have the authority to waive taxes in their localities . . . Nayankaramu must therefore have been some kind of revenue assignment over a fairly limited number of villages . . . Since nayankaramu appears in concert with the new trend in Kakatiya policy of incorporating people of officer status into the networks of power, it was probably a means of recompensing warriors for their military service to the dynasty. Through nayankaramu assignments, officer subordinates without any resources of their own were provided with sustenance. At the same time, the Kakatiya rulers could be assured of a roster of faithful warriors who could be called on for assistance in time of military need. The presence of the nayankaramu holders—who were representatives of Kakatiya might—in diverse localities throughout Kakatiya territory must also have furthered the Kakatiya political and economic agenda. Whether the possessor of nayankaramu rights was expected to maintain a set number of troops and /or a forward position of the revenues he received, however, we cannot say.[10]

To gain the goodwill of the common masses, Rudrama Devi was supposed to have made meeting her subjects and learning about their joys and sorrows first-hand an important part of her state policy. This was another way of circumventing the traditional nobility that was opposed to her and directly establish a connect with the masses and win their love.

To strengthen her position in the wake of repeated onslaughts, Rudrama got the nearly impregnable Warangal fort's construction that had begun under her father's tenure completed. One still sees the concentric circular walls of the fort. There exists a citadel, which is protected by an inner wall that is a kilometre in diameter and made of huge blocks of granite. These blocks are irregular in shape but are perfectly fitted without the use of any mortar. Rudrama Devi had the height of this wall increased to over twenty feet. Forty-five massive bastions, from forty to sixty on a side, project outward from the wall and into the waters of a 150-feet wide moat that she built around the fort.[11] The fort encloses beautiful temples and buildings carved intricately out of single pieces of granite stone. Many of these, stand desecrated today by successive invasions by the Khiljis.

Rudrama Devi was also far-sighted to increase the area under cultivation in her kingdom. The Kakatiyas, by and large, built more than 5,000 reservoirs and tanks by damming streams[12]—many of which are still in use today. This abundant supply of water brought large tracts of land under cultivation and also enhanced the revenues to the royal coffers.

Among other things, Marco Polo during his visit to Warangal also spoke about the diamonds that were found in the kingdom:

> And you must know that in this kingdom there are many mountains in which diamonds are found, even as you shall hear. Know, then, that when it rains in winter, the water runs down the mountains, flowing impetuously in great torrents through deep caverns. When the rain has stopped, and the water has ceased flowing, they go searching in the torrent beds, and find many diamonds. In summer too, when not a drop of water is to be seen, they find numbers of them on those mountains . . . There are certain great, deep gullies, with such precipitous sides, that no one can go to the bottom of them. But this is what the people do: they take many pieces of raw and bleeding flesh, and throw them into the gullies. The places into which the flesh is thrown, is full of diamonds, which get stuck to the flesh. Now you must know that on these mountains there are many white eagles, that feed on the serpents. When they see the pieces of flesh at the bottom of the gullies, they swoop down upon them, and carry them away. Then the men, who have all the time been carefully watching whither the eagles fly, as soon as they see them settled down and tearing the flesh, hasten thither as fast as possible. The eagles fly away, and in their fear at seeing the men suddenly coming upon them, do not carry the flesh away with them; on reaching the spot where the flesh lies, the men take it, and find plenty of diamonds stuck to it . . . when the eagles eat up the flesh of which I have spoken, they also eat up diamonds. So, at night, when they return to their nests, they drop the diamonds they have eaten, together with their dung. Then the people go and gather these droppings, and find quite a number of diamonds . . . and you must know that diamonds are not found in any part of the world except this kingdom alone. But here they are both plentiful and good . . . you must know that in this

kingdom the best and most beautiful, and finest buckrams in the world are made—and the most costly too. For I assure you that they are like tissues of Rheims linen. Indeed, they are so beautiful, the greatest Kings and Queens might wear them as something truly regal. They have quantities of cattle, and the biggest sheep in the world. They have great abundance and plenty of all the necessaries of life.[13]

Marco Polo also states that the fabrics of the Kakatiya kingdom were famed and were an important export item to other kingdoms within and even outside India. The magnificent Kohinoor diamond, too, came from here. It is rumoured to have been the eye of an idol in Warangal during the Kakatiya times. When the Kakatiya kingdom was attacked and ransacked by Malik Kafur, the general of the Delhi Sultan Allauddin Khilji in 1310 CE, he carried away the Kohinoor with him, and it later passed on to the Mughals as part of the Delhi treasury. It later changed hands again, reaching the Punjab rulers and finally the British monarchy, with whom it sits today.

Though not a keen connoisseur of the arts, Rudrama Devi is said to have encouraged the performance of Perini Shiva Tandavam by the soldiers of the army. It was an extremely vigorous and powerful dance performed to the beat of drums by soldiers as a prelude to war and was part of the training for the royal forces.[14] The dance form died down in due course of time, but the several poses and postures have been depicted in the famous Ramappa temple[15] at Warangal. From these sculptural references, renowned dance guru the late Dr Nataraja Ramakrishna reconstructed the dance form in contemporary times. The dance today gives an idea of the athletic nature of Rudrama's army and its war-preparedness.

Skirmishes with Ambadeva and Death of Rudrama Devi

The Kayastha clan were supposedly loyal adherents of the Kakatiya rulers. In the early part of Rudrama's reign, it was the Kayastha chief Jannigadeva who had wrested territories back from the Pandyas. His brother Tripurantaka, or Tripurari, followed him and was the chief of the clan from 1270 to 1272 CE. Like his elder brother, he, too, was seemingly a faithful loyalist to Rudrama. Things, however, changed when his brother Ambadeva succeeded him. He had illusions of grandeur of being able to vanquish a woman who had occupied the Kakatiya throne and kept conspiring for her ouster through all means. To establish his own might Ambadeva began vanquishing several subordinate kings and chieftains, thereby swelling his own importance. The Neela Gangavaram inscription states that Ambadeva was at war with about seventy-five subordinate nayakas whose heads he cut off in battle.[16] All these battles and victories were being achieved on his own accord with no sanction from or credit to the ruler Rudrama Devi. He conquered all of the Pandya-occupied territory that was lost since 1263 CE and extended his sway up to Nellore by 1279 CE. Many faithful loyalists or allies of Rudrama Devi were thus put down, and in due course, by the middle of 1280s, Rudrama Devi seemed to have lost complete control over the southern areas of her domain, beyond the Krishna River. When the Pandyas under Jata Verma Sundara Pandya, Mara Verma Sundara Pandya and Mara Verma Kulashekhara Pandya reattacked southern Andhra in 1282–83 CE, Ambadeva inflicted a crushing defeat on them all. By 1290 CE it was beyond doubt that he had emerged as a powerful, quasi-independent satrap of the Kakatiya throne, defying its authority at every conceivable opportunity.

Finally, Rudrama Devi seems to have decided to take on Ambadeva head-on around 1289 CE. Though she was almost eighty years of age by then, she was at the forefront of her army to defend her kingdom and honour. The outcome of this fierce battle with her loyalist-turned-foe is unknown; the information about Rudrama Devi's death came through the discovery of an inscription in 1994. It was found in Chandupatla in Telangana and was dated to a Saka-calendar day that was equivalent of 25 November 1289. The inscription was laid out by a '*bantu*' or servant of Rudrama, namely Puvvula Mamidi. He might have been a high-ranking official and a favourite of his monarch. The inscription notes the donation of land as grants to the Chandupatla Somanatha temple for the establishment of an '*Annadana Satram*' or food donation counter. He made this donation in the honour and memory of both his queen Rudrama Devi and her general Mallikarjuna

Nayakudu. Since there were no other invasions that occurred during this time, it may be deduced that both the queen and her general died in battle, fighting Ambadeva.

The Tripurantakam inscription has boastful verses from Ambadeva as to how he deprived Mallikarjuna of his seven limbs, which could even mean the seven limbs of the kingdom namely king, minister, friend, treasury, territory, power and forces.[17] Ambadeva could not obviously brag about killing the queen as that would have brought him discredit for slaying an old woman. But when we correlate this inscription with the Chandupatla one, the sequence of events and possible causes of Rudrama's death in battle, along with Mallikarjuna, becomes clear.

And thus, this chivalrous queen passed away into the pages of oblivion with no clear traces of what caused her death. Analysing the possible reasons for the scanty representation of the queen, Cynthia Talbot states: 'Rudramadevi herself is scarcely visible in the historical documentation, for she made only two charitable donations to temples, one directly and another through an intermediary. Rudramadevi also abandoned Ganapati's other efforts to enhance the Kakatiya royal prestige through the appropriation of imperial titles and genealogies. Instead, she concentrated on projecting an image of martial heroism, going so far as to adopt a masculine persona and, it would appear, leading her troops in battle.'[18] But in a time and age when it was uncommon for women to ascend the throne and vanquish foes by leading forces in battle, Rudrama Devi charted for herself an indelible place in the annals of the country.

Notes

1   Perhaps an allusion to the port of Motupalli that was part of the Kakatiya kingdom, which he conflated as the name of the entire kingdom.

2   Aldo Ricci, *The Travels of Marco Polo: Translated into English from the Text of L.F. Benedetto* (New Delhi: Asian Educational Services, 2001), p. 307.

3   *Orugallu* means single stone in Tamil. Another name for Warangal is Ekasi-lanagaram or 'single stone city' in Sanskrit.

4   Cynthia Talbot, *Precolonial India in Practice: Society, Religion, and Identity in Medieval Andhra* (New York: Oxford University Press, 2001), p.144.

5   Alekhya Punjala, *Rani Rudrama Devi* (New Delhi: National Book Trust, 2016), pp. 28–29.

6   Ibid.

7   Evidenced in the Nandaluru Inscription of 1264 CE in J. Ramaiya, *The South Indian Inscriptions, Vol. X: Telugu Inscriptions from the Madras Presidency* (Archaeological Survey of India, 1948).

8   J. Ramaiya, *The South Indian Inscriptions, Vol. X: Telugu Inscriptions from the Madras Presidency* (Archaeological Survey of India, 1948), 10. 423 and 424

9   Ibid.

10 Cynthia Talbot, *Precolonial India in Practice: Society, Religion, and Identity in Medieval Andhra* (New York: Oxford University Press, 2001), pp. 164–66.

11 Archana Garodia Gupta. *The Women Who Ruled India: Leaders, Warriors, Icons.* Gurugram: Hachette India, 2019, p. 47.

12 Ibid. p. 48.

13 Aldo Ricci. *The Travels of Marco Polo: Translated into English from the Text of L.F. Benedetto* (New Delhi: Asian Educational Services, 2001), pp. 307–09.

14 Archana Garodia Gupta. *The Women Who Ruled India: Leaders, Warriors, Icons.* Gurugram: Hachette India, 2019, p. 49.

15 This famous temple was constructed by Recharla Durga, the famous general of Ganapatideva in about 1213 CE. This information is provided in the inscription on the four faces of a polished column within a mandapa, in the northeastern corner of the temple. See Alekhya Punjala. *Rani Rudrama Devi* (New Delhi: National Book Trust, 2016), p. 71.

16 Ibid., p. 34.

17 Ibid., p. 37.

18 Cynthia Talbot, *Precolonial India in Practice: Society, Religion, and Identity in Medieval Andhra* (New York: Oxford University Press, 2001), p.135.

Maharana Kumbha
of Mewar

Expansive, breathtaking, majestic and spectacular—these are some of the adjectives that come to mind when one tries to capture the vision of the stonewalls of this famed fort that embraces the arid, westerly edges of the Aravalli Hills in Rajasthan. Stretching over nearly 36 km, the Kumbhalgarh Fort nestled on the arid hill slopes, about a 100 km from the city of Udaipur, finds a place in the Guinness Book of World Records for being the longest fort wall in the world.[1] Harsh and formidable, like the arid landscapes that it engulfs, the fort—a medieval wonder and a UNESCO world heritage site—was built by the Maharana of Mewar, Kumbhakarna or Kumbha for short. It was completed in 1458 CE after fifteen long years of construction. The palace within the fort stands at 3,568 ft above sea level and commands an extensive and fine view of the wild and rugged scenery of the Aravallis and the sandy plains of Marwar. Below the peak, on every side there are numerous old temples, reservoirs, barracks for the garrison, granaries and domed buildings. Seven gates lead up to the summit of the three-storied fort with the principal exterior one being named as Hanuman Pol (gate). The fort was to be the birthplace of another heroic legend from the same dynasty—Maharana Pratap (1572–97 CE).

It was to this impregnable fortress that the *maharanas* of Mewar always turned to, when either Udaipur became unsafe or Chittor was untenable. From Udai Singh to Raj Singh, every *maharana* of the dynasty sent their royal household for safekeeping to Kumbhalmer, when the aggression of the Mughals was directed against them. Centuries after it was built, Mughal Emperor Akbar coveted the fort and through a large Rajput confederacy, besieged the fort that was then under Maharana Pratap. The fortress briefly fell but quickly recovered and all of Akbar's successors, be it Jahangir, Shah Jahan or Aurangzeb, attempted in vain to capture it. When Rana Pratap's son Amra was attacked by Shah Jahan or Rana Raj Singh was ambushed by Aurangzeb, it was the Kumbhalgarh fort that never failed to shelter and protect its ruler.

Quite like this wonder monument, its builder Rana Kumbha had the unique distinction of being an undefeated hero of Indian history who vanquished every invader, and won every skirmish that destiny put him in.

The Guhilots of Mewar

Maharana Kumbha belonged to the chivalrous dynasty of the Guhilots (Gehlot) of Mewar that ruled the region for fourteen centuries in an unbroken chain. They traced their origin to the Sun God and called themselves *Surya Vamshis* or descendants of the Sun. Kumbha was the eldest son of Rana Mokal (r. 1397–1433 CE) and his Parmar queen Sobhagya Devi (the daughter of Raja Jaitmal Sankhla)[2] and was born on the Makar Sankranti day of 1417 CE. Mokal had seven sons and a daughter Lal Bai. Historians have traced back the story of the heroic Rana Kumbha from the several inscriptions of eulogy written about his life, called *prashastis*—the Kumbhalgarh Prashasti in the Kumbhalgarh fort (1460 CE), the Kirtistambh Prashasti in the Chittorgarh Fort (1460 CE) and the Ranpur Prashasti in the Ranakpur Jain temple (1439 CE), among others.

The political scene in India had seen numerous changes by then. After the first Delhi Sultanate of the Slave Dynasty of Qutub-ud-din Aibak, the Khilji dynasty of Turko-Afghan descent had taken over the reins of Delhi in 1290 CE with is founder Jalal-ud-din Khilji at the helm. One of the most tyrannical and expansionist rulers of the clan, Alauddin Khilji (r. 1296–1316 CE) attacked Chittorgarh, the stronghold of Mewar and its Rajputs, in 1303 CE and laid siege to it.

Rawal Ratan Singh was the ruler then, but the Rajput forces lost to Khilji, and Chittorgarh was ruthlessly ransacked. The legend of the queen of Ratan Singh, Rani Padmavati, committing self-immolation or *jauhar* along with numerous other women to save themselves from the brutalities of the enemy is part of folklore and popular culture in India. The infant Rana Hammir Singh, who was barely a year or two old, was taken away to the Kumbhalgarh fort for safekeeping.

Providentially, the Khilji power in Delhi soon weakened and by 1320 CE they were replaced by the Tughlaqs. Taking advantage of the political flux, Hammir was crowned the Rana of Mewar. Fierce battles ensued between the Tughlaq King Muhammad-bin-Tughlaq (r. 1325–51 CE) and Rana Hammir at Singoli. The sultan's armies were taken aback by the guerilla warfare techniques and clever war strategies of Hammir. What followed was a total destruction of the Tughlaq army and a worse humiliation for the sultan who was taken prisoner for three months. He was released on a bond of five lakh rupees and a promise to never interfere with the independence of Mewar. Hammir became the progenitor of the Sisodia clan, a branch of the Guhilot dynasty and assumed the title of Rana instead of Rawal. Hammir Singh was the great grandfather of Mokal and was succeeded by Kshetra Singh and Laksha Singh (Lakha). Thus, it was the hard-won victory of the brave Hammir that ensured a resurgence of Mewar's supremacy, and his successors proved their mettle to maintain this glory.

While on a battle, Mokal was deceitfully killed in 1433 CE by his own uncles Chacha and Maira who felt inferior and slighted by the Rana as they came of a mother who belonged to the carpenter caste.[3] The young sixteen-year-old prince Kumbha was packed away in haste to a safer location so that he did not fall into the hands of the miscreants who were eyeing the throne. When Mokal's maternal uncle Rao Ran Mal, who belonged to the brave clan of Rathors, heard of the misfortune that had befallen his nephew and the teenaged prince, he was seized with rage and an intense desire to avenge the assassins. Leaving his ancestral place in Nagaur, he rushed to Chittorgarh, drove away the usurpers and placed the infant Kumbha on the throne as the next Maharana. The cowardly usurpers fled to the hills of Pai Kotra, with Ran Mal in hot pursuit along with a force of 1,140 Gehlots and Rathors. With the help of the Bhils, Ran Mal managed to have Chacha and Maira slain. Another accomplice in Mokal's murder, Mahpa Panwar and Chacha's son Ekka however disguised themselves as women and managed to run away to seek refuge in the court of the neighbouring Sultan of Malwa Mahmud Khalji in Mandu.

Sultanates of Gujarat, Malwa and Nagaur

The invasion of India in 1398 CE by the barbaric Timur Lang 'the lame', of the Timurid dynasty of Central Asia was undertaken on the pretext of destroying the infidels and teaching a lesson to the Muslim rulers of Delhi who he felt had been excessively tolerant of their Hindu subjects. Leaving behind a trail of carnage and bloodshed, Timur reached the gates of Delhi. The Tughlaq Sultan Mahmud was defeated at Panipat, and Delhi was reduced to a heap of ruins. Timur's armies ravaged towns and villages that came their way, destroyed crops, and caused untold misery in the country. As Ferishta notes: 'The inhuman Timur . . . gave orders to put all above the age of fifteen to the sword, so that, upon that horrid day, one hundred thousand men were massacred in cold blood. This barbarity, together with his other actions of cruelty, gained him the name of Hillak Chan, or the destroying Prince.'[4]

But Timur had no intention of ruling Delhi or settling in India and left for Samarkand with an immense quantity of spoil. The Sultan of Delhi Mahmud Tughlaq who had fled in fright to Malwa returned to the devastated capital but was weakened beyond imagination as he was stripped of all moral authority to rule. Many hitherto feudatories of Delhi declared their independence, and Gujarat and Malwa were among them.

After the Solanki Chaulukyas, the Vaghela branch of the dynasty had been ruling Gujarat. But in 1297 CE, Alauddin Khilji sent his troops to conquer Gujarat and defeat the Vaghelas. Gujarat was

Delhi's tributary province from 1297 CE to 1407 CE, the year when Zafar Khan broke away from Delhi and declared independence of Gujarat. Zafar Khan was a Hindu of the Tank or Khatri community and after his conversion to Islam he had been appointed as the head of the kitchen of Sultan Firoz Shah Tughlaq, who had made him a subservient viceroy of Gujarat subsequently. However, in 1407 CE following the weakening of the Tughlaq power, Zafar Khan broke away from the shackles of Delhi and declared the independence of Gujarat. He mounted the throne at Birpur taking on the title of Muzaffar Shah I of the Sultanate of Gujarat.

A similar tale occurred in neighbouring Malwa too. Taking advantage of the dismemberment of the Tughlaqs, Dilawar Khan Ghuri who was their governor in Malwa and who had offered shelter to a harried Mahmud Tughlaq during Timur's raid, declared independence in 1401 CE. He founded the Ghurid dynasty of Malwa that was short-lived and was succeeded by the Khaljis of Malwa under Mahmud Khalji (r. 1436–69 CE).

Nagaur, to the north of Mewar, also witnessed a declaration of independence from Delhi by its Governor Feroz Khan. Thus, Mewar was surrounded on all sides by inimical kingdoms—Nagaur to the north, Gujarat to the south-west and Malwa on the south-east. Constant skirmishes between Rana Kumbha and these kingdoms became the order of the day.

War with Malwa

Since the Sultan of Malwa had sheltered the accomplices of his father's assassin, Mahpa Panwar and Ekka, Kumbha demanded these to be handed back to Mewar for suitable punishment. But the sultan refused to give up the refugees forcing Kumbha to declare war on Malwa with 100,000 horsemen and 1,400 horses. The two armies met in 1440 CE between Chittor and Mandsur and after an intense war, the sultan was fully routed. He fled the battlefield and shut himself up in his fort at Mandu. Kumbha pursued him and besieged his fort. Not being able to handle the siege, the sultan finally asked his refugees to leave Mandu as that was the cause of the whole skirmish. Mahpa and Ekka, instead of surrendering, escaped to Gujarat.

But Kumbha was incensed enough to storm the fort and capture it, and take Mahmud Khalji captive, taking him along as a prisoner of war to Chittor. He was imprisoned in the fort for about six months, after which the Rana took mercy on him and released him without extracting any ransom. This was a shortcoming of the Rana—being kind and magnanimous with his enemies to a fault. Far from being grateful, a slighted Khalji vowed to avenge this insult and spent the rest of his life trying in vain to avenge the ignominy and defeat Kumbha by allying with his own former foe, the Sultan of Gujarat. The Rana used the time after the Malwa conquest to strengthen the defence of the kingdom and built numerous forts. Out of the eighty-four fortresses for the defence of Mewar, thirty-two were built by Kumbha.

Mahpa and Ekka meanwhile found no shelter in Gujarat and with few options left they decided to throw themselves at the Rana's feet and seek mercy. The ever-magnanimous Kumbha forgave them and enlisted them in his service. There was, however, political turmoil within Mewar.

The Sisodia–Rathor Conflict

While Ran Mal had been immensely helpful in those dark days following Mokal's murder, he and his clan of Rathors began to strangulate and occupy all positions of importance in the administration and army in Mewar. Taking advantage of the Rana's young age, Ran Mal and the Rathors fancied taking a complete control over the affairs of Mewar—something deeply resented by the Sisodias and the other traditional sardars of the kingdom. A conflict, therefore, was inevitable and it blew up in the face in the most unfortunate manner between the Rathors and the Sisodias. Kumbha was constantly being warned against Ran Mal and he finally allowed his paternal side to exercise whatever resistance they wished to against the Rathors.

The Sisodias used the help of a maid, Bharmali, who Ran Mal was besotted by. She intoxicated him with the choicest drinks and when he was in an inebriated state, tied him to his own cot with his long turban. The assailants were then called in to put an end to him. Though oblivious for a while, Ran Mal who was gigantically built, managed to somehow extricate himself and made a daring attack on the Sisodia assailants but was eventually overpowered and slain. His son Jodha heard the news and fled the palace in fright. Jodha was to later found the city of Jodhpur and the other stream of the Rajput clan. Thus, the Rathors were unceremoniously expelled from Mewar in 1443 CE.[5]

Jodha stayed incognito for over a year in Kahuni and then began to raid the town of Mandor to regain his power, but with little success. Ran Mal's sister and the Dowager Queen of Mewar was naturally aggrieved by the misfortune that had befallen her brother and his family, despite them having helped the Ranas in their time of utmost distress. She pleaded with Kumbha to take mercy on Jodha and grant him a principality that he could live off, in peace. Kumbha relented and promised her that he would not interfere if Jodha won Mandor in war and by his strength. Taking the cue from the queen, Jodha captured Mandor in war. He sued for peace with Mewar and stayed on at Mandor.

The Long-Drawn Battle with the Sultanates of Malwa and Gujarat

In 1442 CE, when Kumbha was away from Mewar on a military campaign in Haravati, the Sultan of Malwa Mahmud Khalji, burning with the fire of revenge for his earlier misfortunes, decided to take advantage and attack Mewar. Arriving near Kumbhalmer, he planned to destroy the temple of the Goddess Bana Mata in Kelwara as popular legend was that it was this deity that protected the fort. For over a week the Rajput chieftain of the fort Deep Singh held the fort and the temple against the designs of Khalji. But he finally fell and consequently the temple fell into Khalji's hands. He ruthlessly razed the temple down and burnt the stone idol of the Goddess.[6]

Buoyed by this easy success, Khalji was emboldened enough to attack Chittor, leaving a part of his army to take the fortress even as he advanced to frontally attack the Rana. Kumbha rushed back to defend Chittor and the two met at Mandalgarh, but the war ended indecisively. The Rana made secret night attacks on the sultan who was vanquished and fled towards Mandu to save his life.

Mahmud Khalji lay low for four years but the itch for revenge got the better of him. In October 1446 CE, he approached Mandalgarh menacingly, with a large army. Kumbha's armies attacked him when he was attempting to cross the river Banas and totally vanquished him yet another time. Khalji fled back to Mandu and for about a decade thence he shelved all plans to attack Mewar.

Ten years later, in 1455 CE, the duo clashed yet again in the war field. The sultan's eyes fell on Ajmer that he wished to control and proceeded to capture it even as he left his armies at Mandsaur to repel any defences from the Rana's side. After putting out a stiff resistance, the governor of the fort, Gajadhar Singh, was killed by the forces of Malwa and the sultan occupied the prized fort. Khwaja Naimatullah was appointed the governor of the fort with the title of Saif Khan. Ajmer was the veritable heart of Rajputana, and Kumbha could not afford to lose it. Hence, with enhanced military strength he launched an offensive against the sultan, thoroughly vanquished him and made him flee again, and occupied Ajmer.

Around this time political instability hit the Sultanate of Nagaur. With the death of Sultan Feroz Shah in 1455 CE his elder son Shams Khan succeeded him. But the younger son Mujahid Khan coveted his brother's throne and plotted to depose him and have him killed. A harried Shams Khan sent emissaries for help to Rana Kumbha. Having had his eyes on Nagaur for long, Kumbha agreed to help Shams Khan in this battle for survival on the condition that the latter would accept the suzerainty of Mewar and also the battlements of his fort demolished.[7] Shams Khan agreed to the terms, following which Kumbha vanquished Mujahid, who fled to Gujarat seeking refuge. Now that he was safely ensconced on his throne, Shams Khan reneged on his promise to demolish the fort battlements and promised the rana that he would do so after a few months of the latter's departure, given the taunts he was being subjected to for having taken help. The rana trusted him and left Nagaur. But far from honouring his word, Shams Khan began strengthening his fortifications. When the news reached Kumbha, he was enraged and he made an attack on Nagaur. He effortlessly deposed Shams Khan, took over Nagaur and its treasury and demolished the fortifications. The *Eklinga Mahatmya* composed during Kumbha's lifetime mentions about this battle thus: '[The Rana] defeated the King of the Shakas [Mussalmans], put to flight Mashiti [Mujahid?], slew the heroes of Nagpur [Nagor], destroyed the fort,[8] filled up the moat round the fort, captured elephants, imprisoned Shaka women and punished countless Mussalmans. He gained a victory over the king of Gujarat, burnt the city[9] [Nagor] with all the mosques therein, liberated twelve lakhs of cows from the Moslems, made the land a pasture for the cows and gave Nagor for a time to Brahmans.'[10] This was perhaps one of the rarest of cases when a Hindu monarch adopted the same policy as the Muslim conquerors or rulers and demolished the latter's place of worship, the mosque, quite like how countless temples had been desecrated. Kumbha was known to follow no ethical codes of warfare that the opponent did not believe in and replied to them in battle in the language that they understood. The gates of the fort of Nagaur were carried away, as also an idol of Hanuman, which got placed on the principal gate of the Kumbhalgarh Fort that thereafter came to be known as Hanuman Pol.

Shams Khan fled to Ahmedabad along with his daughter, whom he readily gave in marriage to the new Sultan of Gujarat Qutub-ud-din Ahmed Shah (Ahmed Shah II, r. 1451–58). The Sultan of Gujarat was now bound to help his harried father-in-law and sent his troops to wrest Nagaur back from Kumbha. A crushing defeat was inflicted on the Gujarat troops by Kumbha and only remnants of the army returned to Ahmedabad to narrate the tales of their misery. The sultan then decided to take things directly under his control and led the army against Kumbha, whom he met at Mount Abu in 1456 CE Sultan Ahmed Shah II sent his Commander-in-Chief Malik Shaaban Imad-ul-Mulk with a large army to capture the fort of Abu and himself marched towards Kumbhalgarh. Aware of this plan, Kumbha came and dealt a death blow on the forces of Imad-ul-Mulk and rushed to reach

Kumbhalgarh before the Sultan of Gujarat could get there. He met the forces of Gujarat under its sultan and vanquished them thoroughly forcing Qutub-ud din Ahmed Shah to retire to Ahmedabad in haste.

The two defeated sultans of Gujarat and Malwa now decided to join forces in an alliance against their common enemy, the Rana. Mahmud Khalji who was keenly watching the war in Abu sent his emissary Taj Khan to meet Qutub ud-din Ahmed Shah on his retreat to Ahmedabad. Fresh from the loss, an angry sultan readily accepted the offer of alliance from Malwa. Towards end 1456 CE, the alliance was formalized at Champaner by Sheikh Nizam-ud-din and Malik-ul-Ulema on behalf of Malwa and by Qazi Hisam-ud-din on behalf of Gujarat. According to this Treaty of Champaner, it was agreed upon that after the confederate forces would defeat Kumbha, the southern part of Mewar that was contiguous with Gujarat was to be attached to Gujarat, while Mewar proper, Ajmer and Ahirwara were to accrue to Malwa. A simultaneous attack was accordingly made in 1457 CE with Qutub-ud din advancing towards Kumbhalgarh in a south-westerly attack and Mahmud Khalji heading to Chittor, mounting an attack from the south. Kumbha decided to adopt the tactics of guerilla warfare as it was not possible for the Mewaris to fight on two fronts at the same time. His aim was to let the enemy forces raid deep into Mewar's territories and then cut off the passage of supply lines for the invading army. The arid and hostile geography of the Aravalli Mountain ranges was also used to inflict these attacks and further harass the enemy forces.

Realizing that the Khalji was probably the weaker link whom he had defeated numerous times in the past, Kumbha first decided to deal with him and intercepted him at Mandsaur, defeating him comprehensively. The Sultan of Gujarat was thereafter dealt another humiliating defeat and he retreated to Ahmedabad, thoroughly discredited. Mahmud Khalji vowed thereafter to never lock horns with Mewar in his life. Qutub-ud din died shortly, in 1459 CE, and his son Daud Shah became the new Sultan of Gujarat. Thus, despite all his opponents combining their forces against him, Kumbha remained an unconquered monarch and Mewar was untouched by the forces of Gujarat and Malwa.

After his earlier triumph over Mahmud Khalji, in 1448 CE Kumbha had commenced the construction of a grand victory tower or Vijay Stambh or Kirti Stambh in the Chittorgarh Fort. By the time the tower was completed in 1458 CE he had not only vanquished the Malwa Sultan but a combined force comprising the Sultan of Gujarat as well. About this spectacular piece of architecture, British Colonel James Tod who chronicled the history of Rajasthan writes: 'The only thing in India to compare with this is the Kootab Minar [sic] at Delhi, but though much higher, it is of a very inferior character. This column is 120 feet in height, the breadth of each face at the base is 35 feet, and at the summit, immediately under the cupola, 17 feet and a half. It stands on an ample terrace, 42 feet square. It has 9 distinct storeys, with openings at every face of each storey and all these doors have colonuaded [sic] porticos.'[11] The whole tower is covered with intricate architectural ornaments and sculptures to such an extent as to leave no plain parts. It has been built largely of compact limestone and quartz rock on which it stands, commanding towering heights just like its builder.

After the campaign against the confederate forces, Kumbha further consolidated his supremacy in the region by subjugating the Deoras of Sirohi and annexing Abu in 1458 CE. In 1467 CE, he decided to assimilate Nagaur and attacked the fort with 50,000 horsemen, killing thousands of the enemy thereby and carrying away several elephants, horses and valuables as war spoils. This was to be among the last major military campaigns of the valorous Rana.

Death of Rana Kumbha

Legend has it that Kumbha was warned by an astrologer that he would die at the hands of a *Chaaran*, a bardic community that remains in attendance on Rajputs and sings their glorious deeds. To pre-empt any harm to himself, Kumbha expelled the entire Chaaran community from Mewar and confiscated their lands. Though a few days before his death, he granted them permission to return to Mewar. On an ill-fated day in 1468 CE when Kumbha was seated meditating and chanting his prayers on the edge of a masonry tank near the temple of Kumbhaswami at Kumbhalgarh that he had built ten years ago, his eldest son Udai Karan treacherously stabbed him to death. Udai Karan apprehended that his father might install his favourite son Rai Mal as heir and not him and hence took this ghastly step. Udai Karan has been castigated in the annals of Rajputana as '*Udo Hatiaro*' or Udai, the killer.[12] It was a sad irony that a man who remained unvanquished in so many fierce battles had to meet his untimely end in this inglorious way, at the hands of his own son and while he was immersed in prayer. Thus, after a reign of thirty-five years of glory, conquests and splendour, the chivalrous Maharana Kumbha departed, but left behind a legacy etched in golden words in the annals of Indian history.

The Great Builder and Scholar

In addition to being the unvanquished monarch, Rana Kumbha was also a master builder whose legacy lives on in the form of innumerable forts, palaces and temples that he got constructed during his reign. Colonel James Tod states: 'He triumphed over the enemies of his race, fortified his country with strongholds, embellished it with temples, and with the superstructure of her fame laid the foundations of his own.'[13] Fortifying the passes between the western frontier of Mewar and Abu, Kumbha erected the fort of Vasanti, founded Vasantapur[14] and also built seven lakes near it. The forts of Machan, Kolana, Vairat and Ahore were some of the other prominent forts that he built. Given the constant skirmishes that Mewar was involved in with the neighbouring sultans, the need to safeguard and protect his kingdom against aggression is what drove this massive fortification drive.

On the peak of Mount Abu, in 1452 CE he built a citadel, which is famous as Ahalagarh. In his travels through Rajasthan, Tod writes about this:

> The traveller would find the ruined towers of Achalgarh (*Ahalagarh*) buried in the dense masses of cloud that surround him. The first pol (gate) of this ancient fortress is the Hanuman Pol, which is composed of two noble towers built with huge blocks of granite, black with rude

blasts of some 1000 winters. The towers had been connected at the top by a guard room, and the gate served as the entrance to the lower fort, whose dilapidated walls are discernable up the irregular ascent. Another portal called the Champa Pol, from a noble Champa tree close to it, which formerly denominated the "Gate of Wisdom" conducts to the inner fortress. The first object that strikes the view on passing the latter gate is the Jain temple to Paraswanath, erected at the sole expense of a banker of Mandoo . . . the upper fortress is attributed to Kumbha . . . there are the ruins of a granary, the Bhandar of Koombha Rana, coated within with a very strong cement. Close on the left is the palace of Oka Rani, his queen, so designated from being of Oka Mandal, near the Land's End of the Hindus. A small lake in the keep is called Sawan Bhadoon, and well merits the name of the two chief months of the monsoon, for in the middle of June it is yet full of water. On the most elevated knoll to the east are the remains of an alarm tower which still bears Koombha's name.[15]

At Abu, Kumbha built the temple of Kumbhaswami that still stands, with a large tank named Ramakund in front of it.[16] He contributed richly to the construction of a spectacular three-storied Jain temple that was built by his favourite architect Dharnak. The temple's foundations were laid in 1438 CE, and it is dedicated to Rishabdeva, the first Jain tirthankara. Kumbha also had the famous Eklingaji temple in Mewar renovated and constructed the Kumbha Mandapa in front of the sanctum.

In addition to his heroic exploits, Kumbha was also a polymath with several scholastic interests ranging from music to drama, poetry and Sanskrit over which he had considerable mastery. Some seminal works on Indian musicology such as *Sangitaraja*, *Sangita Mimansa* and *Rasika Priya* (a commentary on the celebrated *Gita Govinda* of Jaideva) and a commentary on *Sangita Ratnakara* of Sharangadeva are attributed to Kumbha's authorship. These works demonstrate his keen interest and scholarship in both the art and science of Indian classical music. He contributed the last chapter to the famed treatise *Eklinga Mahatmya* and is said to have authored four plays and a commentary on the Chandi Shataka. The Chittorgarh inscription credits him with knowledge of several languages too, including Karnataki (Kannada perhaps) and Maharashtri (possibly Marathi). It is quite amazing that despite a reign splattered with endless conquests and wars, Kumbha managed to nourish his sensitive side through an engagement with the fine arts and literature.

While Indian historiography might not have been kind enough to Rana Kumbha by documenting his life and heroism in the manner that he deserves to be commemorated, folklore and oral history that celebrate the glory of Rana Kumbha, as also the innumerable monuments and works of literature, keep his memory alive. Rana Kumbha became the prototype of the brave Rajput who was unconquerable in the wake of any aggression and who combined deft strategy with raw power to keep all his enemies at bay. That same spirit of valour kept burning relentlessly in the Rajput clan for generations to come.

Notes

1   For detail information of please refer to https://www.guinnessworldrecords. com/world-records/399990-longest-fort-walls (Accessed on 6 May 2022).

2   Chittorgarh Kirtistambha Inscription, Verse 179. Also, Kumbhalmer in-scription of Kumbha. See Har Bilas Sarda, *Rana Kumbha: Sovereign, Soldier* (Ajmer: Scottish Mission Institutions Company Limited, 1917) for more details.

3   Sarda, *Rana Kumbha*, pp. 12–14.

4   Translation from the Persian *Tarik-i-Firishta* of Ferishta: Alexander Dow, trans., *History of Hindostan*, Vol. 2 (London: T. Becket and P.A. De. Hondt., 1768), p. 6.

5   For details, see Sarda, *Rana Kumbha*, pp. 32–35.

6   Ibid., p. 48.

7   Sir Edward Clive Bayley, *The Local Muhammadan Dynasties of Gujarat* (London: W.H. Allen & Co., 1886), p. 148.

8   The Chittorgarh Kirtistambha Inscription repeats these facts and states that he destroyed 'the great mosque built by Sultan Firoz, which showed Moslems the way to Nagor' (Verse 19). Verse 22 says: 'He uprooted the Mussalman tree of Nagor and destroyed it with all its mosques.'

9   Commentary on the *Gita Govinda* (said to have been written by Kumbha himself), verses 60–62, reiterates these.

10   Chittorgarh Kirtistambha Inscription cited in Sarda, *Rana Kumbha*, p. 55.

11 Lt Col James Tod, *Annals & Antiquities of Rajasthan or, the Central & Western Rajpoot States of India*, Vol. 2 (London: Routledge & Kegan Paul Ltd., 1832), p. 761.

12 Sarda, *Rana Kumbha*, p. 65.

13 Tod, *Annals and Antiquities*, Vol 1., p. 290.

14 Chittorgarh Kirti Stambh Inscription.

15 James Tod, *Travels in Western India* (London: W.H. Allen & Co., 1839), pp. 94–95.

16 Chittorgarh Kirti Stambh Inscription, Verses 12 and 13, cited in Sarda, *Rana Kumbha*.

Rani Abbakka Chowta of Ullal

Amidst the expansive green fields of Tulunadu (today's Dakshina Kannada and portions of Udupi districts in Karnataka and Kasargod in Kerala) in coastal Karnataka, in the wee hours of the night, villagers gather to witness a spectacular performance of music, dance and heady vibes. Termed as *bhoota aradhane*, literally a worship of the spirits, it has religious connotations too. The spirit possesses the body of the performer who acts as a medium in this séance and conveys the story to the audience, in a trance. Through verses, singing, storytelling and dance, the story of the spirit invoked is communicated to the spellbound audience through this art form that blurs the horizon between the living and the departed. The performance has definite stages from the invocation to the climatic finale. In these *bhoota aradhane* performances, an oft-invoked spirit is that of a valorous queen of the little town of Ullal, Abbakka Mahadevi, as she is hailed by the locals. Sources, such as archival records, travelogues of several Portuguese travellers and historical analysis point towards the presence of two or three Abbakkas,[1] all of whom fought against the Portuguese army between the 1550s and 1640s CE. Folklore and performances such as the *bhoota aradhane* or *yakshagana* treat all three Abbakkas as one great queen and a brilliant personality Abbakka Mahadevi or Rani Abbakka. In the complete absence of proper archival documentation around the queens, the life stories of the women are interchangeably used and are prone to much error. But more than the details of each individual, what is important is this constant and successful feminine resistance that this small region in coastal Karnataka offered to a mighty European power, the Portuguese, for several decades.

Coming of the Europeans

The end of the fifteenth century saw the advent of the Europeans to Indian shores, in what was to become the first in a series of such expeditions. While initially they were inspired by trade, quickly their motivation metamorphosed into a capture of political power and colonization. Right from the seventh century, maritime trade in spices, textiles, war horses and other commodities flourished between India's western coast and the Arabian Peninsula. This trade was too lucrative to escape the attention of several European powers who were drawn towards it and began a series of discoveries of a sea route to India. It was the Portuguese who first managed to reach the Indian shores in 1498 CE with Vasco da Gama reaching Calicut after a long voyage. Cochin saw the first Portuguese fort five years later, after which a ring of forts came up in the Indian Ocean region—in India, Muscat, Mozambique, Sri Lanka, Indonesia, even as far as Macau in China. These new fortifications and the superior naval technology that was at their command, enabled the Portuguese to completely monopolize all the spice routes to India within merely two decades of Vasco da Gama's historic voyage. This monopoly of the Portuguese remained unchallenged for almost the whole of the sixteenth century, as the other European powers such as the Dutch, the English and the French found their way to India only in the seventeenth century. The Portuguese imposed a paid permit (Cartaz) to trade in the Indian Ocean, which had hitherto been a free trade zone for Indian, Arab, Persian and African ships. Even Mughal Emperor Akbar had to take a Cartaz from the Portuguese for any ships travelling on the Indian Ocean. The naval superiority of the Portuguese enabled them to crush any local rulers and chieftains who rebelled, and this contributed to strengthening their stranglehold in a very short time.

Under one of their most successful Indian governors, Afonso de Albuquerque, the Portuguese captured many territories, including Goa in 1510, from the Bijapur Sultanate. Goa became their capital in the Indian Ocean. Over time, they also created bases at various ports along the Western Indian coast—at Daman, Salsette, Bombay and Diu. The brutalities that the Portuguese inflicted on the people they conquered, especially in Goa under the infamous Inquisition,[2] was blood-curdling due to the kind of atrocities meted out. However, their advances were met with stiff resistance by smaller kingdoms along the western coast like Ullal and Calicut (Kozhikode). These principalities had hitherto traded directly with the Arabs and hence refused to comply with a new player establishing their supremacy over the seas and imposing steep taxes. Constant naval skirmishes and attacks on the towns and ports of these smaller principalities by the Portuguese navy and army became the norm, but the chieftains never gave up. Many of them remained a thorn in the flesh of the Europeans for almost two centuries, till they were finally annexed by the British after the fall of the ruler of Mysore, Tipu Sultan, in 1799 CE.

In 1526 CE, the Portuguese under Viceroy Lopo Vaz de Sampio captured the Mangalore port. Their next target was Ullal, a thriving port town that lay nestled between the verdant peaks of the Western Ghats and the cerulean blue waters of the Arabian Sea. This brought them in direct conflict with the Chowtas who held sway over this principality of Ullal.

The Chowtas of Ullal

The Chowtas ruled over a small but fertile part of coastal Canara—Ullal, which was about 10 km from Mangalore. Mangalore had been an important port for the export of spices and textiles since the beginning of the common era. As mentioned earlier, trade routes with the Arabs from this part of the country were in vogue since the seventh century, with several local Muslim communities such as the Mapillas (Moplahs) in Malabar and the Byaris in Tulunadu carrying on the maritime trade of pepper, ginger and other spices. Indian spices including black pepper, cloth, rice, medicines, jaggery, sugar, among others, were in great demand in Europe and Mediterranean countries. These were produced abundantly in the entire coastal belt. The small coastal kingdoms grew rich on account of maritime trade—the silver and gold that had been looted from the Aztecs and Incas poured into India as payment for spices and textiles.

Mangalore was an important and strategic port for the Raya emperors of Vijayanagara. Along with Bhatkal and Honnavar, they were the empire's international ports. Well-bred Arab and Persian war horses that were their major source of power were brought into the empire by the Arabs through the port of Mangalore. More than a dozen chieftains ruled in this region and their suzerainty often did not exceed more than 100 to 200 villages. Prominent among them were Santras (Bairarasas) of Karkala, the Bangas of Bangadi (Nandavar), the Sawants of Mulki, the Chowtas of Mudbidri and Ullal, the Ajilas of Venur and the Tolahas of Sura. Most of these chieftains either intermarried to forge strategic alliances or kept fighting among themselves and with the local administrators of Vijayanagara to assert their independence or to demand a reduction in the tributes and subsidies that they paid to the empire's exchequers. But the strong central government of Vijayanagara kept them under a tight leash, under the overall supervision of the powerful nayakas of Keladi.

But the Battle of Talikota (or Rakkasatangadi) in 1565 CE dealt a death blow to the Vijayanagara Empire. It was a watershed battle between the Rayas and the confederate Deccan Sultanates. The empire progressively collapsed after this blow and all the subordinate governors and minor chieftains began vying for individual supremacy and independence. Hiriya Venkatappa Nayaka of Keladi (1586–1629 CE) who had annexed Gerusoppa at the time was slowly trying to maintain his hegemony over the entire region, which was by then fully infested with Portuguese pirates, looters and marauders at sea.

The Chowtas were Jain kings who had supposedly migrated to Tulunadu from Gujarat in the twelfth century. The clear documentation around the dynasty is, however, available only from the fourteenth century. One of the earliest rulers of the clan was Thirumalaraya Chowta I (1160–79 CE) who is credited with establishing the dynasty with Ullal as the seat of power. After him, his son-in-law Channaraya Chowta I (1179–1219 CE) made Puttige the capital and built a small palace there. In 1255 CE, Thirumalaraya II built the Somanatha temple in Puttige, despite the clan being Jains by faith. The principality split in 1544 CE with two capitals, one at Ullal and another at Puttige.

Rani Abbakka I[3]

The Chowtas followed a matrilineal system (called *Aliya Santhana Kattu*) but were not matriarchal. This is an interesting system (followed also in some communities like the Nairs in Kerala) wherein the inheritance descends from the female line, but the rule is by the male member. The ruler's sister's son becomes the king. However, in the sixteenth century, the Chowta ruler Thirumala Raya III had no nephews or legitimate heirs. His wife, possibly the first of the Abbakkas succeeded him.[4] She was trained in military sciences, warfare, archery and sword fighting. Folklore depicts her as a prodigious child, unequalled in her military exploits and artistic capabilities. When she was crowned the queen of Ullal (sometime possibly in the 1540s), Abbakka was acutely aware of the threat posed by the Portuguese since they had come so close home to the port of Mangalore that they had annexed in 1525 CE. The annexation of Mangalore by the Portuguese was followed by loot, plunder, burning and pillage that continued till 1531 CE.[5] Given the experience with the Portuguese in the near vicinity, Abbakka had a strong, impregnable fort constructed at Ullal to pre-empt any attacks. She appears in Portuguese records in 1555 CE where she is referred to as 'Bukkorani of Ballala'.[6]

With an eye on Ullal's lucrative trade that had flourished under the queen's able leadership, the Portuguese had been trying to exact tributes and taxes from Rani Abbakka. More than 200 Portuguese landed in coastal areas of Karnataka and demanded goods be sold at a price fixed by them. Abbakka protested the demand and was unwilling to accept the Portuguese embargo since her ships had been travelling to the Middle East to sell spices and fabrics since several centuries. For this trade, she was in an alliance with the Zamorin (the Hindu ruler, the Saamudrin or Protector of the Seas) of Kozhikode. She continued defying the Portuguese diktats and continued trading directly with the Middle East. From Mogaveeras and Billava archers to Mapilla oarsmen, people of all castes and religions found a place in Abbakka's army and navy. The Portuguese captured the trading ship of Ullal that was on its way to the Middle East, in mid-sea. An angered Abbakka attacked Mangalore fort where the Portuguese had built a factory. Infuriated by her effrontery to their authority, the Portuguese began attacking Ullal repeatedly.

Wars with the Portuguese

The first battle between the Portuguese and Abbakka took place in 1555 CE[7] when the former sent Admiral Dom Álvaro da Silveira against the queen with twenty-one battleships. Several innocent people in Ullal were tortured and murdered by the invading fleet. Attempts were made to desecrate the Somanatha temple in Ullal, which was bravely resisted by the nayakas of Abbakka, who died fighting for this cause. Abbakka then formed several strategic alliances with the other chieftains and rulers of the coastal region including the Zamorin of Calicut against the common enemy. She fought with great courage and pushed them back and the war ended in an uneasy truce. As per the agreement, Abbakka was forced to hand over some part of the trade revenue as taxes to the Portuguese. The portions of the temple that had been vandalized were reconstructed and an epitaph in honour of the deceased brave martyrs was installed there by the queen.[8] Though she was forced to give up a portion of her revenue as part of the treaty, Portuguese records have themselves praised the brave fight that the queen put up.[9] But she was determined to undo the terms of the treaty.

Three years later, in 1558 CE, Abbakka had her second brush with the Portuguese as documented by their historian Diogo do Couto in his book *Decada Da Asia*.[10] The trigger for this was the abrupt termination of the tributes by Abbakka that she was supposed to pay the Portuguese as per the earlier treaty and her alliance with the Zamorin to continue trading in the Middle East, Persia and Arabia without the Cartaz. The flashpoint was when the Portuguese attacked Abbakka's erstwhile ally, the Raja of Cannanore, who had assisted her in the earlier battle—she sent him her military support in a naval attack against the invaders. The Portuguese were so incensed at this that they virtually reduced Mangalore to ashes. Thousands of men and women, both young and old, were put to death, temples plundered, ships burnt and finally the city itself was set on fire in the campaign that was led by the viceroy of Goa Antonio de Noronha. Contemporary chronicler Father Francisco D'souza has documented some details of this battle between Abbakka and the Portuguese.[11]

The weakening of the paramount power, the Vijayanagara Empire, after 1565 CE emboldened the Portuguese to make further attacks on the coastal kingdoms. In 1567 CE, a punitive expedition was sent against[12] Abbakka by the Portuguese governor under General Joao Peixoto, who attacked Ullal, captured the city and occupied the palace. However, the queen managed to escape in time and hid in a mosque (some historians say she hid in the hillocks). In the dead of night, with more than 6,000 soldiers comprising Mapillas, Mogaveeras, Billavas and Bunts,[13] she led a frontal attack, riding her horse and raiding the Portuguese in stealth when they were steeped in a victorious, drunken revelry. Launching a surprise attack on them, Abbakka managed to kill General Peixoto and seventy of his soldiers. The invaders fled to their ships, being thoroughly disgraced. Abbakka followed in hot pursuit and killed the admiral of the fleet, Mascarenhas, along with the help of her 6,000 soldiers in 1568 CE, and the foreign army was forced to vacate Mangalore Fort.

The hitherto bonhomie between the rulers of Ullal and Banga deteriorated during Abbakka's time and this division was exploited by the Portuguese to side the Bangas against the Chowtas. The Portuguese and the Bangas under Veera Narasimha Lakshmapparasa reached an alliance in 1567 CE and a new fortification of the foreign powers came up in Mangalore. These caused enmity between the two coastal powers that had been on fairly friendly terms till then. Portuguese records of 1569 CE talk of intense rivalry and skirmishes between the Chowtas and the Bangas that saw the intervention of the Viceroy of Goa Dom Luís de Ataíde who came to settle the matter.

Despite being embroiled in life-long skirmishes with the Portuguese, Abbakka paid a lot of attention to toning the administration of her dominion and to providing care and relief to her citizens. She also made endowments to religious institutions. Her sister Padumaladevi gave a grant to the Basadi (Jain temple) of Tirthankara Parshwanath.

In 1570 CE, Abbakka was part of a major strategic alliance with the Bijapur Adil Shahi Sultan, the Ahmednagar Sultan, the Zamorin of Calicut and Rani Bhairadevi of Gerusoppa. The idea was to forge a united front of all the powers who were opposing the Portuguese. Kutty Pokar Markar, a general of the Zamorin, was invited by Abbakka to Ullal and he fought on her behalf and destroyed the Portuguese fortifications at Mangalore that they had recaptured by 1569 CE along with Kundapura, but while returning he was killed by the Portuguese.

A stunned Portuguese were finally determined to send a considerable force to vanquish Abbakka who had repeatedly handed over humiliating defeats on their troops. Three thousand Portuguese troops supported by a huge armada of battleships attacked Ullal in a surprise predawn attack in around 1584 CE (some say 1588 CE). Rani Abbakka was returning from a visit to her family temple and was caught totally off guard by this sudden attack. But she immediately mounted her horse and rode into the battle, leading her troops in a fierce counteroffensive against the invaders. Her piercing battle cry: 'Save the motherland. Fight them on land and the sea. Fight them on the streets and the beaches. Push them back to the waters', echoed through the winds as she and her soldiers fired several flaming arrows at the Portuguese ships. While many of the ships in the Portuguese armada burnt that night, Rani Abbakka herself was grievously wounded in the crossfire. She was captured by the enemy with the help of a few bribed chieftains. Rebellious till the very end, the fearless queen breathed her last in captivity.

Rani Abbakka II

In the interim, Abbakka's daughter Thirumaladevi is supposed to have taken over the reign of the Chowta dynasty. Some say it was Abbakka's son (name unknown) who succeeded her. The rivalry with the Bangas seemed to continue with a queen there, too, named Veera Narasimha Shankaradevi (around 1587 CE).[14] The Portuguese naturally supported their traditional allies, the Bangas, who managed to wrest some lost territory and power back from the Chowtas. There seems to have been some political vacuum and turbulence in Ullal for a while, and around 1594 CE the deceased Abbakka I's sister Abbakka II took over the mantle of the kingdom. She turned out to be a worse nightmare for the Portuguese than her sister.

Among the first decisions she took after becoming queen was to stop the payment of tribute to the Portuguese, to rebuild and strengthen her fortress in Ullal, build an armoury there and stock explosives, and maintain a regular force of 500 soldiers for its defence and a standing army of 1,100 war-ready soldiers. She also withdrew all the trade concessions that had been given to the Portuguese in Ullal. Only specially invited foreign tradesmen were allowed to carry on commercial activities in her kingdom. Special fleets were designed for the export of rice, textiles, coconuts, spices and sugarcane. Her new fortifications caused an alarm for the Portuguese. Abbakka also renewed the alliance with the Zamorin of Calicut for joint trade expeditions across the seas to Arabia and Persia. She maintained amicable relations with the admirals of the Zamorin's fleet, known by the title of Kunjali Marakkar. The Kunjali Marakkars are credited with organizing the first naval defence of the Indian coast.

Abbakka II was married to Banga ruler Veera Narasimha Lakshmapparasa IV of Bangadi (r. 1613–31 CE) who was obviously predisposed towards the Portuguese and depended on sops offered by them (some scholars like Dr K.G. Vasantha Madhava opine that her husband was Kamarasa (r. 1598–1611 CE) of the Banga clan; we are not sure of the exact name of her spouse). He reigned in his own region that bordered her domain. This was a strategic marriage of convenience rather than one of conviction. Tensions constantly prevailed between the couple, and they hardly lived together, rather in their respective dominions. They met occasionally at the borders of their kingdoms in boats with tents erected over them to see and converse with one another and spend some time. Though this bonhomie prevailed for some time, one does not know what caused a sudden rupture in the relationship—possibly Lakshmapparasa's dalliances with other women. Another reason seems to have been the competition between the parents on controlling their daughter and whom she must wed—which, in the matrilineal system prevalent in Ullal, rested entirely with the mother, and the father had no say. The Banga ruler had made unsuccessful attempts to even have his own daughter kidnapped to have his way.

Abbakka sent back all the jewels that he had given her while taking her as his wife, thereby indicating the intention of a divorce from him. This greatly offended Lakshmapparasa who declared a kind of a war against his estranged wife. One day, when she was on an unguarded cruise on the Netravati River, he sent his soldiers on boats and took her captive. Through her good words and kind behaviour she somehow managed to fool him into forgiveness and to let her off.

On returning to Ullal, Abbakka was burning with the fire of revenge on this humiliation, and she declared a formal war against Bangadi. Lakshmapparasa decided to ally with his friends, the Portuguese, who were only too happy to align themselves against their traditional foe, the queen of Ullal. Lakshmapparasa had rubbed Venkatappa Nayaka of Keladi, too, the wrong way and so he became a natural ally of Abbakka in this war. Thus, all the major powers of the region got sucked into a skirmish that was borne out of a familial dispute. Venkatappa Nayaka sent a powerful army in favour of the queen, defeated Lakshmapparasa, destroyed the fort of Bangadi and rendered them his tributaries. The Banga ruler fled to Kasargod to save his life. The combined forces of Keladi Nayaka and Abbakka defeated the Portuguese in Mangalore, though they did not capture it. The Portuguese army suffered huge losses and a large number of their soldiers were killed in the battle. A treaty ensued with the Portuguese ending the skirmish, whereby Abbakka was allowed to retain her fortifications and also got back her fleet that the Portuguese had wrongfully captured. The battle thus ended conclusively in Abbakka's favour though she was now to be beholden to the suzerainty of the Keladi Nayaka to whom she had to surrender the territory of Bedde (near Moodabidri). But it allowed her to reign over her dominions in peace and quietude, without the interference of either the Portuguese or her estranged spouse. At least for a brief while. After the death of Venkatappa Nayaka, by around 1630 CE, a fiercely independent and self-respecting Abbakka raised an unsuccessful rebellion against Keladi along with several coastal rulers, including her once-rival from Banga, to regain the lost territories.

Egged on by Lakshmapparasa's son-in-law Kamarasa III,[15] the Portuguese, who as it is considered the queens of Ullal as a thorn in their flesh, made another daring attempt on Ullal in 1618 CE. They captured a rich ship of hers that was returning from Mecca. The Portuguese then surrounded Ullal with their naval fleet at sea and waited for a proper opportunity to strike. Abbakka had kept a close watch on the moves of the enemy and wanted to pre-empt any attacks from them. On a dark new-moon night, a band of her fearless Mogaveeras and Mapilla soldiers got into country boats on Abbakka's instructions. They approached the Portuguese warships that were waiting at sea. On receiving a signal, the soldiers threw hundreds and hundreds of burning coconut torches (*agni banas* or *thoote*) simultaneously on the unsuspecting fleet. The sails caught fire and the enemy ships started burning. Those who wanted to save their lives jumped into the sea, only to be killed by the waiting soldiers of Abbakka. Two hundred Portuguese soldiers were killed in this ambush and two warships sank according to Portuguese sources; the Portuguese navy rushed back with huge losses and a bigger loss of face.

The Italian Memoirs

This daring feat made Abbakka famous across the Indian Ocean and beyond, that a queen had managed to burn an entire fleet of the European power. The Persian Emperor Shah Abbas praised Abbakka to everyone he met, including Pietro Della Valle (1586–1652 CE). Della Valle was an Italian composer, musicologist and author who travelled across Asia during the European Renaissance period. His travels took him to the Middle East, Asia and India. Shah Abbas supposedly asked

Pietro Della Valle to specifically go to India and meet the daring queen Abbakka who had ruined the peace of the Portuguese.

And so, on 9 December 1623, Pietro Della Valle reached Ullal (which he called Olaza) and it is in his memoirs that we get a first-person account of Rani Abbakka, whom he met while he was in India. He toured the western coast of India between 1621 and 1624 CE. Della Valle writes that Olaza had a sizeable population of both Hindus and Muslims, and that the queen seldom stayed here, normally holding court elsewhere in her dominion. He then took a boat from Mangalore to Manel where the queen was residing. The country was, according to Della Valle, 'open, fair and fruitful, inhabited by abundance of little Houses and Cottages here and there of husband-men, besides those united to the great street called the *Bazar*, or Market; all which are comprehended under the name of Manel'.[16] While he was at the bazaar, the queen propitiously happened to be coming right there, on foot like a commoner rather than as a regal personality. She had four or five men as foot soldiers who accompanied her and who were 'quite naked after their manner, saving that they had a cloth over their shame, and another like a sheet worn cross the shoulders like a belt; each of them had a sword in his hand, or at most a sword and buckler; there were also as many behind her of the same sort, one of which carry'd [sic] over her a very ordinary Umbrella made of palm-leaves'.[17] Della Valle was rather disappointed by her appearance as she barely looked like a royal personage to him. He wrote:

> Her complexion was as black as that of a natural Aethiopian [sic]; she was corpulent and gross, but not heavy, for she seem'd [sic] to walk nimbly enough; her Age may be about forty years, although the Portugals had describ'd [sic] her to me much elder. She was cloth'd [sic], or rather girded at the waist, with a plain piece of thick white cotton, and bare-foot, which is the custom of the Indian Gentile Women, both high and low, in the house and abroad . . . From the waist upwards the Queen was naked, saving that she had a cloth tied round about her Head, and hanging a little down upon her breast and shoulders. In brief, her aspect and habit represented rather a dirty Kitchen-wench or Laundress, than a delicate and noble Queen; whereupon, I said within my self, 'Behold

by whom are routed in India the Armies of the King of Spain, which
[=who] in Europe is so great a matter!'

Yet the Queen shew'd [sic] her quality much more in speaking
than by her presence; for her voice was very graceful in respect of her
person, and she spoke like a prudent and judicious Woman. They had
told me that she had no teeth, and therefore was wont to go with half
her Face cover'd [sic]; yet I could not discover any such defect in her,
either by my Eye or by my Ear; and, I rather believe, that this covering
the Mouth, or half the Face, as she sometimes doth, is agreeable to the
modest custom which I know to be common to almost all Women in
the East. I will not omit, that though she were so corpulent as I have
mention'd [sic], yet she seems not deform'd [sic], but I imagine she was
handsome in her Youth; and indeed, the report is, that she hath been a
brave Lady, though rather of a rough than a delicate handsomeness.[18]

Seeing her come, everyone in the bazaar stepped aside to give her
place to pass. Noticing the foreigner amongst the gathering, Abbakka
enquired about Della Valle and if an interpreter was there for her to
speak to him. She heard with rapt attention the introduction that
Della Valle gave of himself and his ancestry from Rome and enquired
about the places he had visited already. When told that he had visited
the Great Turks, the Persians, the Mughals and even Venkatappa
Nayaka, she asked self-effacingly what was he, then, doing in her
woods after seeing such splendid places as her dominion was not
worth seeing. Della Valle replied that he had come all the way not to
see her kingdom but to meet her as tales of her bravery had travelled
far and wide. This greatly pleased her. Her maternal instincts then
came to the fore whereby she enquired what he would do in this
distant land, so far away from his near and dear ones and family, if he
fell sick or if any disaster struck, and if he had adequate measures to
take care of himself. To this question of deep concern and compassion
that the queen asked him, Della Valle replied with self-assurance that
wherever he went his God went with him and hence he was not in
the least perturbed about his own well-being. She then asked him if
he had become this aimless wanderlust after losing someone beloved
or suffering a heartbreak, once again with the greatest of concern writ
large on her face. Della Valle assured her that it was none of such

triggers that made him wander but a desire to see diverse countries, cultures and people that made him traverse the world. After several such questions and a long conversation, Rani Abbakka bid him farewell and told him to meet her again on a later date of mutual convenience.

The documentation of this meeting brought to the fore several of Abbakka's qualities as a ruler who had such loving concern, even for a foreigner to her kingdom, and her having kept this softer side of herself alive in spite of being in the rough and tumble of frequent wars. She was a just queen, who also took keen interest in the welfare of her subjects and along with matters of trade that were the mainstay, agriculture and irrigation projects consumed all her personal attention. She was broad-minded and egalitarian and had supported the inter-caste marriage of a Mogaveera boy with a Jain girl, much to the anger of the orthodoxy.[19]

Della Valle was totally taken in by her demeanour. He asked the people of the town to tell him more about the queen and her personal life. From the locals he got to know about her succeeding her sister, her troubles with her estranged husband and that she had a son who was now going to succeed her as per the matrilineal system. He also heard rumours of the queen having an elder son, whom she had wilfully poisoned to death as she feared that the ambitious young man might usurp her throne. But Della Valle dismissed these as Portuguese propaganda to paint the queen as a heartless tyrant and defame her. After all, if she had been so insecure about her throne, she would not have spared her younger son who was now living with her in the palace, he rationalized.

Evidently Abbakka seems to have mentioned about the foreigner she met at the bazaar to her son, who then sent word to Della Valle to meet him. He was called the king though it was his mother who ran the affairs of state. Describing the palace that he went to and his meeting with Abbakka's son, Della Valle wrote (and reproduced here in considerable measure for its delightful details):

> The Palace (which may rather be call'd [sic] a Royal Lodge) is entered into by a Gate like the grate or lattice of our Vine-yards at Rome,

ordinary enough, seated in the midst of a field, which like them is divided by a small hedge from the neighboring fields. Within the Gate is a broad Walk or Alley, on the right side whereof is a spacious plot sown, at the end of which, the Walk turns to the right hand, and there upon the same plot stands the Royal Mansion, having a prospect over all the said great green field. In the middle of this second Walk, you enter into the House, ascending seven or eight wooden stairs, which lead into a large Porch, the length of which is equal to the whole fore-part of the House. This Porch was pav'd [sic] with Cow-dung after their manner, the walls about [=around] shining, and painted with a bad red colour much us'd [sic] by them. The fore-part of it, which is all open, is up-held by great square posts, of no great height (for 'tis their custom to make all buildings, especially Porches, but low in respect of the breadth and length, with very broad Pent-houses; which is, I believe, by reason of the great heat of the Country, where they have more need of shadow and coolness, than of air or light). Directly opposite to the stairs in the middle of the Porch, was another small Porch, which was all the entrance into the inner part of the building.

Within the little Porch was a small room long and narrow, where the King sat near the wall on the left side; and he sat upon the ground after the Eastern manner upon one of those coarse clothes, which in Persia and Turkie are called Krelim [=qilim], and serve for poor people; nor was it large, but only so much as to contain the Person of the King, the rest of the room being bare, saving that it was polish'd [sic] with Cow-dung. Beside the King, but a little farther on his left hand, sat upon a little mat, sufficient only to contain him, a Youth of about fifteen or eighteen years of age, called *Bale Nairu*, who was his Nephew, and is to succeed him, being the Son of his deceased Sister, who was Daughter to the present Queen . . . None other sat with the King, but three or four of his more considerable servants stood in the room talking with him; and in the great Porch, outside the little one, stood in files on either side other servants of inferior degree, two of which nearest the entrance ventilated the Air with fans of green Taffeta in their Hands, as if to drive away the flies from the King or the entrance; a Ceremony us'd [sic], as I have said elsewhere, by Indian Princes for Grandeur; and they told me, the green colour was a Ceremony too, and the proper badge of the King of Olaza, for the King of Bangbel [Bangadi] uses crimson; other Princes, white, as I saw us'd [sic] by Venk-tapa Naieka [Venkatappa Nayaka]; and others, perhaps other colours: A small company indeed, and a poor appearance for a King; which call'd [sic] to my remembrance those ancient Kings, Latinus, Turnus, and Evander, who, 'tis likely, were Princes of the same sort.

The King was young, not above seventeen years of age, as they told me, yet his aspect spoke him elder; for he was very fat and healthy, as I could conjecture of him sitting, and besides, he had long hairs of a beard upon his cheeks, which he suffer'd [sic] to grow without cutting, though they appear'd [sic] to be but the first down. Of complexion he was dusky, not black, as his Mother is, but rather of an earthy colour, as almost all the Malabars habitually are. He had a louder and bigger voice than Youths of his age habitually have, and in his speaking, gestures, and all other things he shew'd [sic] Judgment and manly gravity. From the girdle upwards he was all naked, saving that he had a thin cloth painted with several colours cast across his shoulders. The hair of his head was long after their manner, and tied in one great knot, which hung on one side wrapt [sic] up in a little plain linen, which looks like a night-cap fallen on one side. From the girdle downwards I saw not what he wore, because he never rose from his seat, and the Chamber was somewhat dark; besides that, the painted cloth on his shoulders hung down very low. His Nephew who sat beside him was not naked, but clad in a whole white garment; and his Head was wrapt [sic] up in a greater volume, white, like a little Turban.[20]

It was a brief meeting that Della Valle had with the young man where he kept standing supported by his sword as he did not wish to squat on the floor like his hosts. Identical questions were asked of him as the mother had. Della Valle apologized for not having carried any gift for the king as it had been long since he left his country and so instead, he presented a map of the world from Italy. A hugely impressed king then spent considerable time trying to decipher the various aspects of the map and expressed a desire to travel to several of these countries. Abbakka had once again resumed her travels outside Manel and so he could not meet her while he was at the palace. He did call on her briefly while she was in the middle of commanding labourers, but she told him that she would call him later to meet her. Della Valle waited for a couple of days, soaking in the landscapes of Manel in the meanwhile, including visiting a shrine to a 'devil' that the queen had established and hurling profanities at it. Despite waiting and sending reminders, the queen did not call for him again and so he left Manel without intruding into her privacy again. But these brief accounts of Della Valle give a good picture of Abbakka, her palace, her family and also of her kingdom and its customs.

Abbakka II ruled till about 1640 CE and not much else is known of the rest of her regime or of any more skirmishes with the Portuguese. A third Abbakka is supposed to have ruled from Moodbidri from 1666 to 1671 CE and a fourth one from 1719 to 1725, CE though not much is known about them. Haidar Ali of Mysore subdued the dynasty's power to a great extent, and thereafter the Chowtas became figurehead rulers in the region.

Our historiography might have been unfair to the Abbakkas of Ullal by not resurrecting their stories enough or placing them suitably within the rubric of Indian history. But in 2003, the Indian Post issued a special stamp dedicated to Rani Abbakka, while in 2015 the Indian Navy acknowledged her naval heroics by naming a patrol vessel after her. In today's Dakshina Kannada district in Karnataka, an annual celebration called Veera Rani Abbakka Utsava is held since a few years, and her statue finds pride of place in Bangalore. A few monuments and memorials of her times are still extant—the Abbakka Devi Basadi in Karkala, Shri Adishwara Parshwanatha Basadi in Ullal, the Somanatha temple, a few fortifications and inscriptions.

And of course, most importantly the heroic tales of Abbakka Mahadevi continue to entertain and inspire the people of Tulunadu through their local performances of *yakshagana* and *bhoota aradhane* till this date.

Notes

1   It is unclear if Abbakka was a generic title given to all queens of the Chowta dynasty or a commonly used title for the ruling ladies, possibly like how the rulers of Calicut were known by the title of Zamorin or Saamudrin, and of the Cannanore rulers as Kolathiri. But some past queens had their original names, such as Padumaladevi I (r. 1335–82 CE) and Channammadevi I (1382–1403 CE), and hence it disputes the theory that 'Abbakka' was a title.

2   The Goan Inquisition was set up in 1560, briefly suspended from 1774 to 1778 and then finally abolished in 1812. It was an extension of the Inquisition in Portugal, targeting neo-converts to Christianity accused of secretly practising their old religion and thereby subjected to the most horrific tortures.

3   Scholars like Dr K.G. Vasanta Madhava, V.K. Yadav Sasihitlu, Prof. Tukaram Pujari and others have also referred to an earlier Abbakka who ruled between 1283 and 1316 CE. So, to that extent this Abbakka becomes the second one in the list. But the two queens who ruled in the sixteenth and seventeenth centuries are jointly known as Hiriya (Elder) and Kiriya (Younger) Abbakka and hence they are named here as Abbakka I and Abbakka II.

4   That Thirumala Raya III was succeeded by his wife and not his niece as is commonly believed is borne out by the account of Pietro Della Valle, 'The Queen's Personal History' Excerpt from Letter VI, from Mangalore, 9 December 1623 in *Selections from the travels of Sig. Pietro della Valle, a noble Roman into East-India and Arabia Desert,* trans. G. Havers (London: Printed by J. Jacock, for John Martin, and James Allestry; and are to be sold at their Shop, at the Bell in St. Paul's Church-yard, 1665). However, scholars such as K.G. Vasantha Madhava and Dr Ganapati Rao Aigal in their writings in *Abbakka Sankathana* believe that it was his niece who succeeded him. The actual relationship between Thirumala Raya and Abbakka would never be conclusively understood. An anthology of writings on Abbakka Ranis by various scholars is a comprehensive volume that readers who are conversant in Kannada can access: Dr Amritha Someshwar, ed., *Abbakka Sankathana* (Mangalore: Veerarani Abbakka Uthsava Samithi, 2011).

5   Antono Nune's *Book of Weights and Measures and Coins* and Simao Bothelo's *The Inventory of the State in India* written in 1554 has details of the destruction of Mangalore as also the corrupt trade practices of the Portuguese.

6   Cited in Dr K.G. Vasantha Madhava, *Abbakka Deviyaru* (Mangalore: Karnataka Tulu Sahitya Akademi, 1998), p. 22.

7   Vasantha Madhava's *Abbakka Deviyaru* dates the first battle to 1556 CE.

8   Vasantha Madhava, *Abbakka Deviyaru*, pp. 25–26.

9   K.G. Vasantha Madhava cites these Portugese records as Asia Portuguesa II, pp. 211–12 in *Abbakka Deviyaru*, p. 26.

10 Diogo do Couto, *Decada Da Asia IV*, (Lisboa: Na Regia Officina Typografica, 1790) MDCCLXXXX, p. 91.

11 Cited in Vasantha Madhava's *Abbakka Deviyaru* which also describes the atrocities in Mangalore, pp. 27–28.

12 Cited in Vasantha Madhava, *Abbakka Deviyaru*, p. 28.

13 Vasantha Madhava, *Abbakka Deviyaru*, p. 29.

14 'A Report on South Indian Epigraphy 1968–69 Ap. A. No. 7' *in Annual Report of Indian Epigraphy* (ARIE), (New Delhi: Director General of Archaeological Survey of India, Government of India, 1968-69).

15 Some consider Kamarasa as the spouse of Abbakka. Lack of documentation, however, severely impedes our understanding of the lineage.

16 Edward Grey, *The Travels of Pietro Della Valle in India*, Vol. 2 (London, Hakluyt Society), p. 306.

17 Ibid.

18 Ibid. p. 307.

19 Vasantha Madhava, *Abbakka Deviyaru*, p. 51.

20 Grey, *The Travels of Pietro Della Valle*, pp. 317–20.

Chand Bibi of
Ahmednagar

The Deccan Sultanates

With the death of the Delhi Sultan Muhammad bin Tughlaq in 1351 CE, south India reconfigured itself into several independent kingdoms. The Vijayanagara Empire that was founded in 1336 CE by the chivalrous Hakka and Bukka and the Bahamani Sultanate, established a decade later, in 1347 CE in Daulatabad (in north Maharashtra) by a former governor of the Tughlaqs, Alauddin Hasan Bahman Shah, became the two major powers to reckon with in the south. However, a little over a century later, by 1481 CE, the Bahamani Sultanate splintered into five independent kingdoms, collectively called the Deccan Sultanates, which were constantly at strife with one another. The Sultanate of Ahmednagar (1490–1633 CE) was established by Malik Ambar, the son of a Telugu Brahmin[1] from Vijayanagara, converted to Islam, and who had risen to the position of chief minister in the Bahamani kingdom. This dynasty was known as the Nizam Shahi. The Sultanate of Bijapur (1490–1686 CE) of the Adil Shahis was founded by Yusuf Adil Shah who was believed to be of Ottoman or Persian descent. The Sultanate of Berar (1490–1574 CE) was established by Imad-ul-Mulk, another convert to Islam; he was born a Kannada Brahmin. The fourth dynasty, Qutub Shahi Sultanate of Golconda (1512–1687 CE), was founded by Quli Qutb-ul-Mulk, a Central Asian Turk. Ali Barid claiming Turkic, Armenian or Hungarian descent established the fifth sultanate of Bidar (1489–1619 CE). The history of these sultanates is a record of almost continuous strife, both external and within, through overambitious nobles. Common jealousies not only prolonged the existence of smaller states but saved each of the larger of annihilation, and the usual course of warfare was a campaign of two of the larger states against the third.

These sultanates shared a curious relationship with Vijayanagara too. Bijapur confabulated with the Vijayanagara Empire for help against their rivals in Ahmednagar. When the son of Rama Raya, the de facto ruler of Vijayanagara and the regent of the young king Sadashiva, died, the Bijapur Sultan Ali Adil Shah (1558–80 CE) courageously went to Vijayanagara in person to offer condolences, with a mere hundred horsemen. Rama Raya received the sultan with utmost respect as he and his wife were so taken in by this warm goodwill gesture. His wife in an impulse even adopted Ali Adil Shah as her own son. After three days of staying on to support Rama Raya, Ali Adil Shah took leave. But curiously took great umbrage at the fact that Rama Raya did not see him off from the city and nursed a grouse against his 'adopted father' for this slight. But he had intense hatred and rivalry with the Nizam Shahi of Ahmednagar, Hussain Nizam Shah, with whom there were perennial territorial disputes. In 1558 CE, the combined forces of Bijapur and Vijayanagara had laid waste to Ahmednagar and looted it. A harried Hussain Nizam Shah sent out entreaties to his counterpart in Golconda who initially supported him, but later switched sides.

However, soon bad blood began to brew between the allies—the Rayas and the sultans. Ibrahim Qutub Shah of Golconda tried to play the peacemaker between the warring kingdoms of Ahmednagar and Bijapur by invoking the need for all 'faithful' to ally together, rather than work in cahoots with the infidels (i.e., the Hindu rulers). It was also brought to the notice of Ali Adil Shah that Rama Raya was getting too wealthy and powerful due to the immense revenues that he was collecting from no less than sixty seaports in addition to large territories and dependencies, much to the disadvantage of all the combined Muslim sultanates. Hence, he was urged to give up his enmity with Ahmednagar and forge a joint alliance against the Rayas. To cement this political rapprochement, it was decided that Hussain Nizam Shah would give in marriage to Ali Adil Shah, his twelve-year-old daughter Chand Bibi, born of his queen Sultana Khunza Humayun. Khunza drew her lineage from a Turkic monarchy in north-western

Iran, known as the Qara Qoyunlu tribe. The teenage girl thus became the pawn in the political marriage that welded the unity between Bijapur and Ahmednagar in 1564 CE. The fortress of Sholapur that was constantly eyed by Ali Adil Shah was to be given away as Chand Bibi's dowry. In return, when Ali Adil Shah's sister Hadia Sultana would come of age, she was to wed Chand Bibi's brother Murtaza. Through these double matrimonial alliances, it was hoped that eternal friendship could be brokered between the warring states.

As a child, Chand Bibi had been a precocious learner. She was very interested in the arts, learnt to play the sitar and was also highly trained in painting. But quite unlike several princesses of the time, she was interested in sporting activities such as hawking, usually reserved for men. From a young age, her father had noticed her keen strategical thinking and military acumen, which was found to be promising. Her pursuits of learning continued in Bijapur, even after her marriage to Ali Adil Shah. She was fluent in several languages—Persian, Dakhani,[2] Arabic, Telugu and Kannada. She is also supposed to have accompanied her husband on some of his military campaigns, including the famous Battle of Talikota.[3] Quite contrary to the norms followed by royal women, Chand Bibi was often seen riding astride a richly caparisoned horse, travelling in the city or going hunting with her face covered by a thin veil.

The Battle of Talikota and After

With a strong alliance being forged by the warring sultanates, at the behest of Golconda, the other two kingdoms of Berar and Bidar, too, joined hands in a rare confederacy and with the common goal of vanquishing the Vijayanagara Empire. To save himself the ignominy of betraying a man who had adopted him as a son, Ali Adil Shah hatched a pretense of dispatching an ambassador to Vijayanagara with preposterous demands. When Rama Raya expectedly threw the ambassador away from the court after disgracing him, this became a convenient ruse to launch a combined attack on an unsuspecting Vijayanagara.

The war, known as the Battle of Talikota, began on 25 December 1564 CE, resulting in a total route for the mighty empire. Hussain Nizam Shah cut off Rama Raya's head with his own hand and hung it on to a long spear, exclaiming 'Now I am avenged of thee! Let God do what he will do to me!'[4] Historian Robert Sewell quotes a contemporary chronicler Ferishta, who notes:

> The plunder was so great that every private man in the allied army became rich in gold, jewels, effects, tents, arms, horses, and slaves, as the sultans, left every person in possession of what he had acquired, only taking elephants for their own use . . . The kingdom of Beejanuggur since this battle has never recovered its ancient splendour; the city itself was so destroyed, that it is now totally in ruins and uninhabited; while the country has been seized on by the tributary chiefs, each of whom hath assumed an independent power in his own district.[5]

Robert Sewell details the loot and plunder of Vijayanagara that followed, and of its famed capital Hampi:

> They (the allies) slaughtered the people without mercy; broke down the temples and palaces; and wreaked such savage vengeance on the abode of the kings, that, with the exception of a few great stone-built temples and walls, nothing now remains but a heap of ruins to mark the spot where once the stately buildings stood. They demolished the statues, and even succeeded in breaking the limbs of the huge Narasimha monolith. Nothing seemed to escape them. They broke up the pavilions standing on the huge platform from which the kings used to watch the festivals and overthrew all the carved work. They lit huge fires in the magnificently decorated buildings forming the temple of Vitthalasvami near the river, and smashed its exquisite stone sculptures. With fire and sword, with crowbars and axes, they carried on day after day their work of destruction. Never perhaps in the history of the world has such havoc been wrought, and wrought so suddenly, on so splendid a city; teeming with a wealthy and industrious population in the full plentitude of prosperity one day, and on the next seized, pillaged, and reduced to ruins, amid scenes of savage massacre and horrors beggaring description . . . such was the fate of this great and magnificent city. It never recovered, but remained forever a scene of desolation and ruin. At the present day the remains of the larger and more durable structures rear themselves

from amongst the scanty cultivation carried on by petty farmers, dwellers in tiny villages scattered over the area once so populous.[6]

But the bonhomie among the warring sultanates was short-lived. With the annihilation of their common foe achieved, they resumed their original rivalries. Chand Bibi's father and the Sultan of Ahmednagar, Hussain Nizam Shah died shortly after this battle and was succeeded by his son Murtaza. Contrary to expectations that the matrimonial alliance would broker peace between the two rival kingdoms, Murtaza, egged on by his mother Khunza Sultana, began to open hostile fronts against Bijapur. After a few battles between them, they reached a truce and agreed not to interfere with each other as they extended their respective domains in different directions. Murtaza who ruled for nearly twenty years conquered Berar in 1574 CE and killed its sultan. Ali Adil Shah focused on subjugating the feudatory nayakas of the erstwhile Vijayanagara Empire. He also tried unsuccessfully to wrest Goa from the Portuguese in 1568 CE.

In 1597 CE, Murtaza attacked the Bidar Sultanate and laid siege to its capital. The distraught Ali Barid sent an emissary to Ali Adil Shah seeking help. Quite revealing of his inclinations, Ali Adil Shah responded that he would agree if Bidar handed over to him two eunuchs whom he was totally besotted with. His sexual inclinations were possibly the reason why Ali Adil Shah and Chand Bibi never had children, neither did any of his other wives beget him offspring.[7] The two eunuchs were reluctant to be handed over to the Bijapur Sultan and when the latter took them to his room to enjoy their company, one of them was incensed enough by his sexual advances and stabbed the sultan to death. This occurred on 20 April 1579. Thus, Ali Adil Shah met an inglorious end, leaving Chand Bibi widowed and his kingdom orphaned.

The Regency of Chand Bibi in Bijapur

Following the scandalous and inglorious death of Ali Adil Shah, his nephew, nine-year old Ibrahim Adil Shah II, son of his brother

Tahmasp, was made the new sultan. Just a few months before his death the sultan had proclaimed his nephew as his heir. Chand Bibi, who was about twenty-nine years of age then, was made the guardian of the infant ruler who would look after his education, and nobleman Kamil Khan Dakkhani was appointed the regent. For a brief while, Kamil Khan behaved with moderation but was soon intoxicated with power and began to show utter disrespect towards Chand Bibi. Sensing his evil intentions, Chand Bibi sent a message to Haji Kishwar Khan, who was a high-ranking official of the sultanate seeking his help to overthrow Kamil in whose place she offered to instate Kishwar. Enticed by the offer, he made common cause with several other chiefs, seized Kamil who tried in vain to flee and put him to death. An insecure Kishwar Khan also allegedly slew anyone who he perceived as a competitor including a senior noble Mustafa Khan. When an incensed Chand Bibi protested, Kishwar Khan had her packed off with severe indignities into confinement for a brief while to Satara. However, some of the Abyssinian officers under Ikhlas Khan defeated Kishwar Khan who fled away in fright. Chand Bibi was reinstated as the king's guardian, and Ikhlas became the new regent. At her request, Afzal Khan Shirazi was made the peshwa or prime minister, a position that Chand Bibi introduced in Bijapur on the Nizam Shahi model.

Taking advantage of the political turmoil in Bijapur, Golconda and Ahmednagar (despite the latter being ruled by Chand Bibi's brother) besieged it with a cavalry of 40,000 in 1580 CE. The Abyssinians who were in charge of the fort in Bijapur were at their wits' end since none of the local Bijapur factions came forward to support them during this crisis. They rushed to Chand Bibi to diffuse the situation. She negotiated a deal wherein the Abyssinians, who had grown in power, would abdicate their position and in return she would wedge a deal within the Bijapur establishment for the defence of the fort. Chand Bibi then decided to take on the enemies head-on. As chronicler Cecil Cowley states:

> The queen, accompanied by her nephew the king, used to go from post to post at night, cheering, encouraging and directing all. The weather

was the severest of the rainy season, and after days of drenching rain and bombardment by the enemy, a portion of the city wall gave way. Notwithstanding the torrential downpour the queen guarded the breach in person, collected the masons of the city, and personally superintended the work of repair, leaving the spot neither by day nor night till it was safe against attack by storm. Her devotion and spirited personal valour inspired confidence in all, which now amounted to positive enthusiasm. The leaders of the various factions went to her in a body, and submitted themselves to her authority. In less than a month many thousands of the followers of the different nobles were collected under proper command within and without the city, and the besieging armies thought it advisable to raise the siege. It had lasted a year.[8]

The siege was finally lifted after one long year. With her knack for creating alliances and military strategy, Chand Bibi called on the Maratha forces to cut off the enemy's supply lines, forcing the besieging force to retreat. The troops of Golconda and Ahmednagar were thrown out in hot pursuit by the Bijapur forces under the daring Dilawar Khan who plundered them. On his return, Dilawar felt puffed enough with strength and confidence to claim the regency and captured it to become the most powerful man in Bijapur. He held sway as the regent for the next eight years when Ibrahim Adil Shah attained maturity and took over the affairs of state.

Chand Bibi felt increasingly sidelined in the new polity in Bijapur. To consolidate ties between the kingdoms of Ahmednagar and Bijapur she suggested the marriage of Ibrahim's sister Khadija Sultana with Murtaza's son Meeran Hussain in 1585 CE. As the aunt of both parties, she decided to accompany the bride to Ahmednagar, her paternal home that she had left two decades ago. Only this time, she decided to stay back and never return to Bijapur.

Back in Ahmednagar

On her return to her parental home, Chand Bibi was quite aghast to see that her brother Murtaza had almost become deranged, leading him to be addressed as 'Murtaza Dewana' (or madman), by the masses. He had imprisoned his mother whom he thought was excessively interfering in the matters of state. On one occasion, he asked his chief minister to bring before him all the precious jewels captured in the battle against Vijayanagara and when this was done, much to the shock of onlookers, he set all the jewellery to fire. On another occasion, he allegedly tried to have his teenaged son Meeran Hussain killed by setting fire to the room where he was sleeping. Meeran fled to Daulatabad but returned shortly, arrested his father and soon, allegedly had him murdered by locking him up in a steam room with the fires turned up. Meeran unleashed a reign of terror after assuming the throne in 1588 CE, killing all male relatives whom he viewed as a threat. 'In one day, for fear of treason,' writes Cecily Cowley, 'he put to death 15 princes of the line of succession'.[9] Soon the nobles had had enough of his bigotry, executed a coup and had him murdered. In a short span of six years, from 1589 to 1595 CE. Ahmednagar saw a political flux of the worst kind with over three sovereigns being changed in short succession, accompanied by immense palace intrigues, deceit, murders and coups. Four opposing groups set up rival candidates to vie for the kingship in Ahmednagar. The situation was a political disaster that was any kingdom's worst nightmare. Disgusted by the turn of events, Chand Bibi left Ahmednagar for Bijapur.

The Mughal Attack on Ahmednagar

The intense flux in the Deccan caught the attention of Delhi. Mughal Emperor Akbar had begun to aggressively expand his dominions from 1560 CE onwards. Ahmednagar, which was collapsing with every passing day in view of its instability, was a sitting duck for the Mughals. Being the northernmost among the Deccan Sultanates it attracted his attention more, even as he eyed all the sultanates to gain access to and control over Goa and the Portuguese trade routes. He instructed his son Murad to proceed to wrest Ahmednagar along with his able general Abdur Rahim Khan-e-Khana.

Murad was overjoyed when an olive branch was sent from within Ahmednagar by Mian Manju Dakkhani, the chief minister, who was vying to become the regent by putting his candidate Ahmed on the throne with Mughal help. On 14 December 1595, the mighty Mughal army with a vast retinue on foot and 30,000 cavalry attacked Ahmednagar. In the forty years of his reign, Akbar had remained invincible and not lost any conquest. Ahmednagar was to be one of his challenging encounters. Mian Manju meanwhile fled to Bijapur with Ahmed to seek help, and everyone turned once again to the one person they always turned towards in the face of a crisis—Chand Bibi. She returned to Ahmednagar, had the infant grandson of her brother, Bahadur Nizam Shah, crowned as the king and took over as the regent, stepping up to defend the kingdom, even as the enemy was at the gates.

Chand Bibi sent out requests to Bijapur and Golconda to send help to defeat the Mughals, which they did, especially Bijapur that was under her nephew and erstwhile ward Ibrahim Adil Shah. Ibrahim Adil Shah sent Sohail Khan, a eunuch, with 25,000 horses to her support. She also managed to convince Nehung Khan, the Habshi general who had put up his candidate to the throne of Ahmednagar, to help her withstand the siege. Her allies meanwhile did not make any frontal attack on a beleaguered Mughal army but merely hovered around, stationing at various points leading up to Ahmednagar.

Mughal prince Murad's strategy to take over the fort was to build five saps, mines and trenches around it by 19 February 1596 with the intention to blow up the fort by dawn. When Chand Bibi got to know of this, she personally led the operation to countermine, and along with her generals, dug out two of the five mines before they could explode. They were in the act of removing the powder from the largest mine, when Prince Murad gave orders for it to be sprung. A tremendous explosion caused a huge breach in the fort and its defenders began to flee in fright. This was when, as Cecily Cowley writes:

> ... the queen, clad in armour, with a veil on her head, and a drawn sword in her hand, leaped into the breach and stayed the panic. The Moghuls did not immediately attack, and the defenders, taking advantage of the delay, hurriedly put the breach into a rough state of defence, and trained on to it all their available artillery, loaded as on a previous occasion,

with copper coins. The Moghuls stormed the breach at four o'clock in the afternoon, but the garrison resisted with heroism, inspired by the wonderful example of the queen. Time after time was the attack repeated, and time after time repelled, and it was not till nightfall that the carnage ceased, by which time thousands of dead lay in the ditch. Under cover of the darkness the queen repeated her deed of Bijapur, and personally superintended the repairs to the breach. Working at feverish heat, by dawn she had had the wall rebuilt to a height of seven feet, and felt prepared to resist another attack.[10]

Chand Bibi devised a strategy which allowed them to continuously attack the Mughals exhausting the attackers of their supplies. Ferishta details this in the following manner:

> . . . as the Prince and the Mogul storming party were waiting for the springing of the other mines, time was afforded to the besieged to throw rockets, powder and other combustibels into the ditch and bring guns to bear upon the breach. The Moguls at length advanced to storm. An obstinate defence took place at the foot of the breach, where the assailants suffered severely from the heavy fire of the besieged. The ditch was nearly filled with dead carcasses; and although several storming parties succeeded each other from four o'clock in the evening till night-fall, they were successfully repulsed. The feats of the valiant heroine, Chand Beeby, who had been seen by all defending the breach, became the subject of universal admiration and conversation in the enemy's lines. From that day, the Regent, who had always been called Chand Beeby, now acquired the title of Chand Sooltana.[11]

Prince Murad was now beginning to get worried about a rebellion among his forces as his supplies were steadily diminishing. Hence, he decided to negotiate ceding back the disputed territory of Berar to the Mughals in return for peace. Chand Bibi initially rejected the terms of truce and continued to bravely defend her fort. She later reflected calmly and wondered that if the Mughals regrouped and defeated her allies, she might not receive even these concessions. Hence, she signed the treaty in Bahadur Nizam Shah's name and the Mughals quietly retreated, after feeling much disgraced by a woman defender of Ahmednagar. Murad was heavily criticized back in Delhi for his war strategy and for signing a treaty that was by and large in Chand Bibi's favour.

The allies meanwhile reached three days after the Mughals lifted the siege and retreated. Ibrahim Adil Shah helped his aunt sort out the mess that her paternal kingdom was in. He managed to convince all the contenders to the throne to accept the suzerainty of Bahadur Nizam Shah and Chand Bibi. Mian Manju was invited to join the court of Bijapur to relieve his aunt of the threatening presence. Manju's protégé Ahmed was given an estate to sustain himself. One of Chand Bibi's long-term associates Mahomed Khan was appointed the new peshwa (chief minister), but very soon he, too, turned treacherous, forcing the queen to seek the help of her nephew in Bijapur. Ibrahim Adil Shah sent Sohail Khan again, who sieged the fort for four months, captured Mahomed and installed Nehung Khan as the new peshwa.

In 1598 CE, Chand Bibi is said to have even exchanged letters with the Portuguese Viceroy Francisco da Gama, attempting to strengthen the relationship of Ahmednagar with the Portuguese, seeking their assistance to quell an internal rebellion in her realm.

The Mughals Attack Again

The Mughals were restless on the borders of Ahmednagar. One by one the kingdoms of Gujarat, Malwa and Khandesh fell to their arms, and they began to occupy districts much to the south of Berar. The sultans of Golconda and Bijapur, assisted by troops from Ahmednagar, gave them a tough battle on the Godavari River in the Battle of Sonpeth in January 1597. After a bloody engagement, which lasted two days, the Mughals were victorious. Sohail Khan barely managed to save his own life. This would have been an opportune moment for the Mughals to storm into Ahmednagar and occupy it. But ego tussles and bickering between Prince Murad and his general Abdur Rahim erupted, as they had during the previous siege. Murad's constant letters of complaint exasperated Emperor Akbar who recalled Abdur Rahim and deputed Abul Fazl[12] to the campaign. Murad, by then, had taken to excessive drunkenness and finally died in 1599 CE at the age of thirty-two in Shahpur.

The same year, in 1599 CE, Akbar sent his youngest son, Prince Daniyal Mirza, with Abdur Rahim, to complete the unfinished task in the Deccan. The scale of the challenge that Chand Bibi and Ahmedngar had put to the mighty, invincible Mughal forces was proved by the fact that shortly thereafter, a fifty-seven-year-old Akbar himself moved southwards with about 80,000 horses to fulfil his long-cherished dream of subjugating the Deccan. That a woman was challenging the might of Akbar and the Mughal Empire of Delhi was reason enough for tough action to be taken to quash her permanently.

While Akbar proceeded to conquer Khandesh and besiege Asirgarh, Daniyal and Abdur Rahim marched towards Ahmednagar. He would have joined them later, if need be, even as he was directing the siege from Burhanpur. As Cowley writes:

> Mines were formed from the trenches of the prince, but the besieged broke into them and filled them. One mine was carried under the palace in the fort before being discovered. The queen began to despair of success by arms. The armies of Golconda and Bijapur dare not assist her, and practically no troops were operating on her behalf outside the fort.[13]

Meanwhile, internal trouble as usual brewed in Ahmednagar with the new peshwa Nehung Khan, too, turning upstart against Chand Bibi and leaving the fort with a large section of the army at this critical juncture. Realizing that she had no chance of victory against the mighty Mughal forces that she had withstood for four months now, the astute queen contemplated a truce with the invading forces. However, she made the mistake of discussing these probabilities with a eunuch Humeed Khan. Humeed ran into the streets of Ahmednagar and loudly proclaimed these secret plans of the queen. This aroused the Deccanis, the nobles and others who forgot all about the heroic patriotism that their queen had displayed on multiple occasions in the past. Along with Humeed they rushed into Chand Bibi's private apartments and in an unfortunate manner, put her to death.[14]

Thus, tragically ended the life of Chand Bibi, in the palace where she was born and in the fort that she had so valiantly defended so many times in the past. She was buried within the fort in an unmarked grave, but she still lives in the memory of the people, as a beloved, heroic and honoured queen.

Within a few days, mines were sprung and several breaches made in the fort of Ahmednagar. The Mughals soon occupied it, and the town was sacked. The royal family was taken prisoner and packed off to the Mughal fort of Burhanpur. This was Akbar's last campaign as he died shortly thereafter in 1605 CE.

Though almost erased from history, Chand Bibi's brave exploits and her courage are part of folklore. Between the 1930s and the 1960s, several Urdu biographies of Chand Bibi were published by the Deccan's aristocratic Muslim men. Many of these rely on multiple Persian sources, not just those based in the north. Chand Bibi was held up as role model for Muslim girls, at a time when Muslim women had just begun to attend colleges in larger numbers. Many Urdu biographical plays too were written around her, and they weave in a romance plot about her marriage to Ali Adil Shah.

Most paintings of Chand Bibi emerged long after her death. Paintings of her hawking are found at the Metropolitan Museum of Art in New York. Her image became a popular subject in both Deccani- and Mughal-style painting. She is usually depicted hawking—an activity pursued by princes and sultans, rather than women. She is often shown riding a white horse whose lower half has been coloured red with henna, possibly symbolizing wading through blood unleashed in battle. One of her attendants carries a ceremonial sunshade, which is not only an allegory to her regal status but also doubles up as a euphemism for a halo, all going on to portray her remarkable nature.

Notes

1   John Briggs, *History of the Rise of the Mahomedan Power in India, till the year A.D. 1612, Translated from the original Persian of Mahomed Kasim Ferishta* (Calcutta: R. Cambray & Co., 1910), p. 189.

2   A regional vernacular of the Deccan—a variety of Hindustani spoken in south India; a kind of a hybrid language containing regional and Indic vocabulary.

3   Captain Cecil Cowley, *Tales of Ahmednagar* (Bombay: Thacker & Company Ltd., 1919), p. 51.

4   Robert Sewell, *A Forgotten Empire (Vijayanagar): A Contribution to the History of India,* (London: Swan Sonnenschein & Co. Ltd., 1900), p. 205.

5   Ibid., pp. 130–31.

6   Sewell, *A Forgotten Empire*, pp. 207–08.

7   Archana Garodia Gupta, *The Women Who Ruled India: Leaders, Warriors, Icons* (Gurugram: Hachette Book Publishing India Pvt. Ltd., 2019), p. 97.

8   Captain Cecil Cowley, *Tales of Ahmednagar* (Bombay: Thacker & Company Limited, 1919), pp. 54–55.

9   Ibid., p. 57.

10 Ibid. pp. 64–65.

11 Briggs, *History of the Rise of the Mahomedan Power*, pp. 302–03.

12 The celebrated author of *Akbarnama* and *Ain-i-Akbari*.

13 Cowley, *Tales of Ahmednagar*, p. 69.

14 Gupta, *The Women Who Ruled India*, p. 106.

Lachit Barphukan
of Assam

Being unmindful of the intense fever that had gripped him, even as every limb and sinew of his body seemed to be giving up, he staggered down his war cabin headquarters at Itakhuli. The enemy was in visible distance and were menacingly making their way towards a breach that would eventually result in the fall of Guwahati. If that were to happen, years of planning, penance and resolve would be wasted. History had given him an opportunity to prove himself to his king, his people and land that had reposed so much faith in him. Rest and recuperation could wait; but this battle could not; and it had to be concluded conclusively in his favour. Putting on his armour and tightening the sheath of his glistening gold-plated sword, he boarded his boat that was tethered to the bank of the mighty River Brahmaputra. It was a do-or-die battle for him and his men; their honour, their land and their very lives were at stake in this decisive moment. Seeing him back in action caused an electric wave of excitement amongst the soldiers. They all raised their oars and shouted in unison, cheering their leader: 'Victory to thee, Lachit Barphukan, the invincible commander of the Ahoms!'

The Ahoms of Assam

The name of the dynasty—the Ahoms—and the region that they ruled (Assam) both came from the word *asama* or invincible; without a parallel. The Ahoms ruled for almost 600 years. The dynasty was founded in 1228 CE by Sukhapaa (Chao Lung Siu-Ka-Pha), a Tai prince from present day Mong Mao in China's Yunnan province. Their history is meticulously recorded in chronicles that are still extant, known as *Buranjis*. The establishment of the dynasty united the several ethnic and indigenous groups of the region to create a cogent sense of patriotism for their region, which was quite unparalleled. Assam was invaded several times by the Delhi Sultanate up to the sixteenth century, but this met with no success. The inhospitable and inaccessible terrain and the warrior spirit of the people who fiercely guarded their independence enabled them to maintain their dogged resistance against all attacks.

The first foray that the Mughals made into Assam, at Kajali in 1615, ended in disaster for them. After an initial loss, the Ahoms quickly regrouped, and reoccupied it, sending the Mughals back. While there was a brief lull in hostilities, the conflict began again under Mughal Emperor Shah Jahan's reign.

By the seventeenth century, Assam extended from River Manaha in the west (that was recognized as the eastern boundary of the Mughal Empire) to the hills of Sadiya in the east, wherein are situated several passes that lead to Tibet. The kingdom was more than 600 mi long and the mighty River Brahmaputra ran through it, dividing the kingdom into two main units—*Uttar-kul* (North Bank) and *Dakshin-kul* (South Bank). Kaliabar was the central point that divided the kingdom into two main divisions—western or Lower Assam (from Manaha to Kaliabar) and eastern or Upper Assam (from Kaliabar to Sadiya). The then capital was Gargaon, located in eastern Assam. The famous forts of Samdhara and Simalugarh were located on the northern and southern banks, near Kaliabar.

The independence of eastern Assam remained intact, but western Assam kept changing hands between the Koch rulers, and then the Ahoms and the Mughals. Towards December 1636, Kamrup was occupied by the Mughals, though a gallant resistance was put up by the residents of Samdhara Fort. According to the Treaty of Asurar Ali enacted in 1639 CE between the Ahom General Momai Tamuli Borbarua and the Mughal Commander Allah Yar Khan, the whole of western Assam, beginning Guwahati, passed into Mughal hands.

Taking advantage of the political crisis in Delhi that was caused by the illness of Emperor Shah Jahan and the bitter war of succession among his sons, Ahom King Jayadhwaj Singha (Sutamla, r. 1648–83 CE), expelled the Mughals from Guwahati and chased them beyond the Manaha river. He also destroyed the territory near Dhaka and took several Mughal subjects back to Assam as captives. The principality of Cooch Behar, too, took advantage of the chaos in Delhi—its ruler Pran Narayan declared independence and occupied Kamrup and Hajo. Once things calmed down in the Mughal Empire and Aurangzeb took over after a bloody coup, Delhi's attention was again drawn towards the eastern frontier. Aurangzeb ordered his trusted governor of Bengal, Mir Jumla, to invade Cooch Behar and Assam and re-establish Mughal supremacy in these regions.

After having occupied Cooch Behar, Mir Jumla invaded Assam on 4 January 1662. He easily repulsed the feeble attempts of resistance that the Assamese put up and overran Guwahati. The easy capitulation of the Ahom army was the result of disunity and the resentment that ran deep in the traditional hereditary establishment over Jayadhwaj Singha's appointment of Manthir Bharali Barua as the commander-in-chief. This disaffection enabled Mir Jumla to have a free pass through Assam, lapping up several triumphs. Mir Jumla's daring commander Dilir Khan Daudzai besieged the high fortress of Simalugarh and after facing Ahom resistance for a brief while, easily managed to take it by 26 February 1662. It was only after seeing the enemy so close at their gates that the Ahoms recovered their senses and understood what their disunity had caused them. But by then it was too late. Another combat with the Mughals at Kurkurakata ended in disaster for the Ahoms. So dire was the situation that King Jayadhawaj Singha had to flee his capital Gargaon and run away to the Namrup Hills for shelter. This earned him the opprobrium of 'Bhangania Raja' or the deserting king who absconded, all his life.[1] Mir Jumla triumphantly stormed into Gargaon on 17 March 1662.

A most humiliating treaty was concluded in January 1663 at Ghilajhari Ghat according to which the Ahoms were forced to give up western Assam to the Mughals. They also promised to deliver a war indemnity of three lakh rupees and ninety elephants and an annual tribute of twenty elephants. More disgracefully for the Ahoms, the only daughter of the king, Ramani Gabharu, and his niece, the daughter of the Tipam Raja, were forcibly packed off to the Mughal emperor's harem.[2] The first installment of the war indemnity was collected by Mir Jumla who then left Assam in February 1663 after appointing Rashid Khan as the *fauzdar* of Lower (western) Assam. He took along with him 12,000 Assamese followers and captives. It was the most shameful and dishonorable chapter in the annals of Ahom history—one that would haunt and offend the patriotic sentiments of the Assamese for long.

Once the imperial army left, the king in hiding came back and began conferring with his councillors about regaining their lost territory and honour, even as they maintained a charade of subservience and cordiality with the Mughals, promptly paying the tributes due. Jayadhwaj Singha wrote to the Rajas of Cooch Behar, Jayantia and Cachar to unite with him and form a grand anti-Mughal confederacy in eastern India. They all sent back reassuring promises of help. But just when preparations were beginning to gain momentum, Jayadhwaj Singha died in November 1663, without of course being able to erase the taint that stuck to his name of being a cowardly deserter.[3] But he had surely helped rekindle the patriotic sentiments of the people in what was to prove a long road to recovery of prestige and glory.

The Revival under Chakradhwaj Singha

Since the deceased king had no sons, his uncle's son Chakradhwaj Singha was crowned the successor. The new king was aghast to see the reduction in Ahom prestige and power and their being reduced to almost a vassal state of the Mughals. The new *fauzdar* of Guwahati Syed Firuz Khan had been sending threatening letters as the rest of the war indemnity had not been paid, adding to the humiliation for the Ahoms. Burning with the impatience borne out of the indignity that they found themselves in, Chakradhwaj Singha summoned all his councillors and close confidantes in 1665 CE to strategize on expelling the Mughals from western Assam and launch a military campaign immediately. But his impatience was brought to a timely check by his Prime Minister Atan Buragohain Rajmantri Dangaria who requested him to first inspect their preparedness and take a stock of their military preparedness, stocks and provisions before launching an attack on a major power.

Chakradhwaj Singha was quite astonished to know that there was not even a single box of gunpowder in the army stock; there were not even four boxes of shots or pellets nor a stack of arrows. The death blow that Mir Jumla's invasion had dealt to the Ahoms had thoroughly demoralized them and the army was in a shambles. Hence, thinking of an attack when the army was so ill-prepared would have led to an even bigger catastrophe. Thereafter, the next two years were used by Singha to completely galvanize the army and their stock and prepare for the conflict. He personally supervised the training of soldiers and even taught them the proper method of wielding several weapons. To stock the army's granaries with sufficient foodgrains to face the eventuality of sieges, the cultivation of paddy and other grains was conducted under state supervision. The arsenals and smithies were shifted to within the palace enclosure and under royal supervision, they worked day and night to add weapons to the army's kitty. In addition to fighting on the land, the Ahoms realized the importance of naval conflict given the vast riverfronts that surrounded the kingdom. Hence, they started building a strong naval fleet of big ships and smaller boats where firing cannons could be mounted. Regiments of 1,000 soldiers were divided into smaller battalions of 500 each for greater efficiency, and the regiment was managed by a Hazarika or an Ek-Hazari (1,000) commander. A Phukan was placed in charge of a contingent of 6,000.[4] Thus, a new martial spirit and verve was infused into the hitherto decrepit Ahom army, and military rejuvenation became the common theme of every citizen and arm of government. It was a do-or-die situation for the Ahoms to rebuild themselves and restore their lost glory and territory, and they were willing to do everything under their command to achieve this.

The Ahom kingdom was highly regimented in its structure. The king was known by the exalted title of Swargadeo or the Lord of the Heavens, hailing from the lineage of Sukhapaa, the founder. He initially had two main Gohains or ministers/councillors—Burhagohain and Bargohain. They were given independent territories as veritable sovereigns. A new position was created in 1527 known as Borpotragohain, and later Ahom King Pratap Singha (r. 1603–41 CE) added two more offices, the Borbarua and the Barphukan. The Borbarua acted as a military and judicial head and was in command of the region east of Kaliabar. The Barphukan was the military and civil commander of the region west of Kaliabar and acted as the king's viceroy in the west. Together these five positions constituted the *Patra Mantris* or the Council of Ministers.

While the army was being readied there was a need felt for an able commander who could lead them in this crucial battle too. The Council of Ministers deliberated with the king and the lot fell on a young man, Lachit, to assume the office of Assam's next Barphukan at this critical juncture and lead its armies to victory.

The Rise of Momai Tamuli Borbarua

Lachit, born in 1622 CE, was the youngest son of Momai Tamuli Borbarua, a man who had risen from humble backgrounds to become Assam's general in the wars against the Mughals waged during the reigns of Jahangir and Shah Jahan. Momai's original name was Sukuti and he worked as an ordinary bonded labourer of his nephew for a meagre salary of four rupees. But fortune was destined to smile on him. One day, while he was working in the field, raising bunds for storing rainwater, Ahom King Pratap Singha's cavalcade was passing by. The king saw Sukuti at work and was impressed by the meticulousness of his work in the paddy field and his keen eye for detail. He immediately got him released from his nephew's bondage and took him on the royal pay as Bar-tamuli or superintendent of the royal gardens. Since his nephew addressed him as 'Momai'—Assamese for maternal uncle—that name stuck with him. From a garden superintendent, the assiduous

Momai kept rising from one office to other to the ultimate one of Borbarua that he eventually became. He led the Assam army during the Mughal invasions and was instrumental in enacting the famous Treaty of Asurar Ali with Allah Yar Khan in 1639 CE that became the foundation for Ahom–Mughal relations for decades thereafter. Momai Tamuli's daughter Pakhari Gabharu was thereafter married to King Jayadhwaj Singha, and it was their daughter Ramani Gabharu who was later married off to Sultan Azamtara, the third son of Aurangzeb.

Momai also organized the Ahom administration on the lines of the Mughal *mansabdari* system introduced by Emperor Akbar in 1571 CE. It was a system of ranking the government officials and determining their civil and military duties, along with their remunerations. Similarly, Momai created the functions of the Baras, Saikias, Hazarikas, Baruas, Rajkhowas and Phukans within the Ahom bureaucracy. Assamese rural economy was reconstructed by him on a sound and secure footing and every village and family was to have the goal of being economically self-sufficient.

The main reason of his meteoritic rise within the administration was his deep and enduring sense of duty along with steadfast loyalty to his master. His devotion had been noticed even by the Mughals, who when reporting to their emperor about Assam had said: 'The (Ahom) king is a veritable Mahadeva, and Momai-tamuli is Mahadeva's chief henchman or Nandi. As long as these two wield the affairs of Assam, it is impossible to turn your face to that country.'[5] Lachit had inherited all these qualities from his father, having observed his father closely, in managing the administration. He had the best teachers in his growing-up days and was educated in humanities, military skills and scriptures. Lachit was first made the Soladhara Barua, the scarf-bearer of the king, a position akin to that of a private secretary. In due course, he also held various positions like Ghora Barua (in charge of the royal stable), commander of Simalugarh Fort and later the Dolaksharia Barua (Superintendent of the Royal Household Guards) to Maharaja Chakradwaj Singha. During Mir Jumla's invasion, Lachit had engaged in his limited capacity with the enemy at Dikhowmukh and earned considerable success.

The New Barphukan and the Recovery of Guwahati

Before being formally anointed as the Barphukan, the king wanted to test the man whom he had anyway watched closely in a long time. Lachit was asked to present himself in the royal court before the monarch, and as he knelt before him, in a preplanned and staged move, an attendant rushed from behind and snatched away Lachit's headgear. This was, and still is, considered as a grave affront to a man's dignity and self-respect, in Assamese traditions.[6] The king wanted to check Lachit's sense of self-worth and his reflexes. The young man leapt from his knees, unsheathed his sword and rushed to cut off the head of the errant attendant, who had by now safely plonked himself at the king's feet seeking his shelter. The king was deeply satisfied by this act and he formally installed Lachit as his general and Barphukan, presenting him a gold-hafted sword and the customary paraphernalia of regal distinction.

As the Ahoms were preparing for the combat, King Chakradhwaj Singha renewed the alliances with the Jaintia and Kachari kingdoms. The Garos, the Nagas and the Rani of Darrang were other allies for the Ahoms. Singha had also kept a close watch on what all was happening across the country. His spies and emissaries were gathering information of the movements of the Mughal army, their successes and failures in other wars in order to better prepare themselves. It was the Maratha strongman who later became Chhatrapati Shivaji Maharaj whose successes against the Mughals around this very time— between 1663 and 1665 CE— attracted the Ahoms the most and gave them a sense of hope for their own fortunes. Chhatrapati Shivaji became the role model for them to emulate and to similarly vanquish the arrogant Mughal emperor and his army. In a letter written to the Raja of Cooch Behar, dated 24th Magh 1587 Saka, or 7 February 1666, Chakradhwaj Singha said:

> You have sent the verbal message informing me that war had commenced between Shewa (Shivaji) and the Moguls, and that Shewa having defeated the Moguls has pushed them back to a distance of twenty days' march; that Daud Khan has fallen, and Dilel [Dilir] Khan is wounded,

and that the Badshah has come from Delhi to Agra. It cannot be predicted as to who becomes vanquished and who becomes victorious. You have further informed me that you are engaged in putting your forts and dikes in order; and you have asked us to strengthen our fortifications and to train our soldiers. It is meet and proper that you should give us such advice and encouragement. Because the Moguls have humiliated us once, does it follow that we should make no attempt to throw off this position of subordination to them? They have discomfited us once, and we have dealt them severe blows on repeated occasions, and of this fact you are fully conversant.[7]

By the summer of 1667 CE, the army was completely toned and galvanized and was bursting to set forth once it received the royal orders. On 20 August 1667, the Ahom army under Lachit Barphukan, accompanied by Atan Burhagohain, started from the capital, sailed downstream the Brahmaputra River in two divisions and encamped at Kaliabar at their viceregal headquarters to launch their operations against the Mughals in Guwahati. After offering prayers at the holy shrine of Goddess Kamakhya, they began their offensive. Syed Firuz Khan, the Mughal governor of Guwahati, and his army were ill-prepared for this sudden attack and there was no time for them to seek fresh reinforcements from Rangamati or Dhaka. Dihingia Phukan in the Ahom army led an attack on the Bahbari Fort near the Barnadi, on the northern bank of Guwahati and captured it, along with the fort of Kajali by September 1667. The Shah Buruz and Rangmahal forts, too, fell soon to the Ahom might.

The Ahoms now directed their efforts to the recapture of Guwahati from the Mughals. A fierce battle took place between the Ahoms and the Mughal army detachment issuing out of Itakhuli at Guwahati. Itakhuli was a small hill on the south bank of the Brahmaputra at Guwahati, and it offered a panoramic view and a strategic hold over the valley. The Mughals had established themselves in a fort atop the hill of Itakhuli and this was attacked by the Assamese army in a daring midnight ambush. The Ahom spies had managed to render several of the Mughal cannon as unworthy by filling water in their muzzles. This was led by one Bagh Hazarika, whose real name was Ismail Siddique, and so called because he had once killed a tiger barehanded. When the Ahoms attacked, the Mughals realized to their horror that their cannons were all rendered utterly useless.

The Mughals then advanced with a fleet of boats, but they could not stand or defend the incessant cannonade of the Ahoms. By the midnight of 2 November 1667, Itakhuli and the contiguous garrison of Guwahati fell into Ahom hands and the Mughals were chased out of the region to the mouth of the Manaha river, the original boundary of their empire with Assam. Syed Firuz Khan and several others were taken captive by the Ahoms; many were executed and others sent to the jails in Gargaon. Thus, within a short span of merely two months the Ahoms manage to flush the Mughals out of Guwahati and west Assam and regain their lost glory and possessions. For his chivalry and the first major success, Lachit Barphukan was presented with the *Hengdang*, a gold-plated sword by the king.

The Ahoms knew that the Mughals would not let go so easily and would come back again. Hence, retaining Guwahati that they managed to wrest was essential. Fortifications in Guwahati were strengthened on a maddening war footing. Atan Buragohain was appointed to erect the necessary fortifications on both banks of the river, while Lachit Barphukan was asked to post a contingent of soldiers at all the important and strategic locations. On the pretext of going on a hunt, Lachit would often inspect the passes and defiles in and around Guwahati. Every part of Guwahati was well-covered and protected. Guns were mounted in the ramparts and on hill slopes and valleys in a state of perennial alert. Lachit Barphukan was merciless when it came to dereliction of duty on anybody's part. When his own maternal uncle did not complete the construction of a rampart near Amingaon on the north bank on time, he was immediately sacked. Lachit had remarked that his country was more important to him than his own uncle. This kind of military zeal infused a sense of immense responsibility in the army.

The Ahoms thus kept themselves ready for any further eventualities with the Mughal forces.

The Mughals Return under Raja Ram Singh

Emperor Aurangzeb was enraged to hear the news of the capitulation of Guwahati. He decided to send a strong Mughal force to fight the Ahoms and end the menace for good, establishing the Mughal supremacy in the North-East. He chose to send Mirza Raja Ram Singh, the son of Mirza Raja Jai Singh I, a senior general of the Mughal Empire and a Kachwaha Rajput king of Amber (later called Jaipur). It was largely believed that Ram Singh had played a facilitatory role in the stealthy escape of Shivaji, whom Aurangzeb had got captured and imprisoned in the Agra Fort. Partly to punish him for this act, Aurangzeb deputed Ram Singh to the inhospitable Assam terrains to fight the Ahoms and made it both a matter of prestige, as also life and death for the Raja to win the war. On 6 January 1668, Ram Singh was formally appointed by Aurangzeb as the commander of the Assam expedition. He was obviously deeply upset at this task, which seemed to him as a mighty demotion. Conscious of this disaffection of his lead commander, Aurangzeb sent several other Muslim officers along such as Mirza Said Saif Dewan, Mir Raji Dewan, Bahlol Khan Daroga, Sultan Ali Daroga and Mir Gazar Beg Hazi Waqayanavis. Rashid Khan, the former *fauzdar* of Guwahati, was made the lieutenant of the Raja. Their task was to also watch out closely and report the actions of the Hindu Raja, lest he enters into a secret alliance with a co-religionist king and his officers in Assam.[8]

Ram Singh's army consisted of twenty-one Rajput chiefs with their contingents, 4,000 troopers, 1,500 gentlemen-troopers or *ahadis,* and 500 artillerymen. With reinforcements from Bengal, his total army swelled up to 30,000 infantry men, 18,000 Turkish cavalry, forty ships and 15,000 Koch archers. In addition, the forces of Cooch Behar, too, joined their ranks. It was thus a formidable force to reckon with, far outnumbering the Ahoms. Ram Singh also took along with him Sikh Guru Teg Bahadur who was then living in Patna and also five Muslim *pirs,* to offset any effects of the infamous Kamrupi black arts and witchcraft. The entourage halted at Dhaka for a few days where it was warmly received by the Bengal Governor Nawab Shaista Khan, who happened to be a close friend of Raja Jai Singh. A further detachment of 2,000 soldiers joined this army from the Bengal command.

The swollen Mughal army reached the frontier garrison of Rangamati in February 1669. Raja Ram Singh sent a message to the Ahoms to voluntarily give up their claims over Guwahati and western Assam and to restore the limits that were fixed in 1639 as per the Treaty of Asurar Ali. He also challenged Lachit Barphukan to a combat. A bag of poppy seeds was sent to Lachit with this message, to indicate that the Mughal army was as numerous as the poppy seeds in the bag. Lachit sent a counter-reply that if poppy seeds were well-pounded, in no time they could become a thin paste and that the Ahom army were taskmasters at pounding.[9] This was accompanied with a tube filled with sand indicating that the Ahom army was larger and indissoluble as the sand was. Such bravado and rhetoric continued between the two enemies before any commencement of hostilities.

The War Begins

On 3 April 1669 Ram Singh marched up to Agiahutti on the river bank and the Mughal tent was pitched in front of the Ahom fort of Amingaon. The Mughal–Rajput army was much in awe and apprehension about the vast and intricate fortifications that the Ahoms had managed to erect across their kingdom. The guns then began to blaze on both sides. Ram Singh's nephew was killed in the firing and Ram Singh's tent was breached by a cannon shot made by the Ahoms. The battle ended indecisively. Meanwhile, rifts had begun between Ram Singh and Rashid Khan and the latter slowly then retired with his detachment, to Hazo.

Ram Singh then approached the fort of Sarai through a special underground passage that he had got constructed. But when the Ahoms got wind of this they filled the surrounding moat with water. Ram Singh managed to mount his guns on temporary platforms and fire at the forts causing minor breaches, which were repaired at lightning speed by the nimble Ahom forces. The counter-volley from the Ahom side was impossible to bear for Ram Singh and he beat a hasty retreat. He had the Mughal army divided into four divisions and waited for the appropriate opportunity to break open the fortifications of Guwahati from all four directions. Ram Singh headed the division that was to attack the north bank, Ali Akbar Khan the south bank, Jahir Beg and the Baruas from Cooch Behar headed the division that led to the Sindhurighopa, and Mansur Khan led the naval commanders who guarded the river. The Mughals effected a breach at the Rangaliburuz Fort, near Pandu, on the south bank. But an alert and cautious vassal chief of Rani reported this to Lachit Barphukan, who once again had the repairs made so quickly that it baffled the invaders. The Rani chief also caught several Mughal soldiers as fugitives, and they were allegedly sent to Lachit after their fingers had been chopped off.

In June 1669, just before the monsoons, the Mughals launched several other offensives. A force under Raja Sujan Singh and Raja Roop Narayan engaged the Ahom army at Kaljor Hill and another large contingent manned by Bahlol Khan and others attempted to enter Guwahati through Darrang. The Bahbari Fort at the mouth of the Barnadi, opposite to Guwahati, was attacked. But even here, being tipped off about the moves of the Mughals by the Rani chief, Lachit Barphukan led the army to a rout of the Mughals accompanied with heavy casualties and loss of provisions for them. Dihingia Phukan attacked the Mughals both by land and sea. Sensing a complete debacle of the forces, Ram Singh appeared himself in the field and managed to inflict a devastating defeat on the Ahoms' land force. They dashed into the waters where they were hotly pursued by the Mughals and many slain. Several Assamese war boats were captured.

Just when it seemed things had gone out of the hands of the Ahoms, nature helped them and to their advantage and to the peril of the Mughals, the monsoon broke out. The enemy camps got detached from one another due to the heavy floods, even as the Ahom forces were ensconced in their forts. This gave a huge breather to the Ahoms. Till now, Lachit had avoided making an offensive and proactive attack on the enemy and it was all a reaction to the attacks they were mounting. His idea was to exhaust them and their provisions and used this delay for a frontal offensive to elevate his own preparations to desired perfection.

Intermittent skirmishes accompanied by proposals of sporadic peace continued during 1669 and 1670 CE.

In August and September 1669, there were several naval engagements too. The Mughals, with their warships that were loaded with sixteen cannons, dashed towards the river stockades of the Ahoms. Lachit personally took charge of the naval command and fell upon the enemy, dealing huge casualties. Alongside, the Ahoms also engaged in guerilla warfare (*dagga judha*). They made sudden attacks, mostly in the middle of the night, taking the enemy totally by surprise. Some of their spies were also sent to the enemy camp to loot their treasures and money. Ram Singh wrote a long letter of protest to Lachit against what he termed as unethical war practices that only thieves indulged in.[10] He withdrew himself from the combat trying to earn a high moral ground, from October 1669 to March 1670.

The Assamese, too, were realizing that their guerilla warfare had limited advantages beyond harassing the enemy and pilfering some of their wealth and stock. All along they had been safely shying away from a land fight as much as possible as they were intimidated by the superior Mughal cavalry. The strategy was therefore to pull the opponent to their terms and their comfort, which was naval warfare, and hence the Mughals had to be drawn to the Brahmaputra for combats, rather than on ground. Guwahati with its hilly terrain was also a perfect place that Lachit had drawn the Mughals into, rather than fighting on the plains where the Ahoms would be easily outnumbered and vanquished. Despite being a smaller army, they constantly played to their strengths and literally dictated the terms of the conflict, drawing the Mughals to their weakest point, their navy.

Meanwhile, murmurs began in the Ahom army that Lachit was needlessly postponing a conflict and had squandered away the gains that the timely onset of the monsoons had brought in dissipating the enemy. The Mughal spies caught on to these stories and Ram Singh decided to create further confusion by sending a fake letter to Lachit speaking about an imaginary deal that the two of them had struck.

These murmurs and the letter reached Chakradhwaj Singha, who was temporarily jolted and became suspicious of his Barphukan. It was left to the wise counsel of Atan Burogohain to allay these fevers of the king and pointing to him the conspiracy of the enemy in planting such baseless stories. But there was now increasing restlessness on the part of the king and the army as the hostilities had continued for way too long and a decisive outcome still eluded them.

The Alaboi Debacle

The two armies then met near Alaboi Hill. Ram Singh had posted a heroic female warrior, Madanavati, at the head of the Mughal force, dressed in male attire. Lachit had dispatched a vast force of nearly 40,000 soldiers for this land combat. Madanavati's daring attacks were a huge setback for the Ahoms. She single-handedly managed to vanquish numerous Assamese soldiers and the first three lines of the Assamese army was dispersed away with heavy casualties. Lachit then ordered his men to dig trenches and attack from there. The Mughals were taken by surprise with these new attacks and when some of them rushed to take cover in the river, they were hotly pursued by the Ahoms. Madanavati, too, was shot dead on the bank of the Brahmaputra. The Ahoms under Luthuri Rajkhowa routed the Mughals who were now being led by Mir Nawab. He was captured alive and presented as a fugitive to the king.

But this success was temporary and short-lived. What followed was a terrible disaster for the Ahom army, one that would be remembered for long with deepest regret and dismay. The entire Rajput force fell upon the Ahom army in a sudden burst of surprise attack that the latter was not expecting. This caused a massacre of nearly 10,000 of Lachit Barphukan's brave soldiers in the Alaboi plains. This massive loss hugely dented the morale of the Ahom army and plunged Lachit into great depression.

Enthused by this isolated victory, Ram Singh reiterated his demands to the Ahoms to evacuate Guwahati and call for a cessation of hostilities. He was cognizant of the fact that despite the war having carried on for so long, the Ahoms had managed to hold on and had not surrendered even an inch of their land. He sent out peace negotiations, too, with a promise of three lakh rupees to the Ahoms to cover the expenses of all the fortifications they had erected, if they agreed to hand over Guwahati.

When negotiations and threats failed, he tried to bribe the commanders of the Ahom army through costly gifts. Lachit, too, was presented an exquisite necklace studded with diamonds and gems and was requested to wear it when he appeared on the battlefield. Unfortunately, even this ploy of Ram Singh failed.

His strategists now advised him that there was now only one possible avenue of attack, on account of a slight opening in the ramparts in the sandbanks between Lachit's headquarters at Itakhuli and the foot of the Goddess Kamakhya temple. This sandbank was known as Andharubali. Ram Singh decided that his forces and he would enter Guwahati through this breach at Andharubali, and his men and horses would reach from across the river in boats.

Even as the war was heading to a conclusive finish, tragedy struck the Ahoms. King Chakradhwaj Singha who had galvanized them and made them a fighting-fit force died in April 1670. He was succeeded by his brother Udayaditya Singha. The new king lacked the force of personality and the verve that his predecessor had. But a lot of the heavy-lifting, especially in orienting the army towards a single-minded focus of victory and by placing the right man for the job, had already been done by Chakradhwaj. Udayaditya had to merely follow suit with no major innovations from his side. To demoralize the Ahom army further, Lachit Barphukan fell terribly sick and could barely move, having to be lifted with his cot. But not the one to be easily subdued, he continued to lead despite his ill health.

The Battle of Saraighat, 1671 CE

The death of Chakradhwaj Singha, the illness of Lachit Barphukan and the new glimmer of hope that the breach at Andharubali held out, brightened the designs of a battle-weary Ram Singh. Massive reinforcements arrived in the form of war vessels and imperial officers. He was now determined to bring things to a head-on conclusion. There was talk of how Aurangzeb was threatening to chop his head off and also that of his family if he further delayed a victory in the long and costly Assam expedition.

Moving along the north bank, Ram Singh was joined by ships with artillery and archers under five Rajput Sardars. The battle started on both land and water at Aswarkanta. Laluk Phukan pushed back the Mughals, but their naval forces compelled the Ahom boats to retreat further towards the Amrajuri Ghat. With the Mughals getting dangerously close to Andharubali, the Ahoms retreated further back to Kajali and Samdhara.

And this is when Assam's man of destiny, Lachit Barphukan stood up to be counted and to create history for himself and his clan. Disregarding his illness and fever and the counsel of his confidants, he barged out of his headquarters and boarded the warship, accompanied by six other vessels. He ordered all the land and naval forces to launch a terrible and spirited attack. Lachit's entry had an electrifying impact on the demoralized Ahom soldiers, who now regained their mojo and attacked the Mughals fiercely. Ahom warships, playing on their strength, ambushed the Mughal navy from all sides. Between Itakhuli, Kamakhya and Aswarkranta, one of the fiercest river battles ever was fought. The entire Brahmaputra at the triangle between these three—Itakhuli, Kamakhya and Aswarkranta—was littered with boats and men struggling to escape drowning. The Ahoms created an improvised bridge of boats, by placing one boat over another, over the entire breadth of the river.

The Mughals were then attacked from both the rear and front, their admiral Munnawar Khan was shot dead, totally unnerving them and scattering their forces. Four thousand of the Mughal army lay dead, their navy completely annihilated, and they were hotly pursued and literally pushed away to the westernmost part of the Ahom kingdom, the Manaha river. Darrang also saw a total and complete rout for the Mughals and ending with a decisive victory for the Assamese. This battle is known in history famously as the Battle of Saraighat.[11]

All hopes of Raja Ram Singh were dashed, and the battle ended in a thorough disgrace for him and the Mughals who never made any further inroads into Assam. Lachit Barphukan thus led the Ahom force to victory over a numerically larger and superior Mughal army, in what was to be one of the greatest and most historic military victories. The *Alamgir-Namah* states: 'The Rajas of Assam have never bowed the head of submission and obedience, nor have they paid tributes or revenue to the most powerful monarch, but they have curbed the ambition and checked the conquests of the most victorious princes of Hindustan. The solution of a war against them has baffled the penetration of heroes who have been styled conquerors of the world.'[12]

While the Ahoms were expecting a reattack, Ram Singh had had enough. He ordered the folding up of the tents and prepared to sail down the river. Many in the Ahom army wanted to loot them, but Lachit strongly refused to loot a retreating enemy that had been suitably disgraced in war. Finally on 5 April 1671, Ram Singh left Assam, licking his wounds and cursing his destiny.

Sadly, for the Ahoms the joys of victory were short-lived. The pressures of battle had taken their toll on Lachit Barphukan. That despite running a high fever he had commanded the entire naval attack at Saraighat was something that his body could not possibly take. Shortly after the battle in 1672 CE, Lachit Barphukan passed away at the relatively young age of fifty. His elder brother Nimati succeeded him as the Barphukan and came to be known as 'Metakatalia Laluk Sola Barphukan'.

The legacy and memory of this braveheart is perpetuated to this day at the National Defence Academy, where the best passing out cadet is annually awarded the Lachit Barphukan gold medal. This was instituted by the Government of Assam in 2000 and is a fitting tribute to a brave and loyal soldier, and a brilliant tactician and war strategist.

Notes

1   S.K. Bhuyan, *Lachit Barphukan and His Times: A History of the Assam–Mogul Conflicts of the Period 1667 to 1671 A.D.* (Guwahati: The Department of Historical and Antiquarian Studies, Government of Assam, 1947), p. 11.

2   Manuscript 'Assam Buranji', from the invasion of Mirza Jahina to Swargadeo Siva Singha, 1630–1744 (Guwahati: The Department of Historical and Antiquarian Studies [DHAS], Government of Assam). Also cited in Bhuyan, *Lachit Barphukan and His Times*, p. 8.

3   Bhuyan, *Lachit Barphukan and His Times*, p. 11.

4   Manuscript 'Assam Buranji', from Swargadeo Pratap Singha to Ratnadhwaj Singha Sulikhpa Lora Raja, 1603–1681, DHAS, Guwahati.

5   Manuscript 'Assam Buranji', from the earliest times to Swargadeo Gadadhar Singha's recovery of Guwahati from the Moguls in 1682, with several historical letters; from the earliest times to the death of Swargadeo Rudra Singha in 1714, DHAS, Guwahati.

6   Bhuyan, *Lachit Barphukan and His Times*, p. 23.

7   Manuscript 'Assam Buranji': a collection of 192 letters exchanged between the kings & officers of Assam, and the courts of Delhi, Dacca, Cooch Behar, Jayanta, Cachar, Sylhet etc.; from the earliest times to the death of Swargadeo Rudra Singha in 1714, DHAS, Guwahati.

8   Bhuyan, *Lachit Barphukan and His Times*, p. 34.

9   Ibid., pp. 49–50.

10 Bhuyan, *Lachit Barphukan and His Times*, p. 58.

11 The name Saraighat was loosely applied in those days, and even now to Guwahati and its environs, though Sarai was actually the small village Amingaon.

12 Quoted in Bhuyan, *Lachit Barphukan and His Times* p. 84.

Kanhoji Angre

For close to four decades, his fleet was a terror to the maritime powers in the narrow, but important coastal strip of western India, where he led his sailors from victory to victory; an astute diplomat of uncommon ability, he undoubtedly gave the Maratha navy an unprecedented power after it was envisaged and founded by the indomitable Chhatrapati Shivaji Maharaj; he defied the joint efforts of the English, the Portuguese, and the Siddis in his numerous wars with them, both on land and by the sea, thereby raising the Maratha naval prestige to an extraordinary level. He was Kanhoji Angre, the brave 'Sarkhel', or the Grand Admiral of the Maratha navy, about whom so little is sadly written or spoken about today. His locus of activity was largely the Konkan, the narrow strip of land that lies between the high Sahyadri Mountains and the vast Arabian Sea, stretching from Daman in the north to Goa in the south, and comprising the three main districts of Thana, Colaba and Ratnagiri.

Early Life

The origins of this daring man are obscure, and he did not belong to the nobility of the land. A Portuguese viceroy states that he began his life as a humble servant of other Hindus in the island of Versova.[1] Stories about his origin and exploits were disseminated in the literary works of the English sailor Clement Downing[2] who called him, as his compatriots did, 'Angria the Pirate'. Quite confidently, Downing traces Kanhoji's ancestry to an 'Arabian Cofferey' or the kaffirs of Arab, the pagan non-believers,[3] who abandoned the Mohammedan religion to settle down in western India. From Arabian to Abyssinian origins, there have been varied hypotheses about Kanhoji's ancestry. But according to his family lore, he was a Maratha Kshatriya by birth and his ancestors bore the original surname 'Sankpal'. The new surname of Angrey (or Angria) that stuck with them, came from the village of Angarwadi near Poona, where the family had long resided. His father Tukoji, son of Sekhoji Sankpal, had shown great daring and promise while serving under Shahaji, the father of the great Shivaji Maharaj. Shahaji himself was subservient to the Sultan of Bijapur who held sway over vast parts of the Deccan. Tukoji continued to serve Shahaji's son Chhatrapati Shivaji, who made him a sardar or commander in his fleet. Tukoji must have taken part in the numerous naval skirmishes that formed part of Chhatrapati Shivaji's stormy rule—from the expedition in Karwar in 1665 CE to his lifelong battles with the Siddis of Janjira, whom the Marathas never managed to vanquish. Tukoji was later appointed as the *surnobat* or deputy commander of the seaside fortress of Suvarnadurg, the fort of gold. [4]

Precious little is known about Kanhoji's formative years. He is said to have been born around 1669 CE and when he was eight years old, his father left him under the tutelage of a Brahmin guru in the village of Harnai (in Ratnagiri district). A popular Konkan folktale goes that[5] one day, young Kanhoji who was herding his guru's cows decided to take a short nap under a tree. Since it took long for the boy to return, the guru went looking and was astonished to find a five-headed cobra guarding the boy's head from the harsh sun. This was looked upon as a propitious sign of the boy being destined for a bright future, possibly becoming the ruler of the land someday. During his growing up years, Kanhoji developed a friendship with a studious, bright boy Balaji Vishwanath, who was to later rise to the position of the peshwa or prime minister of the Maratha kingdom.

The Maratha Kingdom and Its Navy

After a series of successful military campaigns, Shivaji Maharaj declared himself as an independent king with the title of 'Chhatrapati' in a grand coronation ceremony held at his new capital of Raigad in the Konkan on 6 June 1674. In the early part of that century, the English had entered the trading scene in India with the East India Company (EIC) that had begun to establish a series of factories on the western coastline of India. They decided to send their emissary Henry Oxenden to the coronation as a goodwill gesture, with precious gifts and shawls, as did the other dominant European power in India then—the Portuguese. The royal proclamation of his kingdom extending up to the limits of the ocean would have caused consternation among the European powers who were vying for a pie in the maritime power of the coast. But it was not an empty, boastful claim that was being made of the Maratha kingdom extending to the oceans. In the fourteen arduous years that it had taken for Shivaji Maharaj to carve out his kingdom, one of his most notable achievements was his visionary role in founding an Indian navy with a formidable fleet. The importance the Marathas gave to the navy is testified in the *Adnyapatra* or a document that gave the tenets of rule, drafted in 1715 CE by the minister Ramachandra Pant Amatya: 'A Navy is a distinct arm of the kingdom. Like the cavalry rules the earth, the one with an armada rules the oceans.'[6] At the time of the coronation, the Maratha navy had fifty-seven major ships of war, excluding smaller craft, with a total fighting strength of over 5,000 men. Five years later there were sixty-six major ships.

The Maratha navy however did not venture out into the oceans and was equipped to escort the merchant ships from one port to another. It patrolled the western coast defying the Portuguese, the Dutch, the Siddis and the English and protected the merchant marine, standing up often to the Europeans in the region. There were various categories of Maratha fighting ships—*ghurab, galbat* or *gallivat, manchwa, shibar* and *paal*. The *ghurabs* (frigates) were the biggest naval ships, with two or three masts and ranged from 150 to 300 ton. They had bigger guns that could fire ahead, as well as deliver a broadside to the enemy ships. The *gallivats* were the real backbone of the fleet and were the smaller ships that generally did not exceed 70 tons, and had two masts. They were basically fast rowboats with sails, with six or eight cannons that could fire pounder shells. The *paals, manchwa* and *shibars* were hybrid vessels, smaller than *ghurabs* but bigger than *gallivats*. The ship was under the charge of the *nakhoda*, the captain. He had one or two assistants knows as *tandales*. But the Maratha fleet fell way short of the seaworthiness of her European counterparts, that excelled particularly in its grand and larger design and the presence of trained gunners.[7] Before Kanhoji, most of the senior officers of the Maratha fleet and in command of the coastal forts, under Shivaji Maharaj, were Muslims.

Shivaji Maharaj was unquestionably the first visionary Indian ruler to have realized the need for protecting the coast. He built several seaside forts along the Konkan and fortified and improved the others. Among the last forts he built was on a rocky outcrop off Alibag, around 32 km south of Bombay. Since the island was nothing more than a vast, bare rock (*kul*), surrounded by water (*aap*), the new fortress came to be called Kul-aap, which came to be known in time as Kulaba or Colaba. In the years to come, Colaba became the headquarters of the Angreys, so much so that they came to be identified as the 'Angreys of Colaba'.

For Shivaji Maharaj who had given the Mughals a tough time, if there was one force that remained a thorn in the flesh and a perennial nuisance, it was the Siddis of Janjira. They owed their allegiance to the Sultans of Bijapur or Ahmednagar or later the Mughals, as and how it suited their best interests. They were of Abyssinian origin and the sailors in their fleet came from Africa. The Siddis were Muslims and held sway over the impregnable island fortress of Janjira, about 50 km south of Bombay and had their capital in close-by Danda Rajapur, a prosperous seaport. Their excellent seamanship and sturdiness had seen them through the greatest of turmoil. They were not hereditary rulers and when an existing Siddi died, the Bijapur Sultan would nominate the most capable of them as the successor. They were given the title of Wazir or Minister by the sultans. Right from 1659 CE, Shivaji Maharaj led a series of attacks on the Siddis who threatened the Maratha suzerainty over the seas but was frustrated each time. After thirteen attempts, he failed to vanquish them. In these attacks, the Siddis had hoped that the Bijapur sultans would send them assistance. When this was not forthcoming, they shifted their loyalties to the

Mughals and sought the help of Aurangzeb who had a long running feud with the Marathas. Aurangzeb readily took them under this fold and gave them a grander title of 'Yakoot Khan'. But the Mughals were no more helpful than the Bijapur Sultans to the Siddis in the long run and they decided to fend for themselves. After a point, Shivaji Maharaj too realized the futility of a conquest over the Siddis and suspended hostilities to focus on his prime enemy, the Mughals.

In 1680 CE, Shivaji Maharaj breathed his last in Raigad. His son Sambhaji was crowned the Chhatrapati of the Marathas. Around this time, young Kanhoji who had also trained to be a powerful swimmer, an excellent swordsman and a skilled horseman, joined Sambhaji's fleet. He was posted at Suvarnadurg, where his father Tukoji had served as the deputy commander. Quite imprudently, Sambhaji, even as he was involved with skirmishes with the Mughals, opened a front with the Siddis as well. In October 1682, about thirty Maratha vessels set out to find and destroy the Siddi fleet. The Siddi Kassam Yakoot Khan himself came forward to lead his squadron against the Marathas, whom he managed to convincingly and disastrously vanquish. Kanhoji must have been a part of this ill-timed naval misadventure and literally learnt the tricks of warfare through a baptism by fire. Aurangzeb egged on the Siddi to carry forward the attack on the Marathas, and a series of forts—Sagargad, Rajkot and Pali in the Konkan—had to be shamefully surrendered to the Siddis, around 1688 CE.

The Attack on Suvarnadurg

The Siddis then attacked the island fort of Suvarnadurg, which was about 160 km south of Bombay. It was commanded by Acholji Mohitay. The Siddi fleet sieged the fort from all three sides and cut off supplies to it. Acholji defected and to save his life was willing to hand over the fort to the invading Siddi forces. Kanhoji, who was the young deputy commander in this fort, was outraged by this defection. He managed to send a secret message to Chhatrapati Sambhaji appraising him of the humiliating turn of events and offered to save the fort if he was given an opportunity. A grateful king granted him all the authority to take whatever steps he deemed fit to save the situation. Aiding Kanhoji was his childhood friend Balaji Vishwanath, who was ostensibly working as a clerk in the Siddis' salt works at Chiplun but doubling up as a spy for the Marathas and passing on military secrets and troop movements to Kanhoji. Buoyed by the Chhatrapati's blessings as also those of a local holy man named Brahmendra Swami, Kanhoji effected a midnight coup, got Acholji arrested and took over the defence of the fort. But quite thoughtlessly Kanhoji launched a cross-channel attack on the Siddi troops, which resulted in a disastrous failure. The stormers were taken captive by the Siddis and Kanhoji himself was imprisoned in the ambush. But he somehow daringly escaped from the Siddi prison in no time, swam the mile-wide channel for several hours and got back to his fort, as an exhausted commander. He then decided to withdraw and fatigue the Siddis by allowing the siege to carry on for as long as possible. This was a gamble that an already defeated Maratha force was taking, under Kanhoji. But after several weeks, the Siddis truly found this to be a wasteful exercise and quietly withdrew from the scene. Kanhoji had beaten all odds to save the day for Suvarnadurg. The Chhatrapati sent his lavish praise and the robes of the commander of the fort to Kanhoji. Balaji Vishwanath, meanwhile, had to flee from the Siddi service given that his dubious role lay exposed. Guru Brahmendra Swami guided him back to Poona safely, where he became a clerk in the revenue office of the Maratha subedar of Poona. By 1695 CE, Balaji Vishwanath ascended to the position of assistant subedar. He was responsible for arranging the supplies of fodder and stores required for the armies that were camped around Poona.

The Murder of Sambhaji and Afterwards

By 1687 CE, Aurangzeb had vanquished the Deccan Sultanates of Bijapur and Golconda and the Marathas were the only long-lasting foes that he was itching to annihilate. A full-frontal attack was launched on the Marathas after that. Sambhaji was captured by the Mughal forces by 1689 CE and taken to the Mughal camp at Tulapur. He was publicly exhibited, bound upon a camel and forced to convert to Islam. Upon his refusal, the worst of tortures were inflicted on him for over thirty-nine days. A red-hot iron rod was thrust into his eyes and his tongue was cut off. On 11 March 1689, his head was then chopped off and paraded from the emperor's camp towards Bijapur, while his body was mercilessly hacked to pieces.[8] This was the darkest hour in the barbarity of the Mughal hegemony, which shook the Marathas to the core and also instilled in them an undying spirit of vengeance for what was meted to their ruler. Sambhaji's son Shivaji II (later named Shahu) was barely six years old. Shivaji Maharaj's younger son Rajaram was nineteen years old and he was made the regent of the Maratha throne. To divide the Mughal forces, it was decided that Sambhaji's wife Yesubai and young Shivaji II would stay on in Raigad and Chhatrapati Rajaram would head towards the fort of Panhala. However, within three weeks of Sambhaji's murder, Aurangzeb sent his wazir Asad Khan's son Itiqad Khan to liquidate the vestiges of the Maratha kingdom too. In April 1689, Rajaram managed to escape from Panhala.

Meanwhile Rajaram's well-wishers advised him to head southwards to a safer place to the fort of Ginjee, 800 km southwards in the Carnatic, which he reached by November 1689 after barely managing to escape several attempts on his life from Aurangzeb's army. There Rajaram created a shadow cabinet of sorts and announced new military commanders with the hope that the Marathas would eventually win back all that they had lost during this darkest period of their eclipse. Siddoji Gujjar was named the new *Surkhail* or Grand Admiral placed in command of the Maratha fleet and given the responsibility of defending the coast from both land and sea. He was to have two deputy commanders—Bhawani Mohitay and Kanhoji Angrey. From Ginjee, Chhatrapati Rajaram wrote letters encouraging men to join the Maratha struggle for regaining their lost glory and kingdom.

The siege of Raigad that was considered to be an impregnable fort carried on for several months. Finally, it fell due to the machinations of a traitor Suryaji Pisal who was bribed. Yesubai and the infant Shivaji, unfortunately, fell into the hands of the Mughals and were taken away as captives to Aurangzeb's camp. The Mughal emperor treated them with a lot more concern and respect, and Aurangzeb's daughter Zebunnissa took the little boy under her care.

Determined to squash Rajaram, too, Aurangzeb sent Itiqad Khan with the title of 'Zulfiquar' Khan to Ginjee to lay siege to the fort there. But the Maratha forces under Santaji Ghorpade and Dhanaji Jadhav with their lightning raids managed to cut off supplies to the Mughal force. By 1693 CE, the Maratha attacks forced them to lift the siege. A couple of years later, in 1697 CE, they returned to lay siege to Ginjee again. But by this time, Zulfiquar had a secret understanding with Rajaram to seek the latter's support to establish his own independent suzerainty in the Deccan after the death of the nonagenarian Aurangzeb. He literally allowed Rajaram a safe passage along with his wives and family before occupying Ginjee, given the repeated pressures from Delhi. Rajaram returned to Maharashtra to take over what he had run away from, into exile. He shifted his capital to the fort of Satara. In his absence, the Marathas, too, had organized a powerful army.

Meanwhile, Kanhoji Angre, in the nine years that his master was in exile, remained steadfastly loyal to the Maratha throne. As commander of the northern fleet that was given to him, under *Surkhail* Siddoji Gujar, he organized it into a compact, powerful striking force of forty assorted vessels, treated with respect along the coast. His ships were already beginning to be known as units of 'Angaria's Navy,' his agents collected revenue in his name as the Lord of the Konkan. He flew his own red standard wherever he lived. He had shown tactical and strategic wisdom, given the doldrums that the Maratha kingdom was in. He had also managed to maintain a surprising neutrality with the Siddis, and all the powers were confined to their respective spheres of influence—the Siddis and the English confined their activities to northern Konkan, the Portuguese in Chaul and Goa, the Dutch in Vengurla, while the Raja of Kudal and Sawants of Wadi were small-time chieftains of the Konkan. In 1695 CE, Kanhoji shifted his headquarters from Suvarnadurg to Colaba. This brought him squarely in the midst of the two major powers, the Siddis at Janjira and the

English at Bombay, a few kilometres away. English records of this time talk about possible naval exploits by people known as 'Shivaji pirates', the term they used derisively for the Maratha navy fleet. It is very likely that Kanhoji was involved in them too, though he is not named directly in them. In February 1694 CE, a letter from Surat to Bombay reported that, 'Ram Rajah's gallvets have been plundering at the river mouth, have taken a boat of Mocho goods, computed worth 80,000 rupees; a boat with ballast we sent to the *William and Mary* they seized, but finding nothing but stones, they beat the poor Lascars and flung their sailes and rigging over board.'[9] On 16 February 1695, the *Emerald* on her way from Calicut to Bombay, met some 'Savajee people south-ward of Danda Rajapoor'.[10] Many such letters are seen narrating with alarm the 'pirate' activities of the Marathas all through the 1690s.

Shortly before the return of Rajaram, the post of *Surkhail* had fallen vacant with the death of Siddhoji Gujar. It seemed like a foregone conclusion that Kanhoji for his deft management of the fleet, in the absence of a central Maratha authority, would be the natural claimant for the position. But Rajaram was somehow reluctant to make such an announcement and he, instead, named both Kanhoji and Bhawanji Mohitay as deputy chiefs of the northern and southern Konkan respectively. This might have been an apt occasion for Kanhoji to revolt and express his displeasure for being short-changed. But he demonstrated remarkable loyalty and placed everything that he had won in the last nine years at the feet of his master and was content to take whatever was offered to him.

Around March 1700–01, the Siddi Kassam Yakoot Khan came charging into coastal Colaba with an intent to plunder. But Kanhoji refused to get drawn in and let the Siddi hang on for more than six months, even as supplies were aplenty in his fort and he himself managed to foray deep into Siddi territory of Thal. The Siddi was once again forced to lift a wasteful siege and return with no achievement.

Kanhoji began offering sea-passports or permits called *dastaks*, similar to the Portuguese Cartaz for all seagoing ships. These were roughly at the same price as the Cartaz and offered more or less the same benefits—protection at sea from pirates and other coastal powers. Ships not in possession of his *dastaks* were to be seized and held for ransom. Given the ownership that both the Portuguese and the Marathas claimed over the waters of the Konkan, prudent traders equipped themselves with both documents to avoid any harassment.

However, gloom quickly set over the fledgling Maratha kingdom as Chhatrapati Rajaram died untimely of a sudden illness in mid-March 1700, in the fort of Singhad. Aurangzeb, who had spent the last eighteen years in a costly Deccan campaign that had caused him to lose more than five lakh soldiers was increasingly beginning to realize its futility and his own pyrrhic victory. Much of the territory he had captured had already been won back by the Marathas even as he camped in their midst. Rajaram had left behind two sons—the ten-year-old elder son Shivaji from his senior queen Tarabai, and the younger one, a three-year-old Sambhaji, from Rajasbai. Tarabai acted swiftly. She got all the chieftains to accept her son's claim to the throne and her own regency, even as she put Rajasbai and her son into prison. Noteworthy was that even after ten years, Sambhaji's widow Yesubai and her son were still in Mughal captivity. Kanhoji, meanwhile, maintained his loyalty to the new sovereign Tarabai.

Kanhoji and the East India Company

There was a gradual hardening of stance of the East India Company towards Kanhoji on the grounds that he was disturbing the peace of the waters around Bombay due to his constant skirmishes with the Siddis. In 1702 CE, Kanhoji seized a private trading merchant ship that had six Englishmen on board. The Company took umbrage at this too. In September 1703, a ship from Aden that was loaded with cargo came to the shores to Bombay and it had Kanhoji's *dastak* for passage. Despite this, to teach him a lesson the English detained the ship. On 13 September 1703, their records at Bombay Castle noted this:

> Yesterday in the evening came into this harbour a grab under Sevajee [Shivaji] colours, being come from Aden, which (on examination) proving to have no pass but to belong to a place Girea, near Rajapore,

under the Government of Conajee Angria (Kanhoji Angrey), and the said Conajee Angria and his people having at sundry times committed many injurious and practical actions on the inhabitants of this Island. In consideration thereof as likewise of the orders lately received from the General and Council at Surat concerning them, 'twas agreed and resolved to embargo and detain here said vessel, cargo and people till we shall receive their orders concerning them.[11]

For almost a year thereafter, Kanhoji kept quiet about the open hostility that the English had shown towards him, making the latter think that their pressure tactics were paying off. By November the next year he sailed with seven *gallivats* and camped at the mouth of the Pane River, close to Bombay. No shots were fired, no offensive messages exchanged. His very presence there blocked off Bombay's communication with the mainland, paralysing all shipping thereby. It was a silent message given to the English that if he chose to become difficult, he could really thwart their trade in ways that they could not imagine. After staying put for a week, he quietly sailed off, but the message had reached the inmates of the Bombay Castle. William Reynolds was sent to wait on Kanhoji 'wherever he might be found, acquainting said chief robber his being sent to him by English General of India, civilly telling him in words neither more or less that he can't be permitted searching, or seizing any boats, groabs [ghurabs] or other vessels, from what port, harbour, place of what nation soever they may be, bringing provisions, timber or merchandize to Bombay, Mahim or other place from whence they came, without breach of that friendship the English nation has always had with Raja Savajee [Shivaji] and all his Captains in subordination to him'. Reynolds was also instructed 'not upon any account, by word or otherwise, to threaten or insinuate any design of hostility against him'.[12]

Kanhoji's reply was straightforward. He told them: 'The Savajees[13] [Marathas] had done many services for the English that never kept their word with him; they had peace with the Portugueze [sic] and every one of their portes [sic] free to them; was known they had held out war with the Mogul forty years, lived now by their sword and would seize what boates [sic] or other vessel belonging to the Moguls vessels from any of his forts or Mallabarr, excepting such as had Conjee Angras passports; the English being at liberty acting as they please.'[14] This was only to be the start of many more clashes between him and the English.

The Return of Shahu

Sambhaji's son who had been captured by Aurangzeb at the age of six was now a young man of more than twenty years. He had nearly forgotten everything of his earlier life as he grew amidst his father's murderers. They had even changed his name from Shivaji II, a name they dreaded and despised, to 'Shahu'. Around this time, in 1707 CE, Aurangzeb died near Ahmednagar, unleashing a war of succession among his surviving sons Sham Alam, Azam Shah and Kam Baksh. Sambhaji's widow used all her diplomatic skills to get herself and her son released from Mughal clutches. They were finally freed, and Shahu marched towards Maharashtra with a view to take over his dead father's erstwhile kingdom. He was joined by several Maratha followers including the Commander Dhanaji Jadhav, Balaji Vishwanath, Khando Ballal Chitnis and others.

But things had changed back home, with the family of Rajaram having taken charge. There was the regent queen Tarabai who was fiercely guarding the throne for her son. She immediately dubbed Shahu as an imposter and a Mughal stooge. She made all her commanders take an oath of loyalty towards her in this claim for succession. Kanhoji obviously sided with the monarch that he had always considered as his master and went with Tarabai's diktats. In return for his loyalty, Tarabai finally made Kanhoji the new *Surkhail* or the Grand Admiral of the Maratha navy, as also the Viceroy of the Konkan.

The two competitors to the Maratha throne met in the battlefield at Khed in October 1707. Shahu emerged victorious in this war and entered Satara triumphantly and was crowned king with the full support of the Mughals. Tarabai meanwhile retreated to Panhala, a fort near Kolhapur, and formed a parallel kingdom from there. The defections of many of her hitherto loyalist commanders to Shahu's side came as a rude blow for Tarabai.

To make herself doubly sure of Kanhoji's loyalty, in 1711 CE, Tarabai placed the fort of Rajmachi, literally meaning 'The Royal Terrace', under his command. Located near Khandala, Rajmachi was technically outside the natural borders of the Konkan. But the fort was of great strategic importance. Along with another fort called Lohgad (fortress of steel), Rajmachi was vital for the defence of north Konkan from incursions from above the ghats. Between these two forts, they commanded the principal pass between the ghats and northern Konkan known as the Bor-Ghat Pass. Anyone who possessed Rajmachi could dominate the pass and paralyse all communication between Shahu's capital Satara and northern Konkan. Tarabai's motives in granting Rajmachi to her most daring and trusted commander, Kanhoji, was thus evident. She also wanted to thwart any fledgling alliance between Shahu and the East India Company in Bombay.

On his part, despite his unswerving loyalty to his queen Tarabai, Kanhoji was reluctant to show any open hostility towards Shahu. He instead decided to wait and watch as the situation emerged. He strengthened his fortifications at Gheria and Colaba. He was almost an independent sovereign as he struck his own coins that were circulated in the Konkan.

The entire coast, from Bombay to Goa, was now in Kanhoji's hands and there was hardly a creek, harbour or river mouth where he had no fortification and a boat station. He had also remodelled his fleet, established five shipyards and employed hundreds of workmen under the guidance of foreign experts to build new ships. His sailors were paid well and regularly with better terms of employment and hence several of them, including foreigners, flocked towards him rather than his rival powers in the region. Kanhoji now possessed ten *ghurabs* (mounting from sixteen to thirty guns each, some of them over 400 ton) and also fifty *gallivats* (of between 60 to 120 ton and mounting four to ten). It was not a formidable naval force by any means, especially in comparison to his European rivals, but it was a well-trained force that was envied by the other powers in the Konkan.[15]

Meanwhile, the tenuous political situation of the Maratha kingdom kept changing. Several disgruntled chieftains of Shahu were defecting to Tarabai and while she was puffing with all the new-found support, she did not know what hit her out of the blue from within her own fold. Rajasbai, the second wife of Rajaram, whom she had imprisoned after the death of Rajaram and assuming power, suddenly struck back. In a sudden and a bloodless coup, Rajasbai managed to imprison Tarabai and her son and instead placed her own son, the seventeen-year-old Sambhaji II on the throne. As ill luck would have it, Tarabai's son Shivaji II died soon after, and she spent the rest of her life, some forty-seven years of it, in prison, cursing the cruel turn that her fate had suddenly taken. Descendants of Sambhaji II ruled from Kolhapur as the direct heirs to Chhatrapati Shivaji and Shahu ruled from Satara, thereby bifurcating the Maratha kingdom.

Skirmishes with the Europeans

Setting aside treaties with the Portuguese signed in 1703 CE, Kanhoji began to adopt a more belligerent attitude towards the main sea power, the Portuguese too. When exactly he challenged the Portuguese supremacy of the seas we do not know, but his first victim was not a merchantman, but a Portuguese fighting ship, *paal*-of-war[16] that was richly laden. It was carrying on board the retired Governor of Chaul whom he imprisoned and who eventually died from the rigours of imprisonment.[17] Kanhoji confiscated all the possessions that he had acquired in his lifetime of service in the Far East. He then fought two fighting ships, *manchwas*-of-war, that belonged to the Portuguese fleet of the north. He burnt one and captured another with twenty-seven Portuguese prisoners. They were all put to death, according to the Portuguese sources, except one who managed to save his life by paying a ransom of 12,000 Xerafins.[18]

In 1712 CE, during the viceroyalty of Rodrigo da Costa, Kanhoji attacked the yearly Portuguese *armado* of merchant ships that was escorted by two powerful warships under the command of Luiz da Costa. Kanhoji fell upon the frigates with his *paals*, dismantled the

Portuguese flagship and captured no less than forty ships. This was a great blow to Portuguese power in Goa since several of their citizens lost all the capital they had invested in the mercantile enterprise.[19] Most of the merchant fleet fell into Kanhoji's hands.

It was the tactics that Kanhoji employed that enabled him to devour the European fleet that were far superior to the Maratha ones in all ways. When the big European frigates came close to the coast, they had to reduce sail and slow down. This was when Kanhoji's ships that were lurking around in a nearby cove would shock them with their sudden swoop and chase them in their row boats, crammed with men. This nullified all advantage of better armaments. Unless the victim put on a burst of speed and got away, he was invariably doomed. The Marathas also indulged in hand-to-hand sword fight in which they were masterful. Hence playing to his strengths and nullifying the opponent's advantages helped Kanhoji gain control over the superior European fleet on numerous occasions.

Turning simultaneously towards the English, in 1706 CE, Kanhoji and his men attacked and captured the East India Company's ship *Monsoon*, off Karwar. In 1707 CE, his ships attacked and sank the Company's frigate *Bombay* and in 1710 his ships had a two-day long gun battle with the Company's ship *Godolphin* within sight of Bombay. In 1712 CE, he captured two more of the Company's ships: one, the Governor's own armed yacht and the other the ketch *Anne*, belonging to the Company's chief factory at Karwar. Both these ships were taken after a hard fight near Vengurla, during which the Company's armed escort *Defiance*, which was a frigate of fourteen guns, had been put to flight. The very next month, two other ships of the Company, *Grantham* and *Somers*, coming from England were attacked by Kanhoji's fleet. All this caused immense discomfiture in the Company headquarters at Bombay Castle. Kanhoji sent a messenger to Bombay in February 1713 with proposals for peace, offering to deliver the captured vessels if an Englishman of credit was sent to Colaba. He was willing to undertake not to molest English ships if the Company promised to assist him militarily in times of need, gave him supplies of gunpowder and also a place in Bombay to manufacture it. The Company ignored several of these proposals and instead listed out six clauses of their own that sought to bind him down:

1. That he deliver [sic] up all that he has taken that belonged to the Company and our people.
2. That upon no pretence whatever he meddle [sic] with any English ships or with the ships belonging to the merchants who live under the protection of the English as Madras, Bengal or any other factories or colonies belonging to the English whatsoever.
3. That whatever ships or vessels belong to any nation whatsoever that are coming into our harbour and in sight thereof he is not (to) meddle with them that is between Mahim stakes and Cundry and at their going out the same rule is to be observed.
4. That he grants our merchants the free liberty of his ports they paying usual customs being conformable to the rules thereof. If any vessels belonging to Sevagee Raza or Sow Razah shall take or molest any vessels belonging to Bombay they having his convoy which he is oblige to give, he shall be answerable for the damage.
5. We on our parts promise that we will permit no ships or vessels whatever to wear English colours, but what belong to the subjects of the English nation, which shall be incerted [sic] in all their ships.
6. We grant him free liberty of our port of Bombay to buy, sell and merchandize he paying the usual custom and observing the rules of our port, which if he complies with that we send the *Blenhein Ann* and *Manchua* to fetch the Company's effects, which he has taken and our people. [20]

Kanhoji accepted these terms in April 1713 and bought temporary truce with the English as he did not want to open multiple fronts of conflict at the same time. He knew that trouble was brewing with one of the Maratha kingdoms for him and hostility with the English, too, at the same time would be imprudent. The fifth clause was important, which obliged the English not to permit foreign ships or vessels to fly their colours. It was the interpretation of this last term that led to hostilities a few years later between Kanhoji and the English.

Peace with Chhatrapati Shahu

The period 1712–13 was turning out to be a busy time for Kanhoji, both on land and by the sea. In addition to the naval skirmishes with the European powers, he had to confront an attack on the land, this time from Shahu in Satara who was keen to punish all the rebel chieftains of his erstwhile rival Tarabai. He sent his peshwa Bahiropant Pingale to reduce Kanhoji and bring the whole of the Konkan under Satara's control. Kanhoji allowed the Maratha column to pass through the Bor-Ghat Pass unopposed and once they penetrated deep inside the Konkan, he went behind the force and occupied the pass, thereby closing down the door of the mousetrap he had set for the peshwa. The Maratha forces were routed by Kanhoji and the peshwa himself was shamefully taken prisoner. Through this battle, Kanhoji reasserted his supremacy over the two strategic forts of Rajmachi and Lohgad once again. From Lohgad, he sent a belligerent note to Shahu that his intent was to march against Satara for the unnecessary hostility that he had opened with him.

A rattled Shahu sent his closest confidante Balaji Vishwanath to win over Kanhoji with the promise that if he succeeded in this mission, he would make him the peshwa. Balaji Vishwanath was, however, a clever man who negotiated that it would make more sense if he was made peshwa first and sent to negotiate with Kanhoji in that formal capacity, rather than be made peshwa post-facto. With few options before him, Shahu agreed and made Balaji Vishwanath his peshwa or chief minister. The two men who were hitherto childhood friends met as rivals at Valvan, near Lonawala. After a lot of discussion, Kanhoji agreed to make peace with Shahu and accept his suzerainty. The Treaty of Colaba was signed between them on 8 February 1714 as per which Shahu granted three districts that comprised the Konkan to Kanhoji; out of the nine forts captured by Kanhoji, five including Lohgad were to be returned to Shahu, and four others including Rajmachi retained. As a result of this treaty, Kanhoji obtained control of ten seaside forts and sixteen land forts. His annual income from the territory that he was placed in command of was now a whopping thirty-six lakh rupees. He was confirmed as *Surkhail* in hereditary perpetuity. From now on, he signed all his correspondences as 'Kanhoji, son of Tukoji, Surkhail by the grace of King Shahu'—'*Shahu-karya dhurandar Tukoji tanujanmanah Kanhoji Surkhailasya Mudrikeyam Virajate* (The seal of Kanhoji, son of Tukoji, Surkhail in the service of Shahu)'[21] was his new official seal.

As an immediate outcome of the truce between Shahu and Kanhoji, the Siddis came to terms with the growing power of Angrey and withdrew from power struggles with him, leaving the Portuguese high and dry in their opposition. This explains the bitter complaints made by the Portuguese viceroy in 1715 CE against the Siddis. In 1716 CE, they tried to seek a new ally in the disgruntled Sambhaji II in Kolhapur, who was enraged at his hitherto loyalist Kanhoji turning his back at him.[22] But they were soon to realize that the ruler of Kolhapur lacked both the energy and the ability to lead a formidable alliance and hence these diplomatic overtures met an untimely death. Kanhoji literally ruled the seas unopposed, and the Portuguese found themselves helpless in being able to circumscribe his activities. Of all their posts on the western coast, Chaul suffered the maximum losses since their main source of income, which was the volume of dutiable commerce, suffered immensely due to Kanhoji. Luckily for the Portuguese, after several years of solo sulking, by 1721 CE, they found an unlikely ally in the English with whom they formed an offensive and defensive alliance to show Kanhoji his place.

Hostilities with Charles Boone

Despite the treaty with the English in 1713 CE, hostilities continued to simmer given the clash of interests between the players. They came to the fore when Charles Boone took charge of the Government of Bombay in 1715 CE. Kanhoji complained to him of the English not reciprocating the amicable terms of the treaty; that the country boats freighted by the Bombay merchants were not covered by the earlier agreement and formed good prizes as long as they were not provided with his passes. Boone strongly protested this claim. Thus began a war that was to last till 1756 CE, long after Kanhoji's death, and eventually ended with the capitulation of Gheria. The matter came to a head with Kanhoji's capture of three ships in quick succession—*Success* (belonging to an Indian broker of the English, Govardhandas), *Robert* and *Otter*, and his forcible appropriation of some timber from some of the Company vessels. The nationality of the three captured ships was a highly contested issue. The owners of the ship were not English, but the cargo belonged to English subjects and Kanhoji contended that they were not entitled to exemption from his *dastaks*. He wrote to the English that while he would abide by the treaty and not molest ships belonging to Bombay, Bengal and Madras, if the English resorted to loading their cargo on other ships and enter through stealth, he would not allow that.

Hostilities were hastened by the detention of a *shibar* at Mahim that belonged to Kanhoji's port Alibag. This elicited an angry letter from Kanhoji to Boone where he proclaimed: 'Our friendship is over and from this day forward what God gives I shall take.'[23] Heated letters followed from both sides, eventually culminating in the declaration of war on 17 June 1718 through a proclamation that the English published at Bombay.[24]

Expeditions were held against Kanhoji through June to October 1718, but they were not always successful. The failure was attributed in some cases to the bad weather and in others the unwillingness of the men to land. The first serious expedition was led by Boone himself and was against the island stronghold of Khanderi. This again ended in failure for the English—something that they pinned on the alleged treachery of a scapegoat, one Ramji Kamathi, a prominent merchant of Bombay, for his treacherous correspondence with Kanhoji revealing the plans, and was imprisoned for life. They then tried to bombard Colaba at different intervals, but this left no major losses for Kanhoji. The English, at best, managed to capture four of his *ghurabs* as a prize for all the efforts they took. Shahu meanwhile intervened and peace was restored and hostilities suspended for the time being. When Kanhoji captured the ship *Charlotte* in 1720 CE, the English decided to ally with the Portuguese and conduct a joint expedition against Colaba the following year.

The Anglo-Portuguese Alliance

In the face of a common enemy, it might have been the most natural thing for the two European powers to ally much earlier, had it not been for the intense mutual suspicion. The Portuguese suspected the English of piratical practices and believed that Kanhoji was secretly getting his artillery and ammunition from them. There was a lot of internal opposition among the Portuguese to sign an alliance treaty with the English. But eventually the English agent Robert Cowan reached Goa and convinced them, with the result that on 20 August 1721 they decided to jointly attack Kanhoji Angrey. The spoils of war and conquered territories were to be equally divided. Colaba was to be awarded to the Porutguese, and Gheria to the English. They were looking for a complete annihilation of Kanhoji and putting an end once and for all to the nuisance and hence no peace treaties were to be entertained.[25] The success of the scheme depended on the secrecy. But sadly for the allies, Kanhoji got wind of the threat and he tried to avert the danger through diplomacy by sending peace proposals to the Portuguese, which were flatly rejected. He began strengthening his position and also sought fresh forces and reinforcements from Chhatrapati Shahu. A week after the Anglo-Portuguese treaty was signed, a squadron of four ships under Commodore Thomas Mathews left England for the East to buttress the strength of the existing forces against Kanhoji.

Without going into the minute details of the joint expedition, it would suffice here to say that once again the combined forces' attack on Colaba and Vijaydurg failed miserably, despite all the bravado. Instead, acrimony and mutual suspicion between the two allies spilt out into the open. The ace diplomat that he was, Kanhoji decided to exploit this split to his advantage and once again sent peace proposals only to the Portuguese. The viceroy was now seeing the futility of aligning with the English. He had seen that Colaba was well-provisioned and strongly garrisoned with 1,000 infantry and 700 cavalry, despite their best attempts to reduce it. Fresh reinforcements were coming in daily from Poona and Satara. Pilaji Jadhav and Baji Rao had come there with an enormous Maratha horde numbering 25,000 cavalry, dimming whatever little chances the allies might have had. When news trickled in of an attack on a Portuguese boat near Diu by the Marathas, the viceroy finally relented, accepted the proposals and quietly returned to Goa. On account of his treaty with the English, there was a logistic error that prevented the Portuguese viceroy from accepting the terms with Kanhoji. So, peace was negotiated not by Kanhoji but by Baji Rao, and the Portuguese came to terms directly with Shahu, thereby cleverly not jeopardizing their treaty with the English as well. A treaty was signed between the peshwa and the viceroy at the camp of Alibag on 9 January 1722, violating thereby the Anglo-Portuguese treaty not in letter, but totally in spirit. The Portuguese undertook not to convoy ships belonging to the enemies of the Marathas but to help them against their foes. The ports of the two nations were thrown open to the merchants of either party and the Portuguese also agreed to furnish the peshwa with ammunition at a just price. The Marathas undertook to restore the Portuguese ships captured by the Colaba fleet.[26] Thus ended the Anglo–Portuguese grand alliance in utter disgrace, leaving the English alone to lick their wounds and also counter an aggressive Kanhoji at sea whose prestige was enhanced manifold.

Buoyed by the success, Kanhoji was relentless against the English. On 14 March 1722, his fleet comprising four *paals* and twenty *gallivats* attached the English *paals* between Chaul and Rajapur. One of the two English vessels was burnt and the other put to flight. Kanhoji also captured an English ship richly laden with coins and valuable goods. Skirmishes and then peace entreaties between the Marathas and the English thus continued. In 1724 CE, Kanhoji wrote a letter to the new Governor of Bombay, William Phipps, proposing peace, but the latter haughtily scoffed at the prospect in his pompous reply. Hostilities continued to simmer between the two rivals, though it secured the release of prisoners from both sides.

The next few years in Kanhoji's life were quiet and uneventful. His rivals at sea did not bother him much and in 1725 CE, he felt emboldened enough to leave his headquarters and journey all the way to Satara to pay respects to Chhatrapati Shahu amidst growing talk of court intrigues against him. He was received at Satara with great pomp and honour. In his illustrious career, Kanhoji Angre had remained an unvanquished Indian naval hero who had managed to keep all the European powers and to a large extent, the Siddis, at bay and enhance the Maratha naval prestige like few other heroes had done.

Kanhoji took ill in 1729 and this brave and daring naval hero of the Marathas finally breathed his last on 20 June 1729.

Kanhoji lived a colourful life, despite being embroiled in innumerable battles and skirmishes. As Manohar Malgonkar mentions, 'born and begotten of the sea, full of its wild and savage energy . . . rocked to and fro by its waves into hardihood and indomitable pluck.'[27] He was fond of both ships and horses and swam as powerfully as he rode horses. He had three wives—Mathura, Lakshmi and Gahina—and several concubines. They all lived in the same house. He was the father of seven legitimate children (a daughter and six sons) and several children from his countless mistresses. There were other dancing girls, too, whom he fancied—the ever-changing objects of a sailor's loveless passion. He was fond of song, dance and drama and often held performances in his court. He was an astute diplomat with great clarity and an abounding sarcasm. He was very fond of feeding Brahmins and showering them with costly gifts.[28] He had brought his family deity Kalimbika from Suvarnadurg to Colaba and installed her with much fanfare at the family temple at Hirakote, across the channel from Colaba. Of his six sons Sekhoji, Sambhaji, Manaji, Tulaji, Yesaji and Dhonji, Sekhoji was perhaps the eldest and succeeded him.

Summing up Kanhoji's glorious legacy, historian Surendra Nath Sen writes:

> Kanhoji Angria may be regarded as the second founder of the Maratha navy, just as Baji Rao I has been styled the second founder of the Maratha empire. He was inspired, as he wrote in his letter to Governor Phipps, by Shivaji's example, and whatever may be said of his naval practices, he undoubtedly re-established Maratha prestige at sea. Even when he was at open war with the Portuguese, their subjects acknowledged his naval supremacy by purchasing his passports for their trading vessels. He defied the joint efforts of the English, the Portuguese and the Siddi,

and in his wars by land and sea he had given evidence not only of good seamanship but also of wise diplomacy. In his foreign relations he could hardly be accused of treachery or faithlessness . . . he left an extensive province and a strong and respectable fleet to his heirs, who had they possessed his prudence and moderation, might have added immensely to the prestige and power they had inherited from their famous father.[29]

Notes

1   J.F. Judice Biker's 'Biker Manuscripts, Archivo Ultramarino, Lisbon; Fundo geral 8548, p. 149.

2   Clement Downing, *A History of the Indian Wars* (London: Oxford University Press, 1924),

3   Ibid., pp. 8–9.

4   For Tukoji's exploits, see Manohar Malgonkar, *Kanhoji Angey, Maratha Admiral: An Account of his Life and His Battles with the English* (Bombay: Asia Publishing House, 1959), pp. 11–12.

5   Ibid., pp. 10–11.

6   Uday S. Kulkarni, *The Maratha Century: Vignettes and Anecdotes of the Maratha Empire* (Pune: Mula Mutha Publications, 2021), p. 30.

7   For more on the Maratha navy, see B.K. Apte, *A History of the Maratha Navy and Merchant Ships* (Bombay: State Board for Literature and Culture, 1973) and O.K. Nambiar, *Our Seafaring in the Indian Ocean* (Bangalore: Jeevan Publications, 1975).

8   Malgonkar, *Kanhoji Angey*, pp. 57–58.

9   Factory Records, Bombay, Vol. 21, India Office, British Library, London, p. 83.

10   Ibid., Vol. 23, Set 2, p. 11.

11   Factory Records, Bombay, Vol. 5, Set 3, India Office, British Library, London, pp. 11–12.

12   Bombay Public Proceedings, Vol. 2, India Office, British Library, London, pp. 15, 17, 21.

13   Meaning adherents of Shivaji, i.e., the Marathas.

14   Bombay Public Proceedings, Vol. 2, p. 90, India Office, British Library, London.

15   For more details on these see Malgonkar.

16   The paals and shibars were hybrid vessels, smaller than ghurabs but bigger than gallivants.

17 J.F. Judice Biker's 'Biker Manuscripts', Archivo Ultramarino, Lisbon, p. 150.
18 Ibid.
19 J.F. Judice Biker's 'Biker Manuscripts', *Tratados da India*, Vol V. Archivo Ultramarino, Lisbon, pp. 292–93.
20 Bombay Public Consultations, Range CCCXLI, No. 4, (Consultation 12 February 1712–13), India Office, British Library, London.
21 Malgonkar, *Kanhoji Angey*, p. 177
22 J.F. Judice Biker's 'Biker Manuscripts', *Tratados da India*, Vol. VI, Archivo Ultramarino, Lisbon; pp. 2–4.
23 Bombay Public Consultations, Range CCCXLI, No. 4, pp. 58–61 (Consultation 13 April 1718) and pp. 77–83 (Consultation 7 May 1718), India Office, British Library, London.
24 Ibid., p. 96
25 J.F. Judice Biker's 'Biker Manuscripts', *Tratados da India*, Vol. III, Archivo Ultramarino, Lisbon, pp. 242–44.
26 Biker, 'Biker Manuscripts', *Tratados da India*, Vol. VI, Archivo Ultramarino, Lisbon, pp. 10–12.
27 Malgonkar, *Kanhoji Angey*, p. 121.
28 For more on the man and his personal life mentioned in this paragraph, see Malgonkar, *Kanhoji Angey*, pp. 120–24.
29 Surendra Nath Sen, *The Military System of the Marathas* (Calcutta: Orient Longman Private Ltd., 1928), pp. 189–90.

Banda Singh Bahadur

The tenth and last guru of the Sikhs, Guru Govind Singh, was hopeful of a rapprochement with the Mughal emperor. After the death of Aurangzeb who had inflicted uncounted miseries on the Sikhs, his son Bahadur Shah who took over the Mughal throne after a war of succession invited the Guru for conciliatory talks. On 2 August 1707, the Guru came to Agra where he was presented with a dress of honour, a jewelled scarf and other marks of respect. But around this very time, a rebellion of the emperor's brother Kam Bakhsh broke out, forcing him to proceed southwards, towards the Deccan. The Guru, too, accompanied the royal entourage, but midway their negotiations broke off causing him to separate himself from the Mughal camp and stop at Nanded.

The Guru had heard from a mahant in Jaipur, Jait Ram, of a curious occultist who lived in Nanded and who practised strange incantations on unsuspecting sadhus and visitors. Jait Ram warned him to beware of the man when the Guru had set out to the Deccan. Disregarding this, in the autumn of 1708 CE, the Guru promptly went calling on the occultist whose name was Madho Das and who had a monastery of sorts in Nanded. Finding him not available at home, the Guru promptly went and plonked himself on Madho Das' cot and also ordered his disciples to cook a non-vegetarian meal for him, knowing pretty well that this was unallowed in the Vaishnava hermitage of the occultist. When Madho Das heard of this strange and ill-mannered visitor who had come into his place and literally usurped it, he was livid with rage and rushed back home hurling invectives at the man. He used all his secret spirits and sorcery tricks to overturn the cot on which the Guru was seated but failed miserably. However, when he came into the Guru's presence and beheld his effervescent visage, his temper cooled, and tears began to flow down his eyes automatically. The following dialogue took place between them, as was recorded in the *Zikr-i-Guruanwa Ibtida-i-Singhan wa Mazhab-i-Eshan* by Ahmad Shah of Batala:[1]

> Madho Das: Who are you?
> Guru Govind Singh: He whom you know.
> Madho Das: What do I know?
> Guru Govind Singh: Think it over in your mind
> Madho Das: (after a pause): So, you are Guru Govind Singh!
> Guru Govind Singh: Yes!
> Madho Das: What have you come here for?
> Guru Govind Singh: I have come so that I may convert you into a disciple of mine.
> Madho Das: I submit my Lord. I am a *Banda* (slave) of yours.

From that day, the occultist was not only a changed man but also bore a new name—Banda Singh Bahadur, the loyal servant of the Guru. From an occult ascetic, he became a brave warrior and a defender of the Sikh Khalsa brotherhood that Guru Govind Singh had established.

Early Years

Banda Singh was born as Lachhman Dev on 27 October 1670 in Rajori, in the Poonch district of western Kashmir. His father was an ordinary Rajput ploughman who belonged to the Bharadwaj clan. It is believed that they belonged to the Sodhi community of the Khatris of Punjab, while according to others, he hailed from Sialkot. Little is known of his younger days except for a life-transforming incident that happened to him in his teens. As a young boy who spent all his time less in education and more in pursuits such as ploughing, hunting, riding and archery, Lachhman had gone hunting once. He had taken aim and hit a doe and given the perfect aim he managed each time, the animal was struck by his arrow. When he went to collect his hunt, he was moved beyond words to see the pitiable eyes of the dying doe who happened to be pregnant. To compound the poignancy, when he slit open the stomach of the dead animal, two unborn young ones fell from her womb. They writhed in pain and died right in front of his eyes in a few minutes, being born prematurely. Something changed inexorably within young Lachhman at that instant. His sense of remorse, repentance and grief grew so strong that his mind took a completely ascetic turn. He began to be disgusted with everything of the material world and started seeking out the larger purpose and meaning of life in the company of sadhus and saints who visited his town on their way to Kashmir. A *bairagi*, a man dedicated to the Vaishnava tradition, Janaki Prasad once came to Rajori and when Lachhman met him, he was so enraptured that he decided to pack his bags and follow him as his disciple. Barely fifteen then, he left home and kept roaming from place to place with a new name that his guru gave him, Madho Das.

In 1686 CE, he accompanied Janaki Prasad to attend the Baisakhi fair at the shrine of Baba Ram Thamman at a village near Punjab's Kasur. Here he met another *bairagi*, Ram Das, and became his disciple as well. But somehow, he felt ill at ease and that something was wanting. He had been on a restless quest and each new guru he took did not seem to satisfy his spiritual thirst. Looking out for a better preceptor he made his way all the way down south towards Nasik. Charmed by its beauty and the spiritual power of the place he selected the woods of Panchvati that had famously sheltered Bhagwan Ram, Sita and Lakshman during their exile, as his abode for meditation. Here he got acquainted with an old yogi, Aughar Nath, who was famous for his tantric achievements and became his steadfast disciple. The old yogi who was in the last stages of his life was deeply moved by the affection and devotion that the young disciple showed him. Being pleased, the yogi bequeathed his entire knowledge and a much-coveted book on the occult and yogic sciences to the young man around 1691 CE before passing away.

Madho Das left Panchvati and decided to establish a monastery of his own, being armed with new magic and tantric tricks. He followed the course of the Godavari and reached Nanded where he set up a humble cottage for himself, in which he immersed himself in the austerities and rigours of meditation and tantric practices. His fame spread soon in the neighbourhood and the village folk gathered to see this man of God and hear his talks or watch the magic he performed, in awe. His monastery grew in stature and attracted large crowds. All the public adulation soon got to his head, and he became puffed up with a sense of his own superiority. His haughty and intemperate remarks and his ridicule and abuse of others made him infamous everywhere. He spent the next sixteen years of his life in this indolent manner before that fated meeting with Guru Govind Singh happened—one that transformed him completely into a brave and daring warrior. Quite ironically, the same man who was so tender and sensitive to be moved to tears by the death of a doe and her unborn kids, was to become a warrior who was to lead bloody conquests.

He began reading up and acquainting himself with everything about Sikhism, its history and its tenets. He read about the pristine teachings of Guru Nanak and the gurus thereafter who raised a nation of saint-warriors, mostly from among the long-downtrodden classes of the Punjab. He heard about how Guru Arjan Dev had fallen a prey to the religious bigotry of Jahangir, while Aurangzeb had brutally executed Guru Teg Bahadur. Stories of persecution of millions of helpless non-Muslim subjects at the hands of the imperial officers riled him up.[2] He was moved to tears to read about the mournful story of Guru Govind Singh's two young sons, Zorawar Singh and Fateh Singh. When Guru Govind Singh was forced to evacuate Anandpur Sahib, in the confusion that ensued, the two young boys and the Guru's old, widowed mother Mata Gujri fell into the hands of Aurangzeb's army. They were forced to convert to Islam and when they refused, their fingers were blown off with firecrackers, they were bricked up alive in a *minar* (tower) on 27 December 1704 in the presence of the old lady, who died on the spot out of the shock and grief.[3] As historian James Browne noted: 'Of all instances of cruelty exercised on the propagators of new doctrines, this is the most barbarous and outrageous. Defenceless women and children have usually escaped even from religious fury.

No wonder then, that the vengeance of the Sikhs was so severe.'[4] Banda was absorbing this long history of strife and persecution that the Sikhs had suffered at the hands of the Mughals. His reverence and admiration for his guru, Govind Singh, was further enhanced as he realized that despite such personal traumas, he had remained so calm and composed.

Just around this time, there was news of an attempt to murder Guru Govind Singh by a Pathan of Sirhind. He was sent by the Mughal Governor Wazir Khan of Sirhind who was becoming increasingly insecure about the peace negotiations between the Mughals and Sikhs, given that he had played the instrumental role in persecuting the Sikhs and also butchering the two young sons of the Guru. Wazir Khan had sent this Pathan to mingle with Guru Govind Singh and join his fold and one day when the Guru was taking a nap, he leapt at him with a dagger that he wanted to strike at his heart. Fortunately, he missed his target, and the other disciples were aroused by the commotion. When Banda heard this news, he was livid with rage, and he begged his Guru to permit him to go the Punjab and seek a retribution for all the crimes committed against their community. The Guru was initially reluctant but given his persistence he finally relented and entrusted the military command of his people to his charge.

Banda Singh Bahadur's Expedition Commences

Before sending him off to the Punjab the Guru summoned Banda to his side, gave him the title 'Bahadur' or 'Brave' and also blessed him with five arrows from his own quiver as an advance token of victory. The *Panj Piaras* or the five favourites who were the first to be a part of the Guru's Khalsa—Bhais Binod Singh, Kahan Singh, Baj Singh, Daya Singh and Ram Singh were told to assist Banda. The flag or *Nishan Sahib* and drums or *Nagara* were given to him as emblems of temporal authority. This anointment by the Guru raised Banda's position as a Jathedar or a leader of the Khalsa and strengthened by the Guru's command letters or *hukumnamas*, Sikhs from all over the country were exhorted to join the expedition. Banda's main target was Wazir Khan of Sirhind and his Hindu secretary or *Peshkar*, Sucha Nand who had cruelly hacked his Guru's sons. With the war cry of '*Wahe Guru ki Fateh*' (Victory to the Holy Guru) on their lips, this modest group set out for the Punjab with the blessings of Guru Govind Singh.

Even as the group headed to the land of five rivers, they sought the reinforcements coming through the joining of the Sikhs from the Malwa, Doaba and Majha districts of Punjab, whose routes were being blocked by the Pathan detachments of Maler Kotla and Rupar. It was decided to commence the operations from the town of Sonepat with their modest group of 500 Sikhs. The faujdar of Sonepat was petrified to see the advancing group that he abandoned the town and fled to Delhi making it an easy fall for the contingent. Samana was the next target. Around here, in the village of Bhuna, a Mughal detachment escorting a treasure of the revenue collections of these villages was to halt. Banda and his men fell upon it and easily took the treasure that was equally distributed among all the members.

Emboldened by these early and easy successes, the group boldly proceeded to Samana. This was where the executioner of Guru Teg Bahadur, Sayyed Jalal-ud-din, and the executioners of the young sons of Guru Govind Singh, Shasah Beg and Bashal Beg, lived.[5] Samana was among the wealthy towns of the district and its faujdar sat in complacent inaction, underestimating the Sikhs. He was however rudely jolted when on 26 November 1709, Banda Singh and his men fell upon the town and encircled it from all sides. Several local folks and peasants and other Sikhs who had been persecuted for the last 100 years saw these as opportunities to vent their frustration, and the rage spilt over. What followed was an unprecedented plunder of Samana. From palatial buildings and domes, by nightfall, the town was reduced to a heap of ruins that was never going to be able to regain its glory. Ten thousand people, mostly Mughals, lost their lives in this bloody conquest. Bhai Fateh Singh, one of the *Panj Piaras*, showed great courage in this campaign and Banda Singh made him the faujdar or commander of this place.

Banda Singh was well aware of the military might of Wazir Khan and hence did not want to attack Sirhind until the Sikh contingent from the northern districts of Majha and Doaba reached him. They therefore decided to move in the eastern direction towards Kiratpur by a long and circuitous route. On the way, several towns such as Ghuram, Thaska, Mustafabad and Kapuri were easily taken and added to the growing Sikh dominion. From there, the contingent moved to Sadhaura. This was the corrupted name for Sadhu-wara, or the place of sadhus, which was once the holy place for the Buddhists. But it had long forfeited its holy nature, being under a despotic tyrant Osman Khan who oppressed his subjects. He had also tortured to death the great Muslim saint Sayyed Budhu Shah, who came in the lineage of Nizamuddin Aulia, simply because he had helped Guru Govind Singh in the battle of Bhangani. The Hindus faced great indignities in Sadhaura and could not even cremate their dead as per their religious injunctions. Even as the Sikh contingent made its way to Sadhaura, the locals and the peasants who had hitherto faced the oppression of Osman Khan felt enthused and rose in revolt. What followed was a free-for-all attack with the overthrow of Osman Khan, followed by an unmitigated rampage of revenge and mass slaughters.[6] Sadhaura had now been added to the Sikh kitty.

Wazir Khan had been keeping a close watch of all these developments. He was dogged in his attempts to prevent the Majha and Doaba Sikhs from joining the group and swelling their numbers and strength. He deputed Sher Muhammad Khan of Maler Kotla to deal with this contingent that was attempting to come from northern Punjab and join Banda Singh. Sher Muhammad Khan, with his brother Khizar Khan and cousins Nashtar Khan and Wali Muhammad Khan, marched to prevent the moving contingent of the Sikhs from the north, who had by then travelled down, up to Rupar. The two unequal forces clashed at Rupar where Sher Muhammad's army comprising of several Afghans of Maler Kotla, the Ranghars of Rupar, detachments from Sirhind, and equipped with two guns and several other weapons fell on the less-armed Sikhs. But the spirit of the holy war that spurred the Sikhs seemed matchless for all the military superiority of their opponents. With limited resources, the brave men managed to give a tough time to Sher Muhammad Khan and his men. Khizar Khan who was leading the attack was killed by a bullet that was shot at him. This led to confusion and disarray among the Afghan ranks that no one could stem. Soon, Nashtar Khan and Wali Khan, too, were killed and by the time Sher Muhammad Khan came in to lead, it was too late. He was severely wounded and had to retreat, allowing the Sikhs to move forward and join their co-religionists under Banda Singh. The Sikhs had won the day and soon, amidst great rejoicings, the Majha and Doab Sikhs merged with their brothers in the Khalsa.

The Battle of Sirhind

As Banda Singh began preparations for the attack on Sirhind, there were three groups of men who came under his command. The first was the loyal and devoted Sikhs who were dedicated to the feet of the Guru and his teachings, and they had rallied around Banda Singh out of this very spirit of self-sacrifice to rid the region of despots and enemies of their faith. Their object was pure devotion, rather than any greed or expectation of the booties of war or self-aggrandizement. On the contrary, several of them sold all that they possessed to purchase arms and flocked around their leader with the singular objective of winning over the enemy or happily embracing death as martyrs. These were the core group of dedicated loyalists. The second group was of paid soldiers who were recruited and sent to aid Banda Singh, by chieftains who had an axe to grind with the Mughals but could not directly jump into the fray and help him. They sympathized and made common cause with Banda Singh and wanted to lend their moral and material support to his crusade. The third group was of irregulars and dacoits who were attracted to the conquest only for their lust for the booty and plunder that invariably came about. This group also had some persecuted peasants and commoners who saw this as an opportunity to wreak vengeance against their hitherto oppressors through indiscriminate pillage and murders. This was the most dangerous and also the least dependable group, as they happily deserted and fled the scene of war in the eventuality of any minor defeat. In all, there were about 30,000 to 40,000 men who had come together by now. Banda Singh had no artillery and elephants, not even the required number of horses for all his men. Only a few of his soldiers possessed matchlocks. Long spears, arrows and swords were their only weapons. But the indomitable courage and spirit of crusade made up for this lack of military resources.

Wazir Khan gave a call to all the noted faujdars and zamindars in the vicinity to send in help, and also declared a *jihad* or holy war against the infidel Sikhs.[7] This religious call led to numerous Ghazis or religious warriors coming to swell his ranks from across the country. With a large army of about 20,000 men of all ranks—cavalry, musketeers, archers and artillery and a train of elephants, he readied himself to battle the Sikhs and check their advance towards Sirhind. The two armies came face to face in the plains of Chappar Chiri on 22 May 1710. The command of the Sikh army was entrusted to Bhai Fateh Singh, Karam Singh, Dharm Singh, Ali Singh and Sham Singh by Banda, who took his place atop a mound to watch and direct the movements of the forces. As soon as the battle began, Wazir Khan opened artillery. Petrified of this, the dacoits and irregulars were the first to flee. Along with them about 1,000 people who had come along with a traitor—a nephew of the Peshkar Sucha Nand who had tried to infiltrate the Sikhs and act as a mole to understand their strategies and pass it to the enemy—fled the field. Such large-scale flight of men away from their side caused considerable confusion among the Sikh ranks. Baj Singh conveyed this to Banda Singh who entered the field and led from the front, thereby enthusing his forces and boosting their morale. With loud cries of *Wahe Guru ji ki Fateh*, they fell on the enemy. Many of the opposing camp, including Sher Muhammad Khan and Khwaja Ali of Maler Kotla, were slain. With a lot of the muskets from the opposing camp having been released, the battle was reduced to a hand-to-hand and fist-to-fist one. Wazir Khan, too, fought courageously and several Sikhs were martyred.

But the Sikhs eventually managed to overpower the opponents and their army was fully destroyed. Wazir Khan was captured and beheaded and made to pay a price for what he had done to Guru Govind Singh's family. The victorious army now marched into the city of Sirhind. The inmates of the fort however still trained their guns at the invaders and a sudden volley of gunshots caused heavy and unexpected losses among the victorious army. About 500 Sikhs were martyred in this and the place where they were cremated has a memorial called Shaheed Gunj. On 24 May 1710, Sirhind was fully occupied, and a loot and plunder of the city followed. Wazir Khan's son fled to Delhi, leaving behind enormous family wealth that the victors made theirs. Sucha Nand, too, was rounded up and killed. An amount of almost two crore rupees belonging to Wazir Khan and Sucha Nand became the property of Banda Singh and his followers. That was the scale of riches they had amassed. Baj Singh was made the subedar or governor of Sirhind, with Ali Singh as his deputy or naib. Bhai Fateh Singh was confirmed as the governor of Samana and Ram Singh (the brother of Baj Singh) was made the governor of Thanesar, along with Baba Binod Singh. Making Sirhind the base camp, the Sikhs now deployed their detachments to occupy regions in and around it. The deputies of the imperial Mughals were so petrified by the occupying force that they readily submitted to them subordinate districts that yielded an annual revenue of thirty-six lakh rupees. Finding few alternatives, several Hindus and Muslims converted to the Sikh faith through the established mechanism of the Guru. As James Browne mentions: 'Neither Hindus nor Mussulmans found any means of safety but in acknowledging and submitting to their authority, and professing to belong to their sect, which disposition, Bunda, who was a man of great art and address, encouraged by every means with a view to increase his force, treating those with the most flattering kindness who came into the sect.'[8]

There was still some unfinished business for Banda Singh, and he proceeded to Maler Kotla to complete this. During the evacuation of Guru Govind Singh, a loyal maid of the Guru, Bibi Anup Kaur, had fallen into the hands of Sher Muhammad Khan who carried her away. The brave Sikh woman held her chastity more important than her life and had stabbed herself to death. Sher Muhammad had then quietly buried her in Maler Kotla. Since she was a Sikh who had not embraced Islam, she needed to be cremated.[9] So Anup Kaur's body was exhumed from the grave and cremated according to Sikh rites. With this, the avenging of his Guru's oppression was complete as all the perpetrators had been brought to book.

Establishment of a Sikh State

With the conquest of Sirhind, Banda Singh made the fort of Mukhlispur that was nearby as his chief headquarters and capital. Sirhind was in the plains and on the Grand Trunk Road, rendering it unsafe and prone to attacks from the Mughal forces who might have wanted to wrest it back. Mukhlispur was a strong hill fort that was constructed during the time of Shah Jahan and had been in a state of disrepair. The Sikhs got it renovated and rechristened it as Lohgarh or the Iron Fort. All the treasures and booty of war were gathered and brought there, to the capital of the Sikh territories. Banda Singh was virtually a king now as he began to be called *Sacha Padshah* or the Real Emperor. He coined a new war cry *Fath Daras* or the Sight of Victory, which the Khalsa later frowned upon as it undermined the traditional Sikh cry of *Wahe Guru di Fateh*.[10] He now struck a coin in the name of both Guru Nanak and Guru Govind Singh. It had the following verse inscribed on it in Persian: Coin struck in the two worlds by the grace of the True Lord, victory to Govind Singh, the king of kings, the sword of Nanak is the granter of desires. On the reverse was written: Coined at the model City, the Refuge of the world, the Ornament of the fortunate Throne. He also introduced an official seal for his *hukumnamas* (command letters) and *farmans* (orders) with the inscription: Kettle (symbol of the means to feed the poor), sword (symbol of power to protect the weak and helpless), Victory and Unhesitating Patronage have been obtained from Nanak Guru Govind Singh. A new calendar was issued with his own year or *sammat* commencing with his victory at Sirhind. Each of these was both an imitation of and a challenge to the Mughal imperial power.

But there was a huge drawback of the fledgling Sikh state. Given that all the conquest and occupation had happened in such a short span, there was absolutely no time for Banda Singh or his group to ideate on the nature of the state, its constitution or the nuances of administration. It was merely a military occupation and thus a shallow establishment that could, at any time, be overthrown by a counter-military campaign. The state did not get the opportunity to dig in its heels and build the foundations that are so important for any new kingdom to come up. The one major administrative or policy decision they took was the total abolition of the zamindari system. This was in keeping with the aspirations of the active constituency that helped the Sikhs during the struggle—the peasantry and the downtrodden—and hence liberating them from these shackles of economic exploitation was important. However small the Sikh state might have been, it brought about a tremendous change in the community's outlook, its notion of its own worth and political consciousness. As historian William Irvine notes:

> In all the *parganahs* occupied by the Sikhs, the reversal of the previous customs was striking and complete. A low scavenger or leather dresser, the lowest of the low in Indian estimation, had only to leave home and join the Guru [Banda Singh here], when in a short time he would return to his birth place as its ruler with his order of appointment in his hand. As soon as he set foot within the boundaries, the well-born and wealthy went out to greet him and escort him home. Arrived there, they stood before him with joined palms, awaiting his orders . . . not a soul dared to disobey an order, and men, who had often risked themselves in battlefields, became so cowed down that they were afraid even to remonstrate. Hindus who had not joined the sect were not exempt from these.[11]

Other Conquests

With the rise in Sikh political power, many Hindus and Muslims began converting to Sikhism in different parts of northern India. This led to societal tensions, especially with the Muslim nobility becoming increasingly hostile to this development. They began to harass the converted and also the missionaries who led the conversions.[12] One such case came to Banda Singh's notice from Unarsa village in the Deoband district (in present-day Uttar Pradesh). Jalal Khan, the faujdar, ordered the neo-Sikhs and the older ones, too, to be persecuted and arrested. Banda Singh marched there with his army to free his brethren from oppression. Towns of Saharanpur, Behat and Nanauta easily fell to the advancing Sikh might. They then lay siege to

Jalalabad, the town and fort founded by Jalal Khan who proved to be a very tough nut to crack. The latter also sent several letters to Emperor Bahadur Shah alerting him of the growing Sikh menace. After nearly three weeks of laying siege and with loss of life on both sides, the Sikhs decided that it was a wasteful campaign and lifted the siege and returned to Punjab to address larger and more pressing concerns that were emerging there. Such impulsive acts, at a time when they should have concentrated on consolidating their newly found kingdom, was another drawback that the new Sikh state suffered from.

A section of the Sikh army felt this overriding need to avenge all the atrocities that the community had traditionally faced since long and they decided to overrun the whole of the Punjab.[13] Accordingly, campaigns were launched for this. The districts of Batala and Kalanaur were occupied first. Batala was an important market for commodities from Kashmir and Kabul and hence conquest of these places added to the heft of the Sikhs. Buoyed by the success they then decided to attack the important centre of Lahore. The Mughal forces and the locals in Lahore put up a tough battle, and despite putting in all the effort and suffering losses of men and material, Lahore could not be taken by the Sikhs. Except for Lahore proper, practically the entire territory in the Majha and the Rearki tracts was now under Sikh occupation.

The next target was the border of Sirhind, known as the Jalandhar Doab region comprising eastern and south-eastern Punjab and the districts of Jalandhar and Hoshiarpur. With a vast army of 70,000 to 80,000, the Sikhs managed to subjugate the local Faujdar Shamas Khan to a nominal position in the Battle of Rahon on 11 October 1710. The Ganga–Jamuna plains had been overrun in the campaign in Uttar Pradesh; to the south of the Sutlej River, the Sikhs now had a complete mastery over the territories of Sirhind, from Macchiwara to Karnal and Panipat, some six districts in all, penetrating to the very borders of Delhi too. At this juncture had Emperor Bahadur Shah not decided to turn away from the Deccan—where he was busy quelling his brother's rebellion—to address this issue, there was every possibility of the Sikh power expanding across northern India and providing a grave challenge to Mughal imperial power. For a rookie army, to grow in strength and shake the foundations of the Mughal Empire was indeed a remarkable achievement.

Emperor Bahadur Shah's Campaign against the Sikhs

Alarmed by the growing power of the Sikhs and the challenge it posed to the Mughals, Emperor Bahadur Shah left the Deccan where he had crushed his brother Muhammad Kam Bakhsh's rebellion and rushed towards the Punjab. The entire imperial force was organized, and orders were sent to Governor of Delhi Nizam-ul-Mulk Asaf-ud-Daula Asad Khan to mobilize an army to hastily advance against the Sikhs. The faujdars and subedars of Oudh, Allahabad, Moradabad, Barha and other places were asked to join this massive expedition, along with their forces. All the Hindus in the imperial forces were given strict orders to shave off their beards, lest any hidden Sikhs might have infiltrated into the forces.[14]

Banda Singh was in Uttar Pradesh at this time. Baba Binod Singh and Ram Singh were alone to face the brunt of the Mughal attack. By the time Banda Singh returned to Sirhind, the Mughal forces had taken over it, along with the surrounding areas, and driven the Sikhs out of there. The Sikhs retreated towards Lohgarh. In the initial conquest they were successful and managed to repel the enemy attacks. But the Mughals called for massive reinforcements and nearly 60,000 troops were sent to the Punjab. The Sikhs were terribly outnumbered in the wake of such strong attacks. The fall of Lohgarh seemed imminent. Gulab Singh, a Hindu convert and a Bakhshi in the Sikh army, offered a great sacrifice. Since he bore physical resemblance to Banda Singh, he offered to act as an imposer, dress himself up in the robes of his leader and thereby distract the besieging forces. Taking advantage of this, it was decided that Banda Singh would slip away with some from his core group and take this time to regroup and reassert himself at a later date. Thus, cutting through a massive siege by nearly 60,000 troops in horse and foot, Banda Singh Bahadur slipped away to a secret hideout in the Shivalik Hills and the Chamba forests. Gulab Singh and others were captured and executed and Lohgarh fell to the might of the Mughals, temporarily extinguishing the Sikh kingdom.

The failure of his army to kill or capture Banda infuriated Bahadur Shah beyond measure and all his officers bore the brunt of his terrible temper. On 10 December 1710, he ordered that wherever a Sikh was found he should be instantly murdered.[15] He was livid with rage. 'It mattered not,' thundered Bahadur Shah, 'where the dog had fled to, whether he was drowned in the river or was hiding in a cave in the hills',[16] he must be produced before him at all costs.

Within barely a fortnight of his escape, Banda Singh issued his *hukumnamas* to the Khalsa across the country to join him and accordingly large forces flocked to him at Kiratpur. One such *hukumnama* addressed to the Khalsa of Jaunpur, dated 26 December 1710 states:

> Ik Onkar Fateh Darshan.
>
> This is the order of Sri Sacha Sahib. The Guru shall save the entire Khalsa of Jaunpur. Repeat Guru Guru; the life shall be purified. You are the Khalsa of the great *Akal Purkh*. On seeing this hukam, repair to the presence, wearing the five arams. Live according to the *Rahit* of the Khalsa. Do not use *bhang*, tobacco, *post* (poppy capsules), wine or any other intoxicant. Do not eat meat, fish and onion. Commit no theft, adultery or any sexual immorality. We have brought about the age of *Sat-yuga*. Love one another.
>
> I enjoin that he who lives according to the *Rahit* of the Khalsa shall be saved by the Guru.[17]

Soon Banda felt emboldened enough to undertake military expeditions against all offending chiefs in the Shivaliks, subjugating Raja Bhim Chand of Kahlur and several others. Around this time, Banda Singh also got married to one of the daughters of the hill chiefs and a son Ajai Singh was born to the couple towards the end of 1711.

Between February and March 1711, barely three months since the fall of Lohgarh, Banda Singh showed up in the hills near Rajpur and Bahrampur and began to slowly expand his influence in the direction of Gurdaspur. Even as news of his reappearance trickled out, the Mughal forces were activated and they began a hot pursuit, but he managed to give them a slip each time. There were strong rumours among the Mughal forces that Banda Singh possessed magical and occult powers and could transform himself to any species, form and shape to escape their attack. Most of the senior Mughal commanders, too, feared a direct encounter with him, imagining that he might perform black magic tricks on them, and constantly pushed their qazis and maulvis to the forefront to offer prayers and counter the enemy's spells. Such was the terror that Banda Singh had instilled in the Mughals.

Political Turmoil in the Mughal Empire

Amidst this, Emperor Bahadur Shah fell ill and quite suddenly passed away on 28 February 1712. His death was followed by a rancid war of succession among his sons and eventually Jahandar Shah ascended the throne on 29 March 1712. But his reign was short-lived and about ten months later, his nephew Farrukh Siyar, with the help of the Sayyed Brothers—Hussain Ali and Abdulla—put the emperor to death and crowned himself on 11 February 1713. If there was one beneficiary of all this confusion and political flux in Delhi, it was Banda Singh who had been pushed to the wall by Bahadur Shah. The Khalsa regrouped and began to reassert itself. The districts of Kalanaur and Batala were overrun, any Mughal faujdars who offered resistance were slain or wounded. Banda Singh and his men reoccupied Sadhaura without further delay, and shortly Lohgarh, too, fell back into their hands. The fort was repaired, and it remained the Sikh capital for the next two years.

During Jahandar Shah's reign, Muhammad Amin Khan was sent to continue the campaign to eliminate the Sikhs, with Zain-ud-din Ahmad Khan under his command. For several months, the men with their troops kept up their attacks on the newly occupied Sikh domains of Sadhaura and Lohgarh but to no avail. With the political churn in Delhi, Amin was recalled and the campaign against the Sikhs was suspended, giving them a further boost and opportunity to strengthen their position.

Within ten days of taking over as emperor, Farrukh Siyar recommenced the operations against the Sikhs. Such was the priority that the Mughal crown attached to this vexed issue. On 22 February 1713, Abd-us Samad Khan Diler-i-Jang was appointed as the new governor of Lahore and his son Zakariya Khan as the faujdar of Jammu. They were given the explicit task of expelling Banda from the region and destroying him completely if possible. Abd-us Samad and the Mughal commanders surrounded Sadhaura from all sides. A pitched battle took place for months. But after holding on for a while, the Sikhs evacuated and moved to Lohgarh where they were hotly pursued. Soon, Lohgarh, too, was captured by the Mughal might. Like the earlier occasion, Banda and his followers once again gave a slip to the imperial forces and retreated into the hills, around October 1713. The evacuation of the Sikhs from Sadhaura and Lohgarh led to a remorseless persecution of the Sikhs in the entire northern districts of Majha and the Rearki.[18]

Banda Singh meanwhile moved to the Jammu hills at a place now called Dera Banda Singh Sahib, about 28 mi north-west of Jammu, waiting for an opportunity to strike back again and achieve the independence of his people and himself. Not much is known of his activities between October 1713 and February 1715, except for the fact that he got married again—this time to the daughter of a Khatri of Wazirabad, Sahib Kaur. A son, Ranjit Singh, was born to them in due course.

In the beginning of 1715 CE, after an exile of nearly fifteen months in the hills, Banda Singh and his followers reappeared in the plain and marched once more towards Kalanaur and Batala to reoccupy them.

Siege and Fall of Gurdas Nangal

Farrukh Siyar had had enough of the problem posed by Banda to Mughal authority and was determined to exterminate it once and for all. The troops under Abd-us Samad were ordered to give a fight to the finish with as much reinforcement as they wished from Delhi. The Sikhs were hounded and were forced to retreat to the old village of Gurdas Nangal, near Gurdaspur. It had no regular fort and the Sikhs sheltered themselves in the *ihata* or enclosure of Bhai Duni Chand.

Fortunately for Banda Singh, the enclosure that had a massive wall around it was spacious enough to accommodate all his men inside it. He made every effort personally to strengthen his defences at Gurdas Nangal and collected stores of rations and ammunition for the long haul. The enclosure was surrounded by a large moat filled with water from the neighbouring canal and also the imperial canal or Shahi Nahar that was cut to feed into this, to prevent the enemy troops or horses from getting close. The courses of small streams in the vicinity too were diverted to the moat to swell it suitably. The Mughal forces soon lay siege to the fort but could not storm inside, both due to the moat and the strong resistance offered by the Sikh troops. Firing continued from both sides for months on end. As William Irvine mentions: 'So bold and indomitable were the Guru's followers, that they impressed their adversaries with the greatest respect for their fighting qualities. It was feared that the garrison might, by a sortie *en masse* and by sacrificing themselves, secure the escape of their leader'.[19] Like always, the Mughals believed in the superstitions about Banda Singh's supernatural powers and that he could turn into a dog or cat or any other living being to escape from the fort. In a bizarre manner, therefore, every dog or cat or animal that moved out of the fort was caught and hacked by the soldiers in the belief that they were actually killing Banda Singh.[20]

The siege continued for several months with immense losses on both sides. The Sikh defence was so strong that they poured a deadly fire out of their ramparts and the Mughal forces dared not to appear in the open to attack and storm their position. Abd-us Samad lost all hopes of a victory and was almost prepared to give up. A ray of hope emerged for them when Qamr-ud-din Khan succeeded in capturing a ditch and bastion in the enclosure, while Zakariya Khan obtained possession of a second gate that was chiefly used by the garrison. The Sikhs realized that they were slowly being hemmed in from all sides. It became increasingly impossible for them to bring in any supplies or arms from outside.

The confinement had continued for nearly eight months now and slowly their stocks and provisions were drying up. They made overtures to the Mughal soldiers from over the walls to allow them to buy a little grain from them at the rate of rupees two or three a seer. But this did not yield fruit and they slowly began to suffer extremities of starvation.

Around this time, some serious differences of opinion emerged between Banda Singh and Binod Singh and the latter stormed out of the enclosure with his followers. In the absence of grains to eat, horses, donkeys and any other animals found within the enclosure were killed for consumption in order to survive.[21] With no firewood to cook the meat, they resorted to eating raw flesh, leading to dysentery which killed many. When this supply of meat, too, was extinguished, they began eating grass to survive and later leaves from trees, or shoots from their bark. Bones of animals killed were pounded and eaten as flour. Obviously, such inedible food wreaked havoc on their system. The putrid and obnoxious odour emanating from dead bodies of men and animals made the place a living hell. Most of the Sikhs were reduced to near skeletons and hence could hardly offer any resistance. The fort finally fell to the Mughals on 17 December 1715. Abd-us Samad cheated them by offering an olive branch of securing an imperial pardon if they submitted, but promptly imprisoned everyone once they opened the gates of the fort. Along with Banda Singh, about 200 to 300 Sikhs were bound and taken away to the Mughal camp.

Imprisonment and Thereafter[22]

Banda Singh and the other Sikh prisoners were taken to Lahore first in a procession and a show of strength. The Mughals were still petrified of his alleged occult powers and the harm he could induce on them through his magic tricks. With fetters tied to his feet, a ring round his neck and a chain round his back, all connected by hammer-like pieces of wood, Banda was thrown into a huge iron cage, chained to it in four places. Two Mughal officers were tied to him on each side of the same elephant to guard against his escape. His officers and principal men were put in irons and marched atop donkeys and camels, with comical paper caps put on their heads. They were preceded by drummers and bandsmen and by Mughals carrying the decapitated heads of Sikhs on spears. The *amirs* and *faujdars* followed this royal procession, with eager spectators flocking on all sides to see this spectacle.[23] Emperor Farrukh Siyar ordered Abd-us Samad to stay on in Lahore to guard against any possible Sikh rebellion in the region and have Banda and his troops sent to Delhi along with Zakariya Khan and Qamr-ud-din Khan. Zakariya thought that it would be an insult to the emperor to just have 200–300 Sikh prisoners marching up to him in Delhi. So, he launched a witch-hunt of common Sikhs in the area, who had nothing to do with Banda or his group. Thousands of them were killed and 700 carts carrying their decapitated heads were dispatched to Delhi.[24]

Quite like how Aurangzeb had publicly humiliated Maratha King Sambhaji in Delhi, Banda Singh and his followers were led in a public procession in the imperial city. It was led by the gory sight of the heads of some 2,000 Sikhs, stuffed with straw and hung on to bamboo spears, with their long hair streaming in the wind like a veil. Along with it came the body of a dead cat, too, to indicate that no living being, human or animal, had been spared at Gurdas Nangal. Banda Singh was the next in the entourage, seated in an iron cage, placed upon an elephant. To mock him, he was made to dress up in a gaudy gold-embroidered red turban and a heavy robe of scarlet brocade embroidered with pomegranate flowers in gold. After this came nearly 740 Sikh prisoners, tied together in pairs on saddleless camels, with comical fool's caps on their heads, made in ridiculous shapes and of sheep skin. One of their hands was pinned to their neck between two pieces of wood which were held together by iron pins. At the end of the procession rode the three nobles, Nawab Muhammad Amin Khan Chin Bahadur, his son Qamr-ud-din Khan and son-in-law Zakariya Khan, the son of Abd-us-Samad Khan.

The road from Agharabad to the Lahori gate was filled on both sides with troops and exultant crowds who mocked Banda Singh and his followers for their ludicrous appearance. Mirza Muhammada Harisi, one of the eyewitnesses, who went to see this *'tamasha'* notes in his *Ibrat Namah*:

There was hardly anyone in the city who had not come out to see the *tamasha* or to enjoy the show of the extirpation of the accused ones. Such a crowd in the bazaars and lanes had been rarely seen. And the Mussalmans could not contain themselves for joy. But those unfortunate Sikhs, who had been reduced to this last extremity, were quite happy and contented with their fate; not the slightest sign of dejection or humility was to be seen on their faces. In fact, most of them, as they passed along on their camels, seemed happy and cheerful, joyfully singing the sacred hymns of their Scripture. And, if any one from amongst those in the lanes and bazaars called out to them that their own excesses had reduced them to that condition, they quickly retorted saying that it had been so willed by the Almighty and that their capture and misfortune was in accordance with His Will. And if anyone said: 'Now you will be killed,' they shouted: 'Kill us, when were we afraid of death? Had we been afraid of it, how could we have fought so many battles with you? It was merely through starvation and want of food that we fell into your hands, otherwise you know already what deeds we are capable of.'[25]

On reaching the fort, Banda Singh, Baj Singh, Fateh Singh and other leaders were packed off to the Tripolia prison. Banda Singh's wife, his four-year-old son Ajai Singh and the child's nurse was handed over to the harem. The remaining 694 Sikhs were sent away for execution that began from 5 March 1716 in batches of hundred every day, going on for a week. Life was promised to anyone who chose to renounce his faith and embrace Islam, but not one among the 700 opted for it or sought pardon.[26] As William Irvine states: 'All observers, Indian and European, unite in remarking on the wonderful patience and resolution with which these men underwent their fate. Their attachment and devotion to their leader was wonderful to behold. They had no fear of death, they called the Executioner *Mukt*, or the Deliverer, they cried out to him joyfully, "O! *Mukt*! Kill me first."'[27] Thus, far from being scared, they jostled with the executioner to be killed first. Decapitated heads were collected in carts daily and hung up on trees outside the city, while their carcasses thrown away ruthlessly to the vultures and dogs to feed on.

A poignant tale during this time was of one young Sikh prisoner who was recently married. His old, widowed mother interceded for his pardon through the Wazir's Diwan, Ram Chand. The old woman was made to cook up a story that her son was not a part of the rebel group but was actually imprisoned by them and hence he should be released. The emperor considered the case favourably and he was pardoned. When the old woman joyously accosted her son with the release letter, handing it over to the kotwal who stood over him with a sword in his hand, the son threw the letter away. He screamed out saying he did not know who this woman was and that she was lying, that he was a true and devoted follower of his Guru and that he should be sent to his companions quickly. No number of tearful entreaties of the wailing mother or persuasion by the imperial authorities could shake the young man's resolve. He quickly met his death without flinching. Such was the devotion and commitment that the Sikhs had towards their faith and their Guru.

For three months Banda Singh and his close associates were kept imprisoned in the fort with the intention that they could extract details of any treasures that he might have had or of the people who had supported him. Finally, on 19 June 1716, Banda Singh Bahadur, his son Ajai Singh, Baj Singh, Ram Singh, Fateh Singh, Ali Singh, Gulab Singh and others were led out of the fort in a procession. He was placed as before on an elephant and dressed in garish costumes. Twenty-six other Sikhs in chains marched behind him. They were taken through the streets of the old city to the shrine of Khwaja Qutab-ud-Din Bakhtiyar Kaki, near the Qutub Minar. Banda Singh was offered the usual option between death or Islam and expectedly he refused to renounce his faith. To compound the brutality, his four-year-old son was placed in his lap and he was asked to kill him. As no father could commit such an act, Banda too refused. The executioner then hacked the little boy to pieces, right in front of Banda's eyes and his quivering liver was pulled out and thrust in his father's mouth, who stood like a statue, unmoved and completely resigned to God's will. [28]

His own tragic turn came next. First, his right eye was gouged out by a butcher's knife and then his left. His left foot was cut off next and then his two hands were severed from his body. His flesh was then torn with red-hot pincers. Finally, he was decapitated and hacked to pieces, limb by limb. But what stunned the barbarians was that all through the ordeal, Banda Singh Bahadur remained alarmingly calm and serene and died with unshaken steadiness. Years of spiritual practices and penance had seeped in deep to make him withstand such unimaginable horrors with surprising calmness and equanimity. The other Sikh prisoners, too, met similar fates. [29]

With the gory murder of Banda Singh Bahadur and his followers a major chapter in the history of the Sikhs came to a sad, abrupt end. Just as their ascent was quick and unexpected, their loss of glory, too, was sudden and unexpected. Despite the short-lived tenure of the Sikh kingdom, Banda Singh's exploits had an electric effect on the psyche of the Sikhs and their military zeal and consciousness. It would not be an overstatement to say that in a way he had laid the foundations for Maharaja Ranjit Singh, who, about eight decades later, united all the warring *misls* or confederacies of the Sikhs under one united, mighty Sikh Empire. The story of Banda Singh Bahadur, his unalloyed devotion to his Guru, his indomitable courage and spiritual strength to face the worst of tortures and a horrifying death make him an inspirational figure for centuries to come.

Notes

1   Ganda Singh, *Life of Banda Singh Bahadur: Based on Contemporary and Original Records* (Amritsar: The Sikh History Research Department, Khalsa College, 1935), p. 14.

2   Ganda Singh, *Life of Banda Singh Bahadur*, pp. 20–21.

3   Ibid., pp. 21, 58.

4   James Browne, *India Tract*, Vol. 2, *The History of the Origin and Progress of the Sikhs* (London: Zogographic Press, 1788), p. 8.

5   Ganda Singh, *Life of Banda Singh Bahadur*, p. 37.

6   For more details on Sadhaura and the atrocities of Osman Khan, see Ganda Singh, *Life of Banda Singh Bahadur*, pp. 46–48.

7   Ganda Singh, *Life of Banda Singh Bahadur*, p. 59.

8   Browne, *India Tract*, Vol. 2, p. 10.

9   Ganda Singh, *Life of Banda Singh Bahadur*, pp. 70, 77.

10 Ibid., p. 85.

11 William Irvine, *Later Mughals*, Vol 1, *1707–1720*, ed. Jadunath Sarkar (Calcutta: M.C. Sarkar & Sons, n.d.), pp. 98–99.

12 Ganda Singh, *Life of Banda Singh Bahadur*, p. 90.

13 Ibid., pp. 100–01.

14 Irvine, *Later Mughals*, Vol. 1, pp. 105–06.

15 Gurbaksh Singh, *The Khalsa Generals* (Vancouver: Canadian Sikh Study & Teaching Society, 1927). p. 10. Also, Surinder Johar, *The Sikh Sword to Power* (The University of Michigan: Arsee Publishers, 2002), p. 27.

16 Quoted in Ganda Singh, *Life of Banda Singh Bahadur*, p. 146.

17 Ganda Singh, *Life of Banda Singh Bahadur*, pp. 152–54.

18 Ganda Singh, *Life of Banda Singh Bahadur*, p. 192.

19 Irvine, *Later Mughals*, Vol 1, p. 314.

20 Ibid.

21 Ibid., pp. 314–15.

22 This section on the inhuman tortures meted out to Banda Singh and his followers draws heavily from Ganda Singh, *Life of Banda Singh Bahadur* and Irvine, *Later Mughals*, Vol 1. Readers may refer to those works for more details on the manner in which the Sikhs were humiliated and eventually massacred by the Mughal captors.

23 See Ganda Singh, *Life of Banda Singh Bahadur* for more details on the atrocities meted to the Sikhs in the procession.

24 Irvine, *Later Mughals*, Vol 1, p. 318.

25 Harisi, *Ibrat Namah,* 52b–53a, quoted in Ganda Singh, *Life of Banda Singh Bahadur*, pp. 220–21.

26 Ganda Singh, *Life of Banda Singh Bahadur*, p. 293.

27 Irvine, *Later Mughals*, Vol. 1, pp. 317–18.

28 Ibid. p. 319.

29 Ganda Singh, *Life of Banda Singh Bahadur*, pp. 233–35 and Irvine, *Later Mughals*, Vol 1, p. 319.

Martanda Varma
of Travancore

The year was 1750 CE. After a string of grand military successes, Maharaja Martanda Varma took a bold decision to dedicate the entire kingdom to the tutelary deity of the royal house, Sri Padmanabhaswamy. In January of that year, on an auspicious occasion when the sun changes its direction northwards, the maharaja, accompanied by his heir apparent and all the other members of the royal family visited the magnificent Sri Padmanabhaswamy Temple. The hoary temple and its deity had been central to the political, social, cultural and religious life of the kingdom since long. He laid his state sword before the family god, and through a holy ablution made over all his existing and newly conquered territories to the deity. From that day onwards, it was Sri Padmanabhaswamy, reclining in divine glory over his multi-hooded Shesha snake, who would be the ruler of the kingdom. He assumed the management of the state as the vassal of the deity, merely officiating on behalf of the divine power. And so it was that from then on, he and every successive king of his lineage were to assume the humble title of *Sri Padmanabha Dasa* or a slave of the God. They carried out the affairs of state in His holy name; all the riches belonged to Him and the rulers were merely the custodians and trustees of the wealth and kingdom. This act of Martanda Varma had a very benign influence on the people, too, who began to regard the kingdom as belonging to their favourite God and viewed the king as His mere representative. None of them would now dare to speak ill of their sovereign as that would be an insult of His master, the deity. For a kingdom that was born amidst strife and intrigue, what better political guarantee to its authority could its ruler seek?

Early History of Travancore

After the decline of the Chera dynasty in Kerala between the eleventh and twelfth centuries, numerous small kingdoms sprang up there. Among these, the kingdom of Venad (later Travancore) in southern Kerala became prominent. The kings of this clan had a mixed lineage from the erstwhile Chera and the Ay kingdoms in the neighbouring Tamil region. Venad was a small kingdom between Edava in the north and Aralvaimozhi in the south. During the fourteenth century, it also instituted the practice of adoption of princesses from Kolathanad in north Malabar. The ruling Venad family then had several maternal branches in the later centuries: Thrippapur, Elayadathu Swaroopam, Desinganad and so on. The fragmented polity led to the tendency among local Nair landlords to grab political power in the region, as also the control of the most important temple there of Sri Padmanabhaswamy. The temple played a pivotal role in the political, social and cultural life of Venad.

By the early eighteenth century, the political structure of Kerala was going through tremendous turmoil. The state had become decentralized with the *Ettuveetil Pillamars* (local landlords) and the *Madampimar* (the barons) calling the shots, even as the *Yogakkars* (council of eight and a half) were throttling the power of the throne. The *Yogakkars* were a body of Potti Brahmins who organized themselves into the management committee of the Sri Padmanabhaswamy Temple. There were eight such Brahmin representatives belonging to eight Brahmin families. Each of them had a vote, while the king himself had merely half a vote. Hence the name of council of eight and a half or *Ettara Yogam*. They soon became a powerful body and wielded enormous clout in the conduct and administration of temple establishments. The king had little or no control over them and was simply allowed to preside over periodical ceremonies.

The *Ettuveetil Pillamars* were the representatives of eight noble Nair families—Martandam, Ramanamatam, Kulattur, Kazhakuttam, Venganur, Chempazahanti, Koduman and Pallichal—and were entrusted with collection of temple revenues. They were initially tillers of the soil as the tenants-at-will of the non-*Ettara Yogam* Potti *jenmis* or landlords. With time, they acquired great wealth and power, defied their *jenmi* landlords and allied themselves with the *Yogakkars*. The king was helpless even vis-a-vis the *Ettuveetil Pillamars*, given the latter's affinity with the *Yogakkars* over whom he had no control. Great chaos and confusion prevailed with this group engineering murderous attacks, conspiracies, palace coups and intrigues against the reigning king whose authority was increasingly subverted with every passing day. During the reign of one Aditya Varma (r. 1661–1677 CE) the feudal anarchy took the most violent form and the very palace of the raja was set on fire and the ruler himself was poisoned.[1] The rebels were virtually reigning as independent monarchs in their little islands of authority. There was no standing army and the various royal lineages kept clashing with one another, leaving the field ripe and open for the European powers—the Dutch and the English—to assert their supremacy over the lucrative spice trade, resorting to blockades of the western coast often.

In the wake of this internal political chaos, the then ruler of Venad, Rama Varma (1724–1728 CE), came under the mercy of the English East India Company and the Madurai nayakas who meddled in the internal affairs of the state. Rama Varma went to Tiruchirappalli and entered into a treaty with the Madurai nayakas to seek their help in quelling the rebellious *Pillamars* and *Yogakkars*. In return, Venad was willing to accept the suzerainty of Madurai and agreed to pay an annual tribute of 3,000 rupees for supplying a suitable force to punish the rebels. A large force consisting of 1,000 cavalry under the command of Venkatapati Nayaka and 2,000 Carnatic sepoys headed by Tirupati Nayaka was brought in from Madurai. While the smaller rebels ran for their lives seeing such a vast army, the *Yogakkars* and the *Pillamars* were too deeply entrenched in the political and temple establishment to be displaced.

Martanda Varma as the Saviour

It was in this turmoil that Anizham Thirunal Martanda Varma was born in 1706 CE to Raghava Varma of Kilimanoor and Rani Karthiga

Thirunal of Attingal. His uncle Ravi Varma was the ruler then. Ravi Varma died in 1718 CE, and the eldest of the adopted princes, Unny Kerala Varma, was proclaimed king. His weak disposition was a boon for the rebels. He ruled for merely six years after which, following his death, his younger brother Rama Varma was crowned king in 1724 CE. Though a teenager then, Martanda Varma detested the stranglehold of the rebels on the kingdom and requested the maharaja to permit him to take more active interest in the affairs of Government. Once he got the requisite permissions from the sovereign, Martanda Varma began taking measures to curb the influence and power of the *Pillamars* and *Yogakkars*, thereby earning their hatred and enmity. In fact, it was on his advice that Rama Varma brokered a treaty with the Madurai nayaka and also forged an alliance with the English East India Company to subdue the rising power of the Dutch in Kerala.

The rebels felt terribly threatened by the young prince and were determined to exterminate him at any cost for their own survival. The prince had to keep shifting from place to place, even stay on treetops in faraway jungles, to escape the nefarious designs of the assassins who were constantly behind him. During one such attempt on his life, legend has it that Lord Krishna helped the prince by appearing in his dream and showing him a hole in a tree (*ammachi plaavu*) inside which he could hide through the night, away from the sight of his assailants. Beside this tree, in remembrance of the incident, he later built the Neyyattinkara Sri Krishnaswamy Temple.

Finding it unsafe to stay in Trivandrum, Martanda Varma shifted his residence, in disguise, moving between the palaces of Sreevalumcode, Neduvangad, Mavellikera, Attingal and so on. He providentially escaped several attempts on his life. During one instance, when the confederacy of the rebels came to know that the prince was in a pagoda, they surrounded it and made preparations to have him slain. It was the sharp mind and the loyalty of the priest that saved the day for Martanda Varma. He quickly transferred his own priestly clothes to the young man, put a pot of boiled rice on his head and asked him to walk out muttering incantations, like a priest would, silently whispering that the prince was lying concealed inside. As he went out, the priest dressed himself up as the prince and kept pacing up and down the pagoda in a state of anxiety. The rebels entered and mistaking him to be Martanda Varma, surrounded him and did the priest to death, even as the prince propitiously escaped. This was the kind of uncertainty that young Martanda Varma's life hinged on.

The Accession to the Throne and Thereafter

When Rama Varma died of a sudden illness in 1728 CE, Martanda Varma ascended the throne the following year, at the age of twenty-three. The kingdom was in a state of utter disarray, but the advantage was that the young king had already experienced the turmoil at first hand in the ten odd years that he had spent, giving a slip to the rebels. This strengthened his resolve to deal with them with an iron fist.

To curb the rebels, the maharaja needed a strong, dedicated and efficient team that he could trust. Arumukam Pillai was made the Dalawah or Prime Minister, Kumaraswamy Pillai the commander-in-chief, the Dalawah's brother Thanu Pillai was made Kumaraswamy's assistant. Rama Iyen whom the maharaja had brought up under his own care and patronage became the palace *rayasom* (Under Secretary of State). Kumaraswamy and Thanu were asked to raise an army of brave soldiers (Maravers and Nairs) and a few hundred horses; to raise up barriers in the form of mud walls and have the gates and passages guarded at the borders to guard against external invaders.

The early years of Martanda Varma's reign were devoted to completely crushing the power of the conniving *Ettuveetil Pillamars*. Secret orders were given to the newly raised military to arrest all the rebel chieftains at a given signal. Horsemen were posted between Nagercoil and Trivandrum for carrying out these orders. Within a few hours of the royal sanction for the arrest of the rebels, the *Pillamars* were seized and bound in chains and brought to the king's presence in Nagercoil. The rebels admitted their crime of sabotaging the state and a few weaker ones among them pleaded for mercy. The king was noble to not be blinded by vindictiveness and ordered a judicial enquiry into all their misdemeanours. After the enquiry, a judgement was pronounced—the four Pottis who were among the conspirators were to be banished from the state and other rebels were to be put to death. The execution of the rebels took place in the Mukhamantapam or Cutchery at Padmanabhapuram. The houses of the *Ettuveetil Pillamars* were razed to the ground and with the materials thereof, the magnificent buildings known as Ramanamatam and Tevaraathukoikal were constructed at Trivandrum. Thus, under Martanda Varma, the long-standing menace of the rebels and the lawlessness of the *Pillamars* and *Madampimars* was eliminated for good.

In 1733 CE, Sri Padmanabhan Thampi, the son of the late maharaja, claimed the throne and appealed to the Nawab of Arcot and the old nobility of Travancore to support his claim against Martanda Varma. An army, too, was sent from Arcot to support him, but the king got it bribed and sent back. The Thampi was now left to the wrath of the king. The same year, the Thampi who was the head of the factions was assassinated while on a friendly visit to the maharaja, and the nobles were all surrounded and arrested at the same time.[2] As a writer puts it: 'Clemency was not one of the virtues of Martanda Varma and the vengeance he enacted was of a nature that struck terror through the whole of Malabar. Forty-two of the proudest nobles were sentenced to death by hanging and their women and children were given away in slavery.'[3]

External Conquests and Their Impact

After the suppression of the internal revolt, the consolidation and the extension of his kingdom attracted Martanda Varma's attention. The area immediately to the north of his own state was partitioned between the rajas of Quilon and Elayada Swaroopam (Peritaly). Martanda Varma began to intervene in their affairs on the grounds of adoption against his interest and liking. The Quilon raja had, in 1731 CE, decided on an adoption from the family of Kayamkulam. Martanda Varma demanded that this adoption be rescinded and on refusal attacked Quilon with a large force. The fort was ably defended by Quilon but could not match up to the superiority of Travancore.

Quilon was annexed and the raja was interned at Trivandrum as a state prisoner. This was the first occasion in which a state was thus dealt with in Kerala history, for until then, the custom was to merely reduce a ruler to a vassal and leave him to enjoy his territory, with regular offerings of tributes and gifts.

This annexation and the attitude of Travancore obviously caused great anxiety amongst the local kingdoms and the European powers who had established control over most of Kerala. The northern princes immediately formed a confederacy to liberate the Quilon raja and reinstall him. The ruler of Kayamkulam persuaded the Dutch to intervene and lead the alliance, but they were hesitant to get into the squabbles initially. The rajas of Kayamkulam, Procaud, Vadakkumkur and Cochin agreed to support each other in the eventuality of a war waged on any of them by Travancore and also resolved to reinstall the raja of Quilon, who by then had secretly escaped from his prison. The allied forces placed a strong army at his command to combat Travancore and they gained considerable success too. Martanda Varma retreated and the Quilon raja was back on his throne, snubbing the efforts of Travancore to topple him. But Martanda Varma beat this retreat only for a strategic reason—to reorganize his army and remedy the defects in his military organization. He had no intentions of giving up the fight and it was a tactical step back. The English merchants at Anjengo and Edavai sold him new and improved war material. Once this was done, he launched a simultaneous dual attack on Quilon and Kayamkulam. Quilon was reannexed easily but at Kayamkulam his army was defeated. However, the raja of Kayamkulam was killed in the battlefield in 1734 CE, and his brother who succeeded him carried on the campaign against Travancore. Martanda Varma was again forced to retreat, though it was a temporary and uneasy peace. In 1734 CE, he annexed Elayada Swaroopam principality that lay to the east of Quilon. The same year the raja of Quilon too died, thus bringing Martanda Varma once again in conflict with Kayamkulam.

On the death of the Quilon raja, the chief of Kayamkulam claimed the territory by virtue of the adoption and immediately took possession of it. Martanda Varma who had already protested against the adoption refused to recognize it and claimed the territory to himself. This brought him and Kayamkulam once again on the brink of war. This time, the Dutch, who had watched with nervousness the exploits of Martanda Varma were not willing to remain mute spectators.

The Dutch East India Company

The Verenigde Oost Indische Compagnie (VOC) or the Dutch East India Company was founded in 1602 CE, and by the early eighteenth century, it had grown to become one of the most prominent organizations in world history. Credited as the first company to be listed on an official stock exchange, the VOC actively expanded its global footprint through the 1600s and 1700s, establishing a foothold across South East Asia, even as it operated from its Asian hub at Jayakarta (Jakarta). Like all other European trading companies of the time, the Dutch East India Company, too, followed an active course of colonization, even as they ostensibly sought to trade. They fought wars, signed treaties at will and promulgated their own laws. As with the other European powers, the Dutch, too, had a strong naval armada that formed the base of their strength and through this established its influence across South East Asia in Indonesia, Japan, Taiwan, Malaysia, Thailand, Vietnam, Mauritius, South Africa, and India. In India, their presence began in 1605 CE from Pulicat and then gradually expanded to Surat and Bengal. They vanquished the Portuguese in Ceylon (Sri Lanka) and took over the administration of that island. Soon, in about fifty years of their establishment they had displaced the Portuguese across most of Malabar too and established their stronghold there.

It was the allure of 'Black Gold'—pepper—that brought several European companies to Kerala, right from the fourteenth century. Pepper's qualities as a preservative were much sought after worldwide, and Kerala being the lead producer attracted traders by the droves. The Portuguese and the Dutch attempted to monopolize the pepper trade by bullying and subjugating the numerous tiny principalities in the region and procuring trade concessions from them.

In 1653 CE, the Dutch laid siege to Cochin, which soon surrendered, and the Portuguese left Cochin according to their terms of surrender. In December 1661, the Dutch Admiral Van Goens appeared with a fleet before Quilon, then the chief Portuguese possession in Kerala. This was opposed by a large body of Nairs, who in spite of their brave resistance had to eventually yield. The Dutch troops marched against the town, which they soon occupied as the Portuguese garrison had fled to the neighbouring woods. In 1663 CE and 1664 CE, alliances were formed between the Dutch and the chief princes of Travancore, the Company being represented by Captain John Nieuhoff, and the kings of Travancore, Karunagapalli, Quilon and Kottarakara being parties to the agreement. According to this, no one could import, sell or exchange opium in these territories, except the Dutch East India Company. Nobody was to be permitted to export any pepper or cinnamon out of the country, or sell them to anybody, except the Company. Thus, by the early 1700s, the Dutch influence over Kerala was at its peak. They had defeated the Zamorin of Calicut and turned Cochin into a vassal state and through these trade agreements with the other powers in the region, guaranteed a monopoly in the lucrative spice trade of pepper and cinnamon emanating from Kerala. They were emerging as one of the most formidable colonial powers in the world.

The animosity between the Dutch and Travancore had its roots in the commercial prospects of the Company and the pepper trade. The Company had entered into a trade agreement with the kingdom of Odanad, from whom they purchased all of their pepper for export to the Netherlands. They were alarmed by the expansionist attitude of Martanda Varma after he came to power. From the small kingdom of Venad, under Martanda Varma, the united and larger Travancore kingdom was slowly but steadily taking shape. His absorption of kingdoms such as Attingal and Kollam, which was a close ally of Odanad, was ominous for the Company. Additionally, his existing alliances with their rivals, the English East India Company, too threatened their prospects. Close on the heels of the Kollam conquest, Martanda Varma also engaged Odanad in a battle, which ended in a victory for Travancore and the death of the Odanad king on the battlefield. In 1737 CE, Martanda Varma marched to attack and annex Kottarakara, the largest pepper-producing region in Kerala during those days. The Dutch interference in the internal affairs and adoption guidelines of local kingdoms of Kerala, contravening Travancore's position, also riled Martanda Varma. On their part, the Dutch were watching in utter dismay how his conquests, one after the other, were directly infringing upon their pepper bounties. This made an ultimate clash between the two an imminent possibility. It was just a matter of time.

Hostilities between Travancore and the Dutch

When Martanda Varma had plans of engaging in a third war with Kayamkulam, which was an ally of the Dutch, Dutch Governor M.A. Maten sent a messenger to Travancore, with a veritable threat laid out of facing dire consequences if Kayamkulam and Quilon were raided. The earlier annexation of Elayada Swaroopam[4] principality (in 1734 CE) into Travancore, after the death of its chieftain Vira Kerala Varma and the prevention its princess from succeeding thereby, was termed as an unjust act. Martanda Varma was livid to receive such a message from the Dutch and sent back a befitting reply stating that they should not trouble themselves with questions and issues that did not concern their commercial speculations or interests, and that while he wished friendly relations with the Dutch, he would not brook any interference on their part in the internal affairs of Travancore. Fishing in troubled waters, the English offered their support to Travancore in its planned conquest against Kayamkulam, which Martanda Varma politely refused stating that he wished to obtain victory single-handedly. The overtures of their archrival, the English East India Company, to Travancore further alarmed the Dutch.

Even as the Travancore forces marched against Kayamkulam, the Dutch Governor of Ceylon, Gustaaf Willem VanImhoff, came to Cochin in 1739 CE and deputed two persons to carry a threatening message, similar to the one that Maten had earlier sent, to Travancore.

On receiving a similar obstinate reply from Martanda Varma, VanImhoff was incensed. In his report to his Supreme Government at Batavia, dated 6 July 1739, he said: 'the king of Travancore, having been successful in the wars, which he had undertaken, had rendered himself so much suspected among the chief kings of the Malabar coast, that he was looked upon by everyone with eyes of jealousy and apprehension.' VanImhoff was hence of the opinion,

> that if it were a requisite for the Company to maintain a balance of power amongst the chiefs of the Malabar Coast, it could never be made to preponderate more to the prejudice or danger of the Company than in favour of the prince, who was almost wholly attached to their competitors and whose increase of power could not but be pregnant with the most alarming consequences to their interests, whilst he at the same time merited some chastisement for his insolence towards them, independent of the primary consideration of maintaining a due balance among the native powers of Malabar.[5]

The Battle of Colachel

The immediate issue that sparked the conflict was that of succession in Elayada Swaroopam, whose chief Vira Kerala Varma had died and its princess whom the Dutch supported for succession was unacceptable to MartandaVarma. Making a case for the Rani, VanImhoff sent a protest letter to Martanda Varma in 1740 CE against his attempts to retain the territory and block her accession. He wanted to take action against Travancore, but without sufficient forces at his command, he decided to try the conciliatory route and sought an interview with the maharaja. VanImhoff was a man of extraordinary personality and courage and was determined to make his point by methods of peace, failing which, through war. Through long experience of diplomacy and warfare in the East, he knew the price he would have to pay for a prolonged campaign in the Travancore hills, away from the range of the guns of his ships. But he also knew that if he allowed Martanda Varma to defy him on a matter on which the Dutch were bound by their treaty obligations with their allies, every petty chieftain in the Malabar would begin defying their writs and disrespecting the Company. Martanda Varma, too, was obstinate. Of his courage and resourcefulness, the Dutch had ample proof of by then. He did not realize the might of the Dutch on the seas but knew that he had all the advantages on his side in a prolonged guerrilla warfare conducted from a well-selected, impregnable base in the hills.

During the meeting, VanImhoff threatened the maharaja with an invasion of Travancore to which he got a cool reply that they were at perfect liberty to do what they wished and that they would get a befitting response to all their actions. He also told the Dutch in plain words that any such attempt by them would most unlikely be crowned with any success, and even if it did in some measure, there were numerous forests in Travancore to which he could retire for safety. VanImhoff scornfully told the maharaja that he would be hotly pursued by the Dutch wherever he chose to hide. This was the last straw, and the Maharaja closed the interview with a sarcastic counter-threat that Travancore, too, had been actively considering an invasion of Europe with his *munchees* (native boats) and local fishermen. It was an unequivocal message to the Dutch that their threat was as ridiculous and far-fetched as his plans. With all hopes of an amicable settlement receding, the Dutch prepared for a war with Travancore. VanImhoff wrote to Ceylon for a detachment of artillery and infantry and told his forces at Quilon to prepare for action in the near future.

In 1741 CE, disregarding Martanda Varma's reservations, the Dutch installed the Princess of Elayada Swaroopam as the next ruler of that principality and obtained tracts of land near Kollam and Bichnor and other advantages from her, in return. This led to the inevitable outbreak of a war between Travancore and the Dutch. Collecting all his troops, Martanda Varma attacked the Dutch and the Elayada Swaroopam princess. The Dutch were completely defeated and 'not one soldier of the Dutch regiments remained to tell the tale of the triumphant annexation'[6] of Elayada Swaroopam to Travancore. The princess fled to Cochin and placed herself under the protection of the Dutch with a pension of two rupees and five annas. The maharaja's army attacked the Dutch forts in and around Travancore and captured all of them, forcing the Dutch to retreat to Cochin. The heroics were achieved under the new Dalawa Rama Iyen.

The Dutch called for further reinforcements from their base in Ceylon. A force of Dutch marines and artillery under Captain Eustachius De Lannoy set sail from Ceylon to capture Padmanabhapuram, the capital of Travancore. They planned it in such a way that Travancore was to be attacked from the south at a time when Martanda Varma was busily occupied in the northern front in his campaign against Kayamkulam. In November 1740, the Dutch ships first reached the coastal town of Colachel (near today's Kanyakumari) and commenced a ferocious bombardment that lasted for three days, causing most of the inhabitants to flee. Colachel became their base in this campaign, and Padmanabhapuram was merely 13 km away. Proceeding from Colachel, they marched deep inside the Travancore territory and attacked it. Several villages fell into their hands, till they reached and besieged the Kalkulam Fort. The Dutch found it hard to proceed further because of the stiff resistance that the local fishermen offered, holding the Dutch off till the time the Travancore army came to the rescue. When the maharaja heard of all this, he reached out to the other major European power that was emerging in the Carnatic—the French in Pondicherry under Dupleix—for their support. Negotiations began for an alliance with the French who were only too glad to get this opportunity to interfere decisively in the affairs of the Malabar. But before this new alliance could take shape the tide of war shifted in Travancore's favour.

Immediately abandoning the northern campaign, Martanda Varma rushed back towards the capital. By when the whole of the territory between Colachel and Kottar had surrendered to the Dutch might. The maharaja, however, arrived just in time to avert the impending capture of his capital. He raised a fresh regiment of the Nairs (*Nair Pattalam* or Nair Brigade) and incorporated them within the regular standing infantry. The Dutch were not expecting to see Martanda Varma back so early. Before commencing the war with the Dutch, Martanda Varma offered his prayers to Lord Adi Kesava at the Thiruvattar Temple (which stands till today) and consecrated his war sword there. He then rode southwards to repel the attack and siege of Kalkulam. The Dutch forces suffered heavy losses in this ambush from the Travancore army and fled back to their base at Colachel. Dalawa Rama Iyen, too, left the northern campaign and joined the king, along with his forces. Martanda Varma and his army now began a relentless pursuit of the Dutch and after having pushed them to Colachel, laid siege to their post there. Getting on to local boats, the Travancore soldiers launched a fierce and unending attack on the Dutch ships.

On 10 August 1741, both armies again engaged in what is famously known as the Battle of Colachel. The Kerala army managed to cut through the formations of the Dutch and destroyed all their defences, taking twenty-four of them as prisoners, including the Dutch Commander De Lannoy and his first-in-command Donadi. About 389 muskets, a few pieces of cannon and a large number of swords from the Dutch side, too, were taken over. Four days later, the Travancore army entered the Dutch positions and took complete control of the area, even as the remaining Dutch fleet deserted their fortifications at Colachel as well as their dead comrades on the battlefield and hastened back to Cochin. Shungoonny Menon writes about the battle:

> On the morning of 10th August, the battle of Colachel was commenced by the Travancore line. The Munchees surrounded the Dutch ship, anchored in the Colachel roads, and watched the landing of men and arms to assist the Dutch detachment then engaged in the battle. Rama Iyen Dalawah's army charged the Dutch line, which was drawn up in fighting order against the Travancoreans. The Dutch line was broken through, the officers and men were driven from their positions and the whole force thrown into confusion and disorder. The Dutch having no cavalry, of which the Maha Rajah's force formed the largest portion, were placed in the greatest peril and after suffering much, they effected a precipitate retreat to the fort, leaving behind them several of their comrades dead, wounded and prisoners . . . the siege of the Colachel fort took place. In the course of a few hours, the fort was taken and the enemy driven to their ships, which sailed to Cochin.[7]

This was a landmark war and a historic victory that an Indian force had registered so convincingly against a European power. Such was the blow that was dealt on the Dutch that their power collapsed thereafter, and they simply could not establish themselves in India and Kerala after that. Their dreams of colonizing India, too, were completely shattered and they just could not recover after this. They did try to align with the Kollam state and other rival kingdoms of Travancore, but each time were thoroughly defeated by Martanda Varma and Rama Iyen, further adding to their decline.

The Dutch prisoners were treated very kindly by Travancore, and they decided to stay on in the service of the maharaja. Among them, both De Lannoy and Danodi were appointed by the maharaja to high military offices within the state with the objective of modernizing the Travancore army and navy. De Lannoy came to be fondly known in Travancore as the *Valia Kappithan* or the Great Captain. He helped in creating a special regiment of sepoys within the Travancore army that became famous for its heroic achievements in times to come. He was made Captain and entrusted the task of constructing forts and the organization of magazines and arsenals. He remodelled the Travancore army on European lines, training them in artillery and weaponry and giving it a smart and efficient new look. De Lannoy was later given the Udayagiri Fort, near Padmanabhapuram, as his residence as he was indispensable for the army. The Travancore army was strong enough in future decades to resist the expansionist attempts in the Malabar by the rulers of Mysore—Haidar Ali and his son Tipu Sultan.

Though the Battle of Colachel was fought in 1741 CE, peace with the Dutch was sanctioned by the Batavian Government only by 18 October 1748 and ratified in 1753 CE.

Shortly after the Battle of Colachel, Martanda Varma notched up several other victories in the major spice-rich regions such as Kollam, Kayamkulam and Purakkad thereby inflicting further losses, both military and financial, on the Dutch.

A Victory Column stands at Colachel, erected later by the Travancore state to mark this triumph with these words engraved on it: 'In remembrance of all the brave men of Travancore Army who laid down their lives in defeating the superior Dutch forces during the Battle of Colachel in 1741.'

After the Battle

Shortly after the Battle of Colachel, in 1742 CE, about 6,000 men of the Travancore army attacked the Dutch fort at Quilon, which was gallantly defended by the Nairs under the command of Achyuta Variyar, chief minister of the Raja of Kayamkulam. The Travancore army was defeated and was forced to retreat temporarily. But they were soon reinforced with about 5,000 Nairs and a corps of Sappers and Miners. Large stores of arms and ammunition were purchased from both the English and the French. Puffed up by the isolated victory, the Raja of Kayamkulam, aided by the Dutch, invaded Travancore but they were thoroughly repulsed by Martanda Varma, his heir apparent Prince Rama Varma, the Dalawa and Captain De Lannoy. The Kayamkulam forces held out for sixty-eight long days, after which they surrendered. The Treaty of Mannar that followed the same year made Kayamkulam a vassal state of Travancore and the raja had to pay annual tributes of 1,000 rupees and an elephant, along with vast areas of his kingdom. Quilon, too, fell to the might of Travancore the same year. Skirmishes with the Raja of Kayamkulam kept continuing each time he conspired or failed to pay the tributes and the Travancore army kept subjugating him, till it was finally annexed in 1746 CE.

In the course of some twelve to thirteen years since his accession, Martanda Varma had suppressed internal rebellion in his state, uprooted all elements that had rendered the kingdom weak and impotent, annexed Quilon and Elayada Swaroopam, defeated the Dutch and established his unquestioned supremacy from Kanyakumari to Camorin. Now he also had a modern and organized standing army that was efficient and powerful enough to help weld Malabar together into a single, powerful state. He had also undertaken numerous administrative and irrigation reforms that made his kingdom the most powerful and progressive one in the Malabar.

Peace with the Dutch

The Treaty of Mannar and the annexation of Quilon had caused great consternation among the Dutch and realizing that pursuing any more hostilities with Travancore would seriously impede their trade prospects that were already in shambles, they now actively sued for peace. In 1726 CE, the Dutch Company had exported 1,952,979 lb. of pepper. By 1746 CE, with the conquests of Martanda Varma in the pepper counties and their own wars with Travancore, this figure had fallen to 541,189 lb. or almost to one-fourth.[8] This was a grievous loss for them and the Batavian Government realized that if their trade was to be re-established in Malabar it could be only through one of two ways: reducing the king of Travancore to a tributary chief (which seemed impossible) or come to an agreement with him. Also, from out of the six Dutch establishments south of Cochin, Quilon, Marta, Kayamkulam and Purakkad had passed under the control of Travancore. The agreements that the Dutch had made with those chieftains for the monopoly of pepper trade thus became infructuous. The Company hence realized that with a hostile Travancore their trade in pepper and cardamom would continue to plummet.

A conference was held at Mavelikara where Rama Iyen and Talavadi Kunju Muthathu Kariakar met Ezekil Rabbi and Silvester Mendes, the representatives of the Dutch. After long discussions, a treaty was drafted in January 1743 and several versions of it kept shuttling between Travancore and Cochin. Briefly, the negotiations also broke down and were revived later. With the annexation of Kayamkulam in 1746 CE, the Dutch lost the final vestiges of hope in being able to revive themselves militarily and commercially against the rising power of Travancore. They knew they could get no pepper from Travancore as the English had already monopolized that trade. The back and forth continued on the treaty clauses and was finally sent to Batavia on 18 October 1747. After five years, it was finally ratified as the Treaty of Mavelikara on 15 August 1753. The Dutch bound themselves to follow a strict peace policy, to keep clear of all disputes and never again resort to force, except in self-defence. The Dutch and

Travancore were to be mutual friends; Travancore was to not permit any other European power to acquire a footing in its territories though it could leave undisturbed the already existing English factories at Anjengo, Edavai and Vizhinjam. The Dutch, too, were not to support or give refuge to the enemies of Travancore. The Travancore State Manual talks of some of the articles of the treaty:

> The ninth article of the treaty does not appear in a light very honourable to the Company; it stipulates that the Company shall recede from all engagements in which they may have entered into with the other Malabar princes whom the King of Travancore might choose to attack, and on no account interfere in their disputes or afford them assistance or shelter; nor in any respect raise any opposition to the enterprises of the king. By the twentieth article, the Company bound themselves to provide that prince annually to the value of twelve thousand rupees, or eighteen thousand gilders, various sorts of warlike stores and ammunition, and the prices of those articles were fixed . . . on the other hand, the king engaged to sell to the Company all the cotton cloths, and every year three thousand *candils* of pepper, of five hundred pounds weight each, together with all the other productions which the lands he already possessed of yielded; and the future quantity of two thousand *candils* of pepper out of those territories, which he might in future conquer. For which the Company . . . engaged to pay, namely for each *candil* of good and sound pepper, properly harped and sifted, from the kingdoms of Travancore and Anjengo sixty-five rupees and for the pepper produced in the countries which the king of Travancore might succeed in subduing, in consequence of the neutrality of the Company, fifty-five rupees per *candil*; and moreover, an export duty of four *fanam rageas* (1 shilling sterling) per *candil* . . . the king shall besides receive an annual douceur or present from the Company, the value however, of which was left to be fixed by them; this was afterwards settled by the Government of Batavia at five thousand gilders (about 454 pound sterling), upon the condition that the stipulated quantity of pepper should be duly delivered.[9]

It was evidently skewed heavily in favour of Travancore, both in terms of its military expansion plans and also its commercial interests that were guaranteed and also rewarded. The ghost of the Battle of Colachel ensured that the Dutch signed this treaty and hastened to make peace with their formidable foe. The extent of this abject surrender of the Dutch can be realized only when it is recalled that the cause of the war between the Company and Travancore was the attempted intervention by the Dutch commander in Cochin in the succession conflicts in Quilon and Elayada Swaroopam. The Dutch had always claimed that they had the right to intervene and were an ultimate arbiter for all disputes. Their surrender of that claim meant giving up all pretensions of political authority and also a perfidious betrayal of all the allies who had hitherto trusted them. Through this treaty, the Dutch literally handed over on a platter, all the petty rajas of the Malabar to Martanda Varma whose military power was becoming irresistible by the day. Many allies like the Cochin raja protested with the Supreme Government at Batavia as to how an old friend and ally had been so treacherously sacrificed. But this had little impact as the Dutch were in no position to dictate terms to Martanda Varma. He was calling the shots.

The Travancore maharaja incidentally never made good on his obligations regarding the supply of pepper, but there was precious little the Dutch could manage to do about it as they had been thoroughly vanquished and dispirited.

Becoming a 'Sri Padmanabha Dasa'

It was at this juncture that Martanda Varma pledged his kingdom to the family deity Sri Padmanabhaswamy and became a mere slave of his. He also got the temple of the deity renovated into the grand structure that one finds it today, building the Ottakkal Mandapam and the Sheevellipura. The construction of the massive *gopuram* or tower of the temple began during his reign. The main deity had been damaged in a fire and so it was redone too. State ceremonies like *Murajapam* and *Bhadra Deepam* that were conducted in the temple were introduced by him. Martanda Varma gave great patronage to various temple art forms such as Kathakali, Koothu, Padhakam, Thullal and Koodiyattam, which are today defining markers of Kerala's rich and vibrant culture. Among his court poets were Ramapurathu Warrier and Kunchan Nambiar.

Martanda Varma also launched a series of administrative reforms in his kingdom, focusing his attention on enhancing trade, water supply and village administration. His efforts to bring irrigation to even the remotest of agricultural lands had a long-term impact on the cultivation of paddy rice in the Nagercoil–Kanyakumari region.

Later Conflicts

Martanda Varma also managed to annex Thekkumkur, Vadakkumkur, Ambalapuzha and Meenachil towards the north of Kerala, bordering Cohin. The anxious Cochin raja and a few other chieftains got together to put up a defence against Travancore, but the campaign went against them. Cochin agreed to pay an indemnity of 25,000 rupees as per a treaty that it signed with Travancore in 1753 CE. It was agreed that all the pepper in Cochin—excepting 500 candies—must be given up to Travancore, and the rights over the important temples of Tiruvalla and Haripad should be surrendered to Travancore. The treaty however was not ratified, and Cochin began to rise in rebellion with a few other chiefs. To put Cochin in its place, Martanda Varma however committed an imprudent act, one that Malabar was to pay a heavy price for in future time. He invited the supreme dictator or *Sarvadhikari* of Mysore Haidar Ali, who had all but taken over the administration of the kingdom from the titular Hindu ruler, the Wodeyars. Haidar's assistance once sought could not be easily shaken off. He wrote to Martanda Varma that he was ready to march on the disaffected people of Travancore, but as the rebellion had quietened down the Maharaja declined Haidar's assistance—quite like what he did with the French. But Haidar was no Dupleix and demanded compensation and deemed the maharaja's excuses as being specious. The future attacks of Haidar's son Tipu Sultan on Travancore and the consequent disasters stemmed from here.

This brave ruler passed away in 1758 CE after a brief illness. He is said to have called his heir apparent over to his deathbed and given him the following instructions:

1. That no deviation whatever should be made in regard to the dedication of the kingdom to Sree Padmanabha Swamy, and that all further territorial acquisitions should be made over to the Devaswam.
2. That not a hair's breadth of alteration or deviation should be made in the established charities and the institutions connected with the same.
3. That no family dissension or quarrel should be allowed in the royal house.
4. That the expenses of the State should not be allowed to exceed the income.
5. That the palace expenditure should be defrayed from the profits of the commercial department.
6. That, above all, the friendship existing between the English East India Company and Travancore should be maintained at any risk, and that full confidence should always be placed in the support and aid of that honourable association.[10]

Ruthless in his ambitions and vendetta, courageous in his military conquests, Martanda Varma left behind a rich legacy of administrative and economic reforms, war triumphs and military might, and cultural renaissance, etching his name in the annals of Kerala's history as the proud builder of a new, expansive and modern Travancore kingdom. Like the Victory Column that stands anonymously, uncared for and uncelebrated in modern India, his place in scripting a unique victory of an Indian sovereign against a powerful European force, ensuring its total collapse thereafter from the country, though forgotten, remains cherished and worthy for all times to come.

Notes

1 For more details on these palace intrigues, see P. Shungoonny Menon, *A History of Travancore from the Earliest Times* (New Delhi: Gyan Publishing House, 2020).
2 Ibid., pp. 123–25.

3   K.M. Panikkar, *Malabar and the Dutch: Being the History of the Fall of the Nayar Power in Malabar* (Bombay: D.B. Taraporevala Sons & Co., 1931), p. 62.

4   This was the principality that comprised the modern taluqs of Shencottah, Valliyur, Kottarakara, Pattnapurom and Nedumangad

5   V. Nagam Aiya, *The Travancore State Manual*, Vol. 1 (Trivandrum: Travancore Government Press, 1906), p. 341.

6   Ibid., p. 342.

7   P. Shungoonny Menon, *A History of Travancore from the Earliest Times* (New Delhi: Gyan Publishing House, 2020), pp. 135–36.

8   Panikkar, *Malabar and the Dutch*, p. 81.

9   Aiya, *The Travancore State Manual*, Vol. 1, pp. 348–49.

10 Menon, *History of Travancore from the Earliest Times*, pp. 174–75.

Devi Ahilya Bai
Holkar of Indore

Scottish poet and dramatist Joanna Baillie was enamoured by the magnetic and saintly personality of an early modern Maratha queen from India of the eighteenth century. In glowing terms, she praised her thus:

> For thirty years her reign of peace,
> The land in blessing did increase;
> And she was blessed by every tongue,
> By stern and gentle, old and young.
> Yea, even the children at their mother's feet,
> Are taught such homely rhyming to repeat.
> In latter days from Brahma came,
> To rule our land, a noble Dame,
> Kind was her heart and bright her fame,
> And Ahilya was her honored name.[1]

Even to this day, everywhere one goes to in the city of Indore that she nursed with maternal concern, one encounters the smiling and angelic visage of 'Punyashlok' Maa Saheb Devi Ahilya Bai Holkar, lovingly holding her favourite god Lord Shiva in her hand and exuding a beatific, radiant aura. She was everyone's mother first, queen later. The golden era and a civilizational revival that she ushered in are part of folklore, centuries after her death.

The House of the Holkars

The founder of the Holkar state of Indore, Malhar Rao, was born on 16 March 1693 at a village called Hol, on the banks of River Nira in Poona district. His father was Khanduji Virkar, though Malhar Rao later in life used the surname 'Holkar' instead—the one who came from Hol. The Virkars belonged to the Dhangar or shepherd caste and served as village officers under the Patil.[2] Malhar Rao's mother was a Bargal from Talode in Khandesh, belonging to a well-to-do family which held lands and served as soldiers under Maratha Sardar Kadam Bande. Khanduji died when his son was only three. His paternal relatives seized Khanduji's property and drove out the helpless widow and son from the village, whereupon she returned to her father's house seeking shelter. Her brother Bhojraj treated them well and the little boy was soon put to the task of looking after the sheep. As he grew up, he was taught to use the lance and enlisted as a trooper in the service of Kadam Bande. He married Bhojraj's daughter Gautama Bai and joined the Chief of Burwani as a soldier. His military talents soon attracted the attention of his superiors, including that of Peshwa Balaji Vishwanath's son Baji Rao I, who befriended the young man. When Baji Rao became the new peshwa, he confirmed the services of Malhar Rao and gave him the right to collect the taxes of Chauth and Sardeshmukhi in Central India, thereby giving Malhar Rao his first foothold in the Malwa region. From the humble background that he came, he steadily climbed the ladder of professional success. In 1732 CE, when Baji Rao I first distributed territories among his chief generals—Shinde (Scindia), Holkar, Gaikwad and Pawar, as the senior-most, Malhar Rao received the best territories that remained after the peshwa had kept aside the crucial ones for himself. In 1728 CE two-fifths of Malwa, with about twelve districts, was granted to the Holkars as *saranjam* or territory for the maintenance of the army. Soon, in 1731 CE, Malhar Rao was also rewarded with more *saranjams* in western Khandesh, as well as revenue from other conquests.

Once, on his way back to his capital of Indore, Malhar Rao spent the night in the village of Chaudi in his kingdom. There he saw an eight-year-old girl (born in 1725 CE), who was the daughter of the village chief Mankoji Shinde of the respectable Dharnagar family residing in the Beed district[3]. He was struck by the little girl's behaviour and intelligence and proposed an alliance with his son Khande Rao who was ten years old then. Mankoji readily agreed and the little girl Ahilya became the daughter-in-law of the Holkar family.

Quite contrary to the times, Malhar Rao took an active interest in the girl's education. Ahilya Bai was given the best of education in religious texts, scriptures and also in warfare, accounting, statecraft and administration. This was a very progressive move by her father-in-law, who noticed her potential and wanted to nurture it well. By the time she was twenty in 1745 CE, Ahilya Bai was a mother to Male Rao and three years later, to a daughter Mukta Bai. Khande Rao had married several other women, but these were his only offspring.

Khande Rao was a man given to pleasures, who did not involve himself too much in matters of state, though he did accompany his father on his numerous wars.[4] Malhar Rao was constantly on wars led by the peshwa in different parts of India and in his absence, he began to rely heavily upon his daughter-in-law and his diwan, Gangadhar Yashwant Chandrachur. Malhar Rao played a prominent role in Baji Rao's march on Delhi in 1736 CE and in the siege of Bassein with the Portuguese along with Maratha Commander-in-Chief Chimnaji Appa. Even after Baji Rao's death and the succession of Balaji Baji Rao, his son as the peshwa, Malhar Rao Holkar's eminence remained intact in the Maratha kingdom. In 1750 CE, he overran Rohilkhand along with Jayappa Shinde, and in 1754 CE, he accompanied the peshwa's brother Raghunath Rao or Raghoba on the northern campaigns. As British General Sir John Malcolm states in his memoirs: 'Mulhar Row Holkar, encouraged by the wretched condition of the Moghul Empire, appears to have entertained the design of fixing the power of his nation permanently over Hindustan; and we find him, both alone, and in combination with other chiefs, endeavouring to affect this object, by operations which extended from the province of Oude to the Indus, and from the hills of Rajpootana to the mountains of Kumaon'.[5]

Life after Khande Rao

Two noblemen in Delhi, Imdad-ul-Mulk and Safdarjung, were vying with each other for control and the former sought Maratha help against the latter's ally Surajmal Jat, the ruler of Bharatpur, in capturing Kumner. The fort of Kumner was sieged. Khande Rao had accompanied his father on this expedition, but unfortunately, he was killed by an accidental stray shot during this campaign. Ahilya Bai was thus widowed at the age of twenty-one. All of Khande Rao's wives (nearly ten more) rushed to commit sati, but Malhar Rao prevented Ahilya Bai from this self-immolation as her presence was indispensable in the administration.[6] Thus, while all the other queens ended their life on the pyre of their husband, Ahilya Bai lived on to take care of her two children and the Indore state. In the regular letters that Malhar Rao wrote to his daughter-in-law, he kept her informed about all the latest political developments in the country and also gave her advice on administrative matters.

In 1757 CE, the peshwa entrusted his younger brother Raghunath Rao along with Malhar Rao Holkar as his second-in-command with the conquest in Punjab. The Afghans who had occupied Lahore were driven out and forced to withdraw into Afghanistan. Though militarily the campaign was a huge success, it led to a massive financial loss for the Maratha Empire. Raghunath Rao had to deal with a huge deficit. The campaign also sowed the seeds of strife between the peshwa's first cousin Sadashiv Rao and Malhar Rao, when the latter was accused of siphoning off rupees eighty lakh of the treasury. These dissensions were to have a disastrous effect a few years later at Panipat.

Ahmad Shah Abdali, the ruler of Afghanistan, had learnt with bitter anger about the eviction of his troops from northern Punjab. He invaded India and overwhelmed the Marathas. Jotiba and Dattaji Scindia fell in action and Malhar Rao Holkar, taken by surprise, was badly beaten at Sikandra. To restore Maratha prestige, a grand army marched northwards under the command of Sadashiv Rao. The differences of opinion between Sadashiv Rao and Malhar Rao, who was part of this grand army, continued to grow. While the Afghan and Maratha armies clashed at the Third Battle of Panipat in 1761 CE, Malhar Rao retreated with his troops and left for Gwalior—an act that earned him the opprobrium of several of his contemporary sardars. Elaborating on this, Sir John Malcolm writes:

> The early escape of Mulhar Row, on a day so fatal to his nation, has given rise to some reproaches; but his advocates ascribe his safety to his superior knowledge as a leader, which made him, when he saw the action lost, keep his party together, and retreat with an order than none of the others preserved. This account will be more probable, if we credit the statement given of his quarrel with his commander, on the morning of the day on which the battle was fought. He had, it is affirmed, intreated Sesasheo Bhow [Sadashiv Rao] to delay the action for one or two days; but the latter whose pride and vanity exceeded all bounds, impatient of the advice, exclaimed, 'Who wants the counsel of a goatherd?'. . . at all events, he was one of the few that escaped; and he retreated into Central India, where he employed himself in setting his possessions.[7]

The Marathas were devastated at the Battle of Panipat, death tolls mounted in the lakhs, and they were pushed back to the south of the Narmada River. Malhar Rao's domains that were to the north of the Narmada became the seat of conflict, with the Jats, Sikhs and Bundelas often converging there for conflicts. The deaths of Sadashiv Rao and the peshwa's son Vishwas Rao in the battle, and the massive loss at Panipat jolted the Marathas and the peshwa, who too died shortly, mourning the grief of the horrific loss. The peshwa's second son Madhav Rao was made the new peshwa and he viewed Malhar Rao with contempt and suspicion for the latter's conduct during the battle. But Malhar Rao soon regained his master's confidence by his gallantry at Rakshasbhawan where he guided the Marathas to victory. He then became a part of several of Madhav Rao's campaigns, including those against Haidar Ali of Mysore. Incessant fighting and expeditions tired Malhar Rao, who was now ageing. On his deathbed, he managed to extract the promise from Mahadji Scindia of Gwalior, who was at that time one the most powerful Maratha sardars, that after his death, Scindia would protect the Holkar family and Ahilya

Bai. Mahadji kept his word all his life and remained a trustworthy ally of the Holkars.[8] Malhar Rao, the man who had risen from penniless dependence to the head of a royal house, finally breathed his last on 20 May 1766 at the age of seventy-six. He had been a commander of repute for more than forty years of his life, in the later part of which he was one of the most distinguished amongst the Maratha confederacy.

Succession Woes

After Malhar Rao's death, Ahilya Bai's son Male Rao was invested by the peshwa as the subedar. But unfortunately for Ahilya Bai, Male Rao was mentally infirm and this caused her great consternation. Sir John Malcolm elaborates this:

> He had always been considered of weak and unsettled intellect, but no symptom of positive insanity had appeared before he came to the head of the government, when every action displayed it. His conduct was at first more marked by extremes of folly than of guilt. The life of his mother was devoted to acts of charity and benevolence, and she was particularly kind to Brahmins. This tribe became objects of Mallee Row's [Male Rao] malicious ridicule. It was a common usage with him to place scorpions in clothes and slippers that he gave them [Brahmins]; he also put these venomous reptiles in pots filled with rupees, which he invited the holy mendicants to take; and when their eager cupidity caused them to be stung, his joy was so excessive, as the grief of the pious Ahalya Baee, who used to lament aloud her hard destiny, in having a perfect demon born to her as a son.[9]

Within a year of coming to power, Male Rao died at the age of twenty-two. Malcolm states the insinuations that surrounded Indore was that Ahilya Bai perhaps accentuated the 'death of her own offspring',[10] but he thoroughly and completely rejects these rumours as baseless. In a fit of rage, Male Rao had killed an embroiderer who he believed had an intimate relationship with a female attendant whom he fancied. This liaison was later proved to be false and the remorse of his own crime against an innocent man is said to have taken Male Rao to extremes of hysteria. There were all kinds of wild talks that the spirit of the murdered man had occupied Male Rao to seek revenge. Poor Ahilya Bai sat for days and night on end by the bedside of her afflicted son, in chants and prayers and supposed communions with the aggrieved soul, seeking its pardon and redemption. She even offered to build a shrine for the deceased and settle some estates upon his family, if only the spirit would leave her son, but none of these worked and he eventually died.

The issue of succession came up after his untimely demise. Diwan Gangadhar Yashwant Chandrachur advised her to adopt some male child of a distant relative as an heir, so as to also confirm his own authority as minister. But he realized to his horror that Ahilya Bai had no such intention and she intended to carry on the affairs of the state as its ruler. Diwan Chandrachur wrote to Raghunath Rao (Raghoba), the uncle of the peshwa and the de facto regent, to annex Malwa for this intemperance of the queen and promised Raghoba a substantial gift in return. Raghoba was known to be avaricious and was delighted to hear of this instability in Indore that he could use to his advantage. He decided to attack Indore with 50,000 troops and camped near Ujjain, on the banks of the Shipra River.

Ahilya Bai decided to fight back on multiple fronts. She sent emissaries to all the Maratha sardars—Scindias, Dabhades, Bhonsales, Pawars and Gaikwads—reminding them of the immense favours bestowed upon them by her deceased father-in-law and the bonhomie that existed among them. She wrote to Peshwa Madhav Rao explaining that it was her due right to decide who would rule after her son's death. Malhar Rao's deputy in war, a young man Tukoji Holkar, who was just a couple of years older than Ahilya Bai, was someone who was brought up as a member of the family, though he was not related. Ahilya Bai called upon Tukoji, too, for his support, even as she tactfully packed off the venal diwan on a pilgrimage. She then sent a letter to Raghoba urging him not to make war on a woman, from which he might incur disgrace, but could never derive any honour. To show Raghoba as an oppressor of women and widows, she created a contingent of some 500 women, gave them elementary training in warfare and sat them on horses. She herself got her favourite elephant readied for a combat, with quivers of arrows placed on all four corners of the howdah, declaring her intent to lead the battle with an army fully composed of women.

Raghoba had not expected this kind of pushback from a woman whom he assumed would meekly surrender to the peshwa might. Other Maratha commanders including Mahadji Shinde, too, were putting pressure on Raghoba to withdraw and not cause further disgrace by attacking a noble lady from amongst them. Finally, a letter from the peshwa to his uncle to desist from all attempts against the respectful lady, sealed the deal in Ahilya Bai's favour. She had demonstrated that despite her image of being a virtuous lady, she was no pushover and could stand up to oppression when the need arose. To save his face in the wake of such widespread opposition to his foolhardiness, Raghoba sent a message to Ahilya Bai through Tukoji that he had not come there with the intention of war but to merely convey his condolences on her son's death. He was asked to leave his troops behind and was warmly welcomed and hosted at Indore for a week, before he meekly retreated to Poona.

Heralding a Golden Era

This marked the beginning of the independent rule by Ahilya Bai Holkar as Indore's sovereign, sharing the responsibilities of running the state with Tukoji whom she deeply trusted. Tukoji was to command the armies of the state. On his part, Tukoji was deeply reverential and loyal towards Ahilya Bai and addressed her as mother, though she was two years younger than him. Territories south of the Satpura Range were managed by him, while those to the north came under Ahilya Bai, to whom the different tributaries also made their annual payments. The treasures of the family, around two million, remained with Ahilya Bai, besides personal estates that yielded annually above four lakh rupees of revenue. She shifted the capital from Indore to Maheshwar, located about 95 km away on the banks of the Narmada River. One of the most iconic images of Maheshwar are the flight of steps or the ghats that she got constructed on the banks of the holy river. She had a traditional Maratha-style mansion or *wada* for residence that was simple, yet regal and elegant.

The thirty years that she ruled Indore were a golden period, and a blessing for the Holkar state as it was an extraordinary administration by every stretch of imagination. She had a very modern perspective to governance. During her regime, she strove to provide excellent physical and institutional infrastructure to her subjects, was moderate when it came to taxation policy, strictly imposed the rule of law, vehemently defended individual rights to property and strove to resolve issues amicably among people through settlement, with coercion as the last resort. The first principle of governance for Ahilya Bai seems to have been moderate assessment, and a sacred respect for the native rights of village officers and proprietors of lands. She personally heard every complaint and though she referred cases to courts of arbitration and to her ministers, she made herself accessible to anyone seeking recompense. So strong was her sense of justice and duty that she patiently sat through even investigations of several cases. Alongside, she also had a deep sense of religion and consciousness of God that guided her worldly duties. She was known to often say that she 'deemed herself answerable to God for every exercise of power' and when her ministers took extreme steps, she would gently admonish them saying, 'Let us, mortals, beware how we destroy the works of the Almighty'.[11] She had a unique way of dispensing justice and settling conflicts. Once, for instance when there was a conflict with the Bhils and Gonds, she resolved it by granting them those waste hilly lands and right to a small duty. They also had an obligation to protect the roads, and recover any property that was stolen within their respective limits. It was only when gentle methods of persuasion failed that the extreme step of death penalty was taken.

Regarding her daily schedule, Malcolm gives us details that she rose daily about an hour before daybreak to begin her prayers and other customary rituals. She then heard the scriptures for a fixed period, distributed alms to the needy and personally fed a large number of Brahmins. It was only after this that she had her own breakfast, which was a simple vegetarian meal. Though her family had no compunctions about non-vegetarianism, she eschewed meat completely. After her breakfast Ahilya Bai once again went for her prayers, took a short nap and by about two o'clock in the afternoon went to her darbar or court, where she stayed on till about six in the evening. Taking a short break thereafter, she reassembled at the darbar by nine in the night and continued till about eleven, listening to people's grievances or attending to matters of administration, before finally retiring for the day at about eleven. This regimen that was replete with piety, prayers, abstinence and hard work was maintained on all days, except on religious fasts and festivals that she observed very diligently.

Ahilya Bai saw herself as a trustee of the people and not as their ruler. In cases when the state had appropriated the properties of men who had died without heirs, she had these properties returned to their widows—something that was unheard of in her times. She refused the bequeathing of private property to the state, even if it were for endowment purposes, urging the individual to carry out whatever charitable works they wished to, themselves. Indore, her capital, was raised literally from a sleepy village to a wealthy city, teeming with mercantile activity pouring in from across the country. Numerous instances abound of her maternal concern for Indore and its citizens and these have all become part of folklore. Ahilya Bai's good management and financial control helped Indore to increase its revenue from seventy-three lakh rupees when she took over to more than one crore rupees, during a time when constant wars had bled most princely states and their income.[12]

Harbinger of a Civilizational Reawakening

One of the towering legacies of Ahilya Bai's munificent rule was the enormous works of charity that she undertook all her life. These were not restricted to her kingdom or Indore alone but were pan-India. She liberally gave grants to build and restore pilgrim centres, *dharamshalas* or places of rest for weary travellers, ghats on riverbanks, educational institutions and temples and monasteries that had fallen under disrepair during the several centuries of Islamic conquests in India. Right from the invasion of the Arabs to the despotic reign of Aurangzeb, several thousands of Hindu temples had been desecrated and Ahilya Bai as this beacon of Hindu renaissance and resurgence across the country, re-established them to their former glory from their pitiable ruins. Shaivite and Vaishnavite temples, the twelve Jyotirlingas[13] spread across the country, the four *dhaams*[14] and the seven Puris[15] were all beneficiaries of her benevolence.

Her acts cannot be construed as merely disbursement of money in charity to build structures. But they contributed in an unprecedented cultural and spiritual renaissance through the medium of pilgrimage and sacred geography, one that was so inherent to the Indic way of life since the ancient times. This common unified sphere of cultural circulation had been a part of the ethos of Bharat since the times of the Epics, Puranas, the *digvijaya* of Adi Shankara who established his cardinal *mutts* in the four directions—all earmarking the civilizational contours of the land, which obviously did not have the same political boundaries as of today and as is the case with any modern country. That there were so many sacred spots scattered across the length and breadth of the subcontinent also guaranteed a sense of expanded geographical consciousness and also helped prevent regional parochialism—if anyone felt a sense of jingoism that their part of the country was the most sacred, there were hundred other, equally, if not more, sacred spots elsewhere too. In reinforcing this civilizational renaissance in the early modern history of India, Ahilya Bai's contribution is second to none. The temples that she got constructed—from Srinagar, Haridwar, Kedarnath, Badrinath, Rishikesh, Prayaga, Kashi, Naimisharanya, Puri, Rameshwaram to Somnath, Nasik, Omkareshwar, Mahabaleshwar, Pune, Indore, Srisailam, Udupi, Gokarna, Kathmandu—united the subcontinent in a unique, sacred manner. It is said that at Somnath, which had borne the brunt of attacks from Mahmud of Ghazni and several other invaders and fanatics, she was shocked to see the temple's dilapidated condition. She, therefore, decided in 1783 CE to install an idol underground in a secret shrine so that it could remained undefiled. Today the new, magnificent shrine that came up at Somnath after independence overshadows Ahilyabai's modest one, though it is still termed as 'Old Somnath' or 'Ahilyabai Mandir' by the locals. At Gaya, the iconic figure of her holding adoringly the idol of her favourite deity Lord Shiva in the linga form, is the one with which she is recognized and canonized across India even today.

The hoary and ancient city of Kashi (Varanasi or Banaras) was home to innumerable holy temples and sacred spots, principal among them being the temple of Lord Shiva as Vishweshwara or Vishwanath. It was destroyed at least thrice from the twelfth century onwards. It was first attacked by Qutub-ud-din Aibak in 1194 CE and later Queen Raziya Sultana appropriated the site and had a mosque constructed there.[16] The temple then became an important symbol of Hindu resistance. Another temple that was built on the site was pulled down during a wave of iconoclasm during the medieval times. In 1585 CE, Narayana Bhatta was involved in the reconstruction of the Vishwanath temple along with Todar Mal's son who was a Mughal official in the Bundelkhand region. This temple was ruthlessly pulled down by Aurangzeb in 1669 CE. A portion of the temple was intentionally retained as the rear wall of the mosque that he got constructed at the site, naming it as Gynavapi, deriving its name from its hitherto sacred spot. The Shiva linga was, however, safeguarded and reinstalled in an inconspicuous corner south of the Gyanvapi well with no structure built over it, lest it attract the attention and ire of the emperor. Several Rajput rulers are said to have visited the place in stealth to offer their obeisance to the displaced deity. However, it was not until 1777 CE, when Ahilya Bai took the lead, that Kashi Vishwanath got a permanent structure, a temple atop the linga. She requested the local mahants to allow her to construct this new shrine on their land and they readily agreed. Located south of Aurangzeb's mosque, the temple built around the displaced deity was a modest one with a small spire and a domed *mandapa*, that was later gold-plated by Maharaja Ranjit Singh.[17]

Ahilya Bai also made fixed annual disbursements to support the holy shrines that she established or renovated. There were other occasional gifts and presents that were showered on these temples.

She also had water from the holy River Ganga regularly delivered to more than thirty temples in south India to conduct their rituals. Her genuine humanity and maternal care are exemplified in the manner in which persons were stationed during the hot months of the year to provide water to the thirsty and weary travellers and the poor, and warm clothes disbursed during the harsh winter months to the needy. Portions of daily food were also reserved for birds and animals and the fish in the Narmada ghats, which she visited to have a ritual bath. The numerous roads that were constructed in the kingdom were all lined with shady trees and wells dug at intervals to quench the thirst of people.

Maheshwar became a melting pot of art and culture under Ahilya Bai. The doors of her court were thrown open to stalwarts like Marathi poet Moropant, Shahir Anantaphandi and Sanskrit scholar Khushali Ram. The capital was also famous for its distinctive craftsmen, sculptors and artists who were handsomely remunerated. Famously, she invited weaver communities to come and settle down in Maheshwar and teach her people the craft of weaving. Originally, it is said that the community of weavers that settled in Maheshwar due to her efforts, hailed from Mandu, weaving for the Mughals what was known to be the finest fabric of Madhya Pradesh. Soon a large community of weavers settled down in Maheshwar and the famous sari and textiles that emerged from here is well known till date as 'Maheshwari'. At one time, even the peshwas were supposed to have ordered their dhotis from Maheshwar. The town is today a teeming hub of weaving activity and artisans, all thanks to the foresight and vision of Ahilya Bai Holkar.

The Maheshwari handlooms derived their fine simplicity from the queen who patronized it. Under her artistic guidance, the weavers made light fabrics, detailed with motifs derived from carvings on the Maheshwar Fort, which became a kind of a design directory in stone that they regularly consulted for inspiration. Maheshwari saris were traditionally made in colours like peacock blue, bright yellow, forest green and an Indian red dye called *Aal*. The *pallus* or side drapes were designed with stripes of red, white and gold (*zari*). Borders like *Leheriya* (wave), *Narmada* (the sacred river), *Rui Phul* (cotton flower), *Eent* (brick), *Chatai* (matting), *Heera* (diamond) were all drawn from the fort and the adjoining river and woven seamlessly into the fabric. Originally, the classic Maheshwari saris were only woven in pure cotton, nine-yards long like how the Marathi women wore, and with *pallus* at both ends—so when they frayed, the sari could be reversed and worn some more. Its elegant versatility and durability made the Maheshwari sari unique.

Ahilya Bai's charities, temple constructions and compassion gave her a saintly aura all over the country and thereby also protected Indore from any invasion. She wrote to several of her contemporaries from the Raja of Odisha to the nawabs of Hyderabad and Awadh, seeking their permission to build temples in their kingdoms. Given her reputation as a saint-queen, they readily agreed. This unique nature of her diplomacy and statecraft also helped cement friendly relations between Indore and contemporary princely states.[18]

Ahilya Bai had a good grasp of the political affairs of the time and was wary of the British, about whom she warned the peshwa in a letter in 1772 CE. British historian and journalist John Keay called her a 'Philosopher Queen' and quoted this letter of hers to the peshwa:

> Other beasts, like tigers, can be killed by might or contrivance, but to kill a bear it is very difficult. It will die only if you kill it straight in the face. Or else, once caught in its powerful hold, the bear will kill its prey by tickling. Such is the way of the English. And in view of this, it is difficult to triumph over them . . . it behoves the Peshwa to enlist good number of Silhedaars and increase the standing army and Nawab, Bhonsle and the rest should make a common cause and crush the English.[19]

Towards the End

For a woman as pious and saintly as herself, Ahilya Bai's personal life was unfortunately a source of great grief for her. Having been married off to a carefree, pleasure-loving man who died early, leaving her widowed, and having a son who was mentally imbalanced and who too died early, it was her daughter Mukta Bai on whom she had pinned all her hopes. When the kingdom faced the menace of dacoits, she threw an open and quirky challenge that any youngster who would tackle this problem and rid the kingdom of it would win her daughter's hand in marriage. A chivalrous poor commoner Yashwantrao Phanse picked up the gauntlet and with the help of the kingdom's troops and funds managed to quell the trouble. In her customary generosity, she pardoned the dacoits and made them guardians of the highway who could collect the highway toll, instead of punishing them or slapping the death penalty on them. Keeping her promise, Yashwantrao was married to Mukta Bai and they had a son Nathyba, who in due course grew up to have two wives. Things were going well at the domestic front for a while, before tragedy struck once more. In 1789 CE, Nathyba died untimely of some unknown malady and his two wives committed sati. The following year Yashwantrao, too, died of cholera. Ahilya Bai was horrified to know that the only person whom she could call as her relative, her daughter Mukta Bai, was firm in her resolve to commit sati. Sir John Malcom describes the heart-wrenching scene where Ahilya Bai tried her level best to dissuade her daughter from self-immolation:

No efforts (shorts of coercion) that a mother and a sovereign could use were untried by the virtuous Ahalya Baee to dissuade her daughter from the fatal resolution. She humbled herself to the dust before her, and entreated her, as she revered her God, not to leave her desolate and alone upon earth. Muchta Baee, although affectionate was calm and resolved. 'You are old, mother, (she said), and a few years will end your pious life. My only child and husband are gone, and when you follow, life, I feel will be insupportable; but the opportunity of terminating it with honour will then have passed.' Ahalya Baee, when she found all dissuasion unavailing, determined to witness the last dreadful scene. She walked in the procession, and stood near the pile, where she was supported by two Brahmins, who held her arms. Although obviously suffering great agony of mind, she remained tolerably firm till the first blaze of the flame made her lose all self-command; and while her shrieks increased the noise made by the exulting shouts of the immense multitude that stood around, she was seen to gnaw in anguish those hands she could not liberate from the persons by whom she was held.

After some convulsive efforts, she so far recovered as to join in the ceremony of bathing in the Nerbudda [Narmada], when the bodies were consumed. She then retired to her palace, where for three days, having taken hardly any sustenance, she remained so absorbed in grief that she never uttered a word. When recovered from this state, she seemed to find consolation in building a beautiful monument to the memory of those she lamented.[20]

It was perhaps one of those rare occasions when Ahilya Bai had let go of her characteristic poise and composure and actually lost all self-control in full public glare. She became a recluse thereafter and the grief seemed to slowly seep into her vitals. She did not live long after this. She subjected herself to innumerable fasts and prayers that further sapped her vitality. Five years later, in 1795 CE, at the age of seventy, Devi Ahilya Bai Holkar, a mother for all her subjects of Indore state, breathed her last. Since she had no blood heirs, Tukoji took over the kingdom and ruled for another two years, and after his death his successors became the rulers of Indore.

The Woman and Her Legacy

About her appearance and nature, Malcom writes glowingly:

Though at no period of her life handsome, her complexion, which was of a dark olive, was clear; and her countenance is described as having been to the last hour of her existence agreeable, and expressive of that goodness which marked every action of her life. She was very cheerful, and seldom in anger; but when provoked by wickedness or crime, the most esteemed of her attendants trembled to approach her. The mind of this extraordinary woman had been more cultivated than is usual with Hindus; she could read, and understood the Puranas, or sacred books, which were her favourite study. She is represented as having been singularly quick and clear in the transaction of public business ... After her husband's death she never wore coloured clothes; she always dressed in plain white, nor any jewels except a small necklace, and indeed, remained, amid every temptation, unchanged in her habits or character ... a female without vanity, a bigot without intolerance; a mind imbued with the deepest superstition, yet receiving no impressions except what promoted the happiness of those under its influence; a being exercising, in the most active and able manner, despotic power, not merely with sincere humility, but under the severest moral restraint that a strict conscience could impose on human action; and all this combined with the greatest indulgence for the weakness and faults of others . . . her name is sainted, and she is styled an Avatar, or Incarnation of the Divinity. In the most sober view that can be taken of her character, she certainly appears, within her limited sphere, to have been one of the purest and most exemplary rulers that ever existed; and she affords a striking example of the practical benefit a mind may receive from performing worldly duties under a deep sense of responsibility to its Creator. [21]

Neither did she appreciate flattery, nor could she take an unwarranted unkind comment. Once a Brahmin had attempted to write her biography and offered to read it out to her. She patiently heard the narration, including the high praise that was inherent in the hagiographical narrative. At one point where the text inadvertently mentioned that 'she was a weak sinful woman, and not deserving such fine encomiums', she had the book seized and thrown into the Narmada, though no punishment awaited its author.[22]

Paying the perfect tribute to Devi Ahilya Bai Holkar, theosophist and women's rights activist Annie Besant summed up her legacy thus:

This great ruler in Indore encouraged all within her realm to do their best, merchants produced their finest clothes, trade flourished, the farmers were at peace and oppression ceased, for each case that came to the queen's notice was dealt with severely. She loved to see her people prosper, and to watch the fine cities grow, and to watch that her subjects were not afraid to display their wealth, lest the ruler should snatch it from them. Far and wide the roads were planted with shady trees, and wells were made, and rest-houses for travellers. The poor, the homeless, the orphaned were all helped according to their needs. The Bhils who had long been the torment of all caravans were routed from their mountain fastnesses and persuaded to settle down as honest farmers. Hindu and Musalman alike revered the famous Queen and prayed for her long life. Her last great sorrow was when her daughter became a Sati upon the death of Yashwantrao Phanse. Ahalya Bai was seventy years old when her long and splendid life closed. Indore long mourned its noble Queen, happy had been her reign, and her memory is cherished with deep reverence unto this day.[23]

Notes

1   Joanna Baillie, *English Poem* (1849). https://www.webnovel.com/book/the-maharani-ahilyabai-holkar_20309005606244905/an-english-poem-written-by-joanna-baillie-in-1849-reads_54519571641588394

2   Muntazim Bahadur Mukund Wamanrao Burway, *Life of Subhedar Malhar Rao Holkar, Founder of the Indore State (1693–1766 A.D.)* (Indore: Holkar State Printing Press, 1930), pp. 1–2.

3   N.N. Nagrale, 'Ahilyabai and Her Benevolent Administration', in *Proceedings of the Indian History Congress*, 40 (1979), pp. 700–06.

4   Archana Garodia Gupta, *The Women Who Ruled India: Leaders, Warriors, Icons*. (Gurugram: Hachette India, 2019), p. 193.

5   Major General Sir John Malcolm, *A Memoir of Central India including Malwa and Adjoining Provinces: With the History, and Copious Illustrations of the Past and Present Condition of That Country*, Vol.1 (London: Kingsbury, Parbury & Allen, 1824), p. 150.

6   Ibid., p. 195.

7   Malcolm, *A Memoir of Central India*, Vol. 1, pp. 153–54.

8   Gupta, *The Women Who Ruled India*, p. 196.

9   Malcolm, *A Memoir of Central India*, Vol. 1, p. 157–58.

10   Ibid., p. 159.

11   Ibid., p. 177.

12   Gupta, *The Women Who Ruled India*, p. 201.

13   Somnath (Gujarat), Mallikarjuna (Srirsailam, Andhra), Mahaakaal (Ujjain), Omkareshwar (Omkar, MP), Kedarnath (Himalayas), Bhimashankar (Khed), Vishweshwar (Kashi), Tryambakeshwar (Nasik), Vaidyanath (Beed), Nagesh (Darukavan, Maharashtra), Rameshwaram (Tamil Nadu) and Grushneshwar (Verul, Maharashtra)

14   Badrinath (north), Dwarka (west), Rameshwaram (south) and Puri Jagannath (east).

15   Ayodhya, Mathura, Kashi, Haridwar (Maya), Kanchipuram, Ujjain (Avantika) and Dwarka as stated in the Garuda Purana: *Ayodhya Mathura Maya Kashi Kanchi Avantika Puri Dwaraavati chaiva saptaita Moksha daayika.*

16   Meenakshi Jain, *Flight of Deities and Rebirth of Temples: Episodes from Indian History* (New Delhi: Aryan Books International, 2019), p. 93.

17 Ibid. See this book for more details of the iconoclasm that Kashi suffered under Aurangzeb.

18 Gupta, *The Women Who Ruled India*, p. 202.

19 John Keay, *India: A History* (New York: Grove Press, 2000), p. 425.

20 Malcolm, *A Memoir of Central India*, Vol. 1, pp. 190–91.

21 Ibid., pp. 192–95.

22 Ibid.

23 Annie Besant, *Children of the Motherland* (Banaras: Central Hindu College, 1906), pp. 290–91.

Rajarshi Bhagyachandra Jai Singh of Manipur

His favourite deity Lord Krishna appeared to him in his dream in a vision and directed him to go back to his kingdom and search for the divine presence, which would be found in a *theibong* (jackfruit) tree at the Kaina Hill. 'Make an idol for me,' he was guided in that vision, 'and celebrate my arrival through song and dance.' Upon waking up, he had a clear memory of what he was directed to in his dream. Summoning his learned assistant, Pandit Gopiram Singh Patchahanba, he narrated everything that he was told to execute. The learned Patchahanba ably recreated the vision that his master had seen in his dream into a beautiful idol, which came to be known as Shri Govindaji. The song and dance celebration that he was guided to create in the divine honour was to become the embodiment of Manipur's culture and tradition, the Raas. The dance and its mellifluous music are considered as the highest spiritual expression of worshipping Krishna in the performing arts of the country. And for this unique benediction and fortune that accrued to him of being able to see the Lord Himself in his dream, the king of Manipur, Jai Singh, came to be known as Bhagyachandra—the lucky one.

The Royals of Manipur: 'Garib Nawaz' Pamheiba

The beginning of the eighteenth century saw the dawn of a new era in the annals of Manipur. This came about in c. 1709 CE with the ascension to the throne of one of the illustrious rulers of the Meiteis, Pamheiba (born in 1690 CE), popularly known as Garib Nawaz or the protector of the poor. In the four decades that he ruled, till 1751 CE, he styled himself as a mighty monarch of Manipur. Fascinating tales abounded his childhood and growing up years. He was born to King Charairongba and Nungshel Chaibi, one of his several queens. There was a barbaric custom among the Manipur royals those days that every son born to a queen who was not the chief queen would be slain, so as to prevent later fratricidal power plays and wars of succession among rival princes.[1] Pamheiba was not born to the chief queen and so was fated to be killed at birth. But his mother was determined to save his life and secretly shifted the child to the house of a Naga chief with the help of her father.[2] The chief queen kept trying to have the baby boy slain when she came to know that he had escaped the sword, but he somehow kept escaping the attacks, rather miraculously. King Charairongba, meanwhile, had no other sons and was longing for a successor. Once, on a visit to a village, he happened to see a beautiful and bright boy playing with his mates and wished to adopt him. As destiny would have it, the boy was none other than his own offspring Pamheiba and that is how the prince re-entered the royal house in a twist of luck. After his father's death, he ascended the throne.

Relations between Manipur and Burma had been hostile since time immemorial. The Burmese army had invaded and ravaged Manipur on numerous occasions. In 1562 CE, Bayinnaung, one of the most powerful rulers of Burma's Toungoo dynasty, had reduced Manipur to the status of a mere vassal state. However, in time Manipur began to flex its strength and gradually asserted its independence and even made counter-raids on Burma. In 1725 CE, Pamheiba launched his first offensive against Burma and defeated the Burmese forces. The vanquished ruler Tanninganwe negotiated for peace but haughtily put a request to wed Pamheiba's beautiful daughter Satyamala, despite being the defeated party. Pamheiba made a pretense of accepting the offer but on the day of the marriage, instead of the bride's party, it was the army of Manipur in disguise that caught the Burmese camp and made a huge slaughter of them.[3] During subsequent years, Pamheiba defeated the Burmese twice, and the conflicts kept simmering.

One of Pamheiba's enduring legacies was the introduction of Hinduism, in particular the Ramanandi order of Vaishnavism, as the state religion in 1717 CE.[4] He also changed the name of his kingdom to a more Sanskritic name of 'Manipur' in 1724 CE. Pamheiba had seven sons—one of them, Shyam Shah, was born of the chief queen, while the rest—Ajit Shah, Ugat Shah, Nun Shah, Tong Shah, Sarbosache, Bharat Shah and Satrughna Shah—were the sons of the second queen. He had abolished the cruel practice of slaughtering the non-heir apparent male issues and hence all the sons survived. However, when Pamheiba and his heir apparent Shyam Shah were on an expedition, they were treacherously murdered in 1751 CE by his own son Ajit Shah who was eyeing the throne. Ajit Shah's reign, however, lasted for merely five years as the public got wind of his heinous crime and he had to abdicate the throne to his younger brother Bharat Shah and retire to the forests. Bharat Shah ruled for just two years, after which he died in 1759 CE.

Political Unrest after Pamheiba

The deceased elder brother Shyam Shah's two sons Gaur Shah and Jai Singh were to be the next contenders. In their childhood, they had to flee with their mother from one hill village to the other to live incognito in order to avoid the assassination plots of Ajit Shah and Bharat Shah. The stories of Jai Singh's adventures in the hills during the early phases of his life and the struggle for resistance, when he risked his life on numerous occasions, is a moving saga in itself. Jai Singh endeared himself to everyone in the hills and he had several aliases—the fellow ethnic brethren in the hills called him by the Meitei name *Ching-Thang Khomba* (meaning hill-range gatherer), the British and the people of Assam called him by his name of Jai Singh and the Vaishnavas addressed him as Karta Maharaj.

Since the elder brother Gaur Shah was a cripple, he came up with an ingenious solution of a shared, rotatory rule with his younger sibling. While this agreement seemed to last for a year or two, Gaur Shah could not bear the idea of sharing power with his younger brother and on some provocation that led to a severe misunderstanding, he had Jai Singh exiled from the palace. The latter then took shelter in the house of his maternal uncle Kheli-Nungwa Telheiba, the feudal chief of Moirang. But to get rid of Jai Singh forever, his brother managed to win over the maternal uncle and tried to have his sibling killed. Getting to know of this hideous plan in time, Jai Singh slipped away to Thigomei (modern Kohima) and from there to Tekhao (Assam). The Ahom king Swargadeo Rajeshwar Singha gave him shelter. But his detractors tried to poison the Swargadeo's mind against the refugee by stating that he was an imposter and not the king of Manipur. This created doubts in the Swargadeo's mind, and he came up with a strange challenge that was thrown at Jai Singh to prove that he was a true king and not an imposter. They decided to let loose the palace's wild elephant and have Jai Singh tame it and capture it, all in the full glare of the public. If he won this challenge, he was to be given refuge in Assam.

Jai Singh, who was an astute devotee of Lord Krishna, was deeply hurt by this and remonstrated with his deity, spending the night in prayers and fasting. Folklore has it that Krishna appeared in his dream the night before the spectacle in his cowherd form and assured him of his grace. In the morning, crowds had gathered in large numbers to see the man taming the wild beast in the colosseum. Taking Krishna's name, a bathed Jai Singh wore a pure-white attire, a tilak on his forehead and a rosary in his hands, as he approached the elephant. To the great surprise of everyone, it is said that the animal miraculously changed its demeanour, kneeled on his forelegs, with his tusks deeply embedded in the ground. Jai Singh stepped on to the tusks of the animal and sat on it. The elephant then stood up and trumpeted loudly, almost in obeisance. The Ahom king realized his folly and profusely apologized to his Manipur counterpart and continued to shelter him.[5]

As luck would have it for Jai Singh—and as his favourite deity had prophesized to him in his dream about returning to his homeland soon and victoriously—Gaur Shah died in 1763 CE and Jai Singh made his way back as the undisputed ruler the following year. The maternal uncle Telheiba was encountered in battle for his treachery and defeated, thereby integrating Moirang into the Meitei state. Jai Singh felt the need for total integration of different ethnic groups within Manipur to create a larger state where they all could live together bonded in common destiny. He travelled incognito through the hill ranges that he was familiar with as a child growing up there and managed to stitch together a unified state. He then began contemplating a new political order for the governance of this state that was made of diverse entities and ethnic groups.

Conflicts with Burma

But all the political instability following the death of Pamheiba had emboldened the Burmese who were itching for revenge. Hence, from 1755 CE till the Treaty of Yandabo in 1826 CE, the history of Manipur is replete with the stories of bloody, successive invasions by Burma, but Manipur managed to push back each time, even if temporarily vanquished. Within the short period intervening Pamheiba's murder and the accession of Jai Singh, Manipur was invaded twice by the Burmese. Burma itself was in a state of political flux at that time. The Tungoo dynasty was axed by the Mons in 1752 CE, but their hold over the region was short-lived as the chivalrous Alaungpaya vanquished them and established the Konbaung dynasty. After consolidating himself in upper and lower Burma, he sent a massive army to subjugate Manipur in 1755 CE. This campaign resulted in what the Manipuri records call as 'Koolthan Kahalba' or primary destruction, and a subjugation of Manipur.[6] Two years later, Alaungpaya once again invaded Manipur briefly and had to retreat in the midst of the campaign due to internal revolts back home. But these repeated invasions of a land that was ruled by weak and ineffective rulers laid threadbare the weakness of Manipur, for external and internal aggressors to manipulate to their advantage.

These weaknesses did not go unnoticed by Ajit Shah, the deposed ruler of Manipur who had been forced into exile in Cachar for murdering his father and brother, to come to power. He began his machinations to regain his lost power and sent feelers to the English, through the Raja of Tripura. He represented that he was the rightful claimant of the throne and that he had been wrongly dispossessed of this, thereby seeking their help in his restoration. Getting wind of his uncle's activities, Jai Singh deputed his ambassador Haridas Gossami to both the English in Chittagong and the Raja of Tripura detailing the reasons for Ajit Shah's displacement. The English badly needed an ally in the eastern frontier. The Anglo–French rivalry had spilt over in the region as well, with Burma allying with their archrival, the French, and creating havoc for the English. At the instigation of the French, Alaungpaya had destroyed the English settlement in Nagrais, an island at the mouth of the Irrawaddy River in 1759 CE. Being hemmed in from all sides, finding a possible ally in the ruler of Manipur seemed propitious. After elaborate confabulations, the terms of an alliance between Manipur and the English were stitched together by 14 September 1762. Jai Singh was promised that a contingent of British troops comprising six companies of sepoys would be sent to aid him in the recovery of lost territories. In return, Manipur was to offer rent-free land of 8,000 cubits to install a factory and a fort, and also facilitate promotion of their trade with China. But to the disadvantage of both parties, all of this concluded just before Jai Singh's banishment by his brother Gaur Shah and consequently the alliance was stillborn even before it could take off.

Jai Singh regained the throne of Manipur in 1764 CE, but during his reign from then until 1793 CE, he lost and regained power at least three times. Several internal rebellions and external aggression caused this. Alaungpaya's son Hsinbyushin had succeeded his father as the ruler and continued the policy of aggression towards Manipur, forcing Jai Singh to retreat to Cachar. Burma put one of their stooges and a member of the Manipur royal family, Wangkheimayum Eringba, as the titular head. Large numbers of Manipuris were ruthlessly deported to Burma as slaves.

Jai Singh shifted from Cachar to his old ally the Ahom king of Assam, Swargadeo Rajeshwar Singha. To strengthen their friendship, Jai Singh offered the hand of his daughter Kuranganayani (the doe-eyed one) in marriage to the Swargadeo, which he readily accepted. She soon became his chief queen and was to play an important role in Assam's history. When Singha died and a usurper took over by stealth, Kuranganayani engineered a palace coup, got him murdered and helped restore the throne to the Ahoms. Jai Singh sought his son-in-law's help to regain power. The combined forces of Assam and Manipur made a couple of unsuccessful attempts, but eventually with the Nagas too joining them, they managed to crush a feeble resistance put by the Burmese-backed King Eringba, and Jai Singh was crowned again in 1767 CE. He built a palace in Sangaithel and started ruling the land. The following year he shifted the palace to Sangaiprou. The pattern with Burma was repeated twice over in 1770 CE and 1782 CE with the Burmese invasions resulting in the retreat of Jai Singh, followed of course by a subsequent recapture with armed resistance. Time and time again, the king used his strength, bravery and diplomacy to rescue his land from the hands of the enemies. Eventually, an agreement was reached with Burmese ruler Bodawpaya to retreat from hostilities and restore tranquility in the region.

In the course of these conflicts with Burma, the Assam–Manipur bonhomie was solidified through several matrimonial alliances. Jai Singh gave his granddaughter in marriage to the next Ahom king Swargadeo Lakshmi Singha. When rebellions broke out in Assam in 1786 CE, Manipur sent all its forces to help the king crush them. Commercial relationships between the two neighbours, too, flourished.

The Advent of Gaudiya Vaishnavism in Manipur

During one of his exiles in Cachar, Jai Singh visited Dacca Dakshin in Sylhet, the ancestral home of the fifteenth-century mystic and saint Chaitanya Mahaprabhu (1486–1534). His stream of intense devotion-laden service to Lord Krishna had a profound influence on the Vaishnavism in Bengal, leading to the establishment of the Gaudiya Vaishnava school. It laid stress on the '*madhura rasa*'—Radha's self-effacing love for Krishna and the equally self-abnegating devotion of every soul (seen as one of his *gopis* or cowherd girls) yearning for the ecstatic union of the blissful couple. While in mundane parlance, this seemed like romantic love between people, in spiritual essence it was the longing of the soul to merge with the super-soul, its maker.

Jai Singh came in contact with one of the descendants of Mahaprabhu's family, Ramnarayan Shiromani. His detailed expositions of the philosophy of Chaitanya completely swayed Jai Singh, who was already a devout Krishna devotee. The latter persuaded Ramnarayan to accompany him to Manipur and preach this philosophy to his subjects. Along with Ramnarayan, several other Vaishnavas migrated to Manipur. These included Paramananda Thakur, Ganganarayan Chakravarty, Krishnanarayan Charavarty, Kunjabihari Nidhiram Acharya Thakur, Ram Gopal Bairagi, Adhikari Kamdeb Brajabasi, Krishna Das Thakur and others. The prevailing Ramanandi school of Vaishnavism of venerating Lord Rama, that Pamheiba had popularized, slowly gave way to the Gaudiya school that became the new state religion.

Based on the vision he had of Lord Krishna, Jai Singh got a beautiful idol of Shri Govindaji sculpted. As per the directive to use a jackfruit tree for the idol, he had the tree cut into seven pieces for the seven images of Vijaya Govinda, Gopinatha, Madanamohana, Shri Govindaji, Adweitya, Nityananda and Shri Radha. At the chosen auspicious date for the installation of the idols, while the first four were ready, that of Shri Radha remained incomplete. This caused a lot of consternation among the king and his ministers. Jai Singh then came up with an ingenuous suggestion. He dedicated his own eight-year-old daughter Bimbavati (Lakshmi Priya) to the holy feet of Shri Govindaji as his divine consort. The princess thereafter came to be known as 'Sija-Lairoibi' or 'She who became a Goddess'. The installation (known as *Govinda Nirupon)* in the grand temple in Kanchipur within the palace occurred in 1776 CE. The other idols were consecrated in different places and the king entrusted them with tax-free landed properties and paddy fields as honorarium for running the temples. This convention and practice carry on till date.[7]

The Manipuri Raas Leela and Other Arts

As further directed by the divine, in 1779 CE, Jai Singh introduced a dance form that later was to become one of the eight prominent classical dances of India—the Manipuri Raas Leela. In this dance form, the philosophy of the pre-existing Meitei beliefs forms the basis on which the Vaishnava and Bhagavata theories and philosophies are constructed around in an aesthetic and pleasing manner. The king, along with Kabo Khumbong Ngangbam Swarupananda, Premananda Thakur and Ananta Sai Mantri conceptualized a new synthesized dance form with unique compositions. The essential elements and the mode of dancing were drawn from Laiharaoba, while technical aspects such as head, body and neck movements, intricate footwork were drawn from the Thengou-rol (sword play), Khu-Sa-Rol (spear play) and Paphal-graphs (charts of graphic movement). Thus, broadly the choreography is a spectacular combination of Thang-Ta (martial arts of Manipur), Sarit-Sarat (unarmed Manipuri martial arts) and Mukna Kangjei (war exercises), all of which emanated from the pre-Hindu culture of the state. The *pung* (drum) of Nata Sankirtana came to be used as a musical instrument, along with the conch, Mandira, and Manipuri bamboo flute. The vocal music of Raas Leela was composed in a specialized and typical tune but based within the structures of the raga and ragini of Nata Sankirtana (a devotional art form that Jai Singh established, as explained later). The whole of the Raas Leela is composed in Bengali and Brajbuli verse, but the dance is uniquely Manipur's own. The king composed the three forms of Raas Leela: Maharaas, Kunjaraas and Basantaraas. The Maharaas was based on the theme of *Ras Panchadhyayi* of the Srimad Bhagavatam where the narratives are represented through songs and exquisite body gestures. Kunjaraas was a more playful, mirth-filled form depicting Krishna playing with all the other gopis, with Radhaas the kunja. The third form of Raas celebrating the advent of spring and its beauty drew heavily from the Shringara rasa depicted in Jaideva's *Gita Govinda*.

When the temple of Shri Govindaji was completed, Jai Singh became universally known and hailed by a new name—Bhagyachandra, the fortunate one who was blessed by God. His daughters supervised the worship protocols of Govindaji in the palace. Among them, Sija Lairoibi (Bimbavati) was the foremost. She was completely dedicated to the worship of the deity and donned the role of the first Radha (or Raseshwari) when the Raas Leela dance was performed. She eschewed material life and marriage and was wedded to her God and the art that venerated him. She also composed several devotional songs in Bengali for the pleasure of her beloved Govindaji.

Bhagyachandra also went on to establish the Nata Sankirtana (also called *Nupa Pala*), a very crucial form of worship in Manipur. It is an intricate combination of rhythmic movements, music and rituals and is something that permeates every aspect of Manipuri life and culture, till date. It synthesized several elements of the pre-Vaishnava, indigenous Meitei culture, beliefs and rituals. Ujha Rasanand was employed to incorporate Manipuri ragas into the Sankirtana. Besides being a religious performance, it regulates day-to-day activities of one's journey from cradle to grave. The beginning of *Cholom / abhinaya* or emoting in the Nata Sankirtana was also made with necessary adaptations to the art form. To foster research and development and regulate this nascent art, Bhagyachandra institutionalized it by establishing a Pala Loishang of Nata Sankirtana, which encompasses a wide array of arts performed to mark religious occasions. In 2013, the UNESCO's Intangible Cultural Heritage of Humanity included the Nata Sankirtana in its list of global cultural treasures. The Sankirtana, 'establishes and reinforces relationships between the individual and the community through life-cycle ceremonies. It can also be regarded as a vibrant practice promoting an organic relationship with people. Sankirtana works in harmony with the natural world, whose presence is acknowledged through its many rituals ... the blending of the native pre-Hindu religious elements and cultural traditions with the great tradition of Hinduism led to the birth of a state deeply rooted in a unique form of Hindu Vaishnavism. This was aptly described as the 'Meiteisation of Hinduism'.[8] Thus, it seemed like a new civilizational renaissance were heralded in Manipur under Bhagyachandra. Old values were transmuted; old materials reorganized to yield new meanings. A new society thus emerged from the old, but without a break in continuity of tradition, rituals and customs.

Bhagyachandra's work to promote Vaishnavism through the arts also included *Wari-Liba* or Storytelling from the Epics and the Puranas, as well as *Lairik-Thiba-Haiba* or recitation of Hindu scriptures. Some of these practices were also inspired by Assam and its traditions. He did this with the intention of making the lofty ideals of the scriptures and epics easily accessible to everyone. Through all these efforts, especially of integrating Vaishnavism through the arts, he made it not just a state religion but a way of life, a part of everyday existence. He patronized scholars such as Pandit Gopiram Singh Wangkhei and Madhav Ram Wahengbam to get various manuscripts dealing with genealogy, Ramayana and Mahabharata themes and chronicles were resurrected. Madhav Ram wrote many books including *Langlon, Sanakashi, Mahabharata, Virat-Parva, Sanamanik* and other milestones in Manipuri literature. The coins of the kingdom were inscribed with the titles '*Shri Govinda Padasuman Madhukarasya*' or the bee at Shri Govindaji's lotus feet. Madhav Ram had described the king and his reign as follows:

> The Lord Incarnate King Jaisingh, is a true Vaishnav who knows all the religions and looks upon his subjects like the sky from above. Justice is being administered with a stern hand, with dignified knowledge, defying all evils, ruling as a supreme head of the state. He is the sheltering tree of 'Kalpataru' for the Brahmins and saintly persons. He seems to be the origin of happiness for his people. The nectar from within, but at times the poisonous of all poisons. An invincible warrior for the enemy, who routed a great enemy by storm. The bejewelled sword, burning bright in his hands defeated the rebelling people of the hills. He is aptly given the title of 'Khongjaingamba' by all.[9]

For his enormous contributions to the spread of Vaishnavism, the congregation of Shreepat Kheturi Sammelan honoured him by bestowing on him the *Joypatra Khunti* (meritorious honour or title) of 'Raja Rishi' or a sage among kings. This soon became the prefix to his name as 'Rajarshi' Bhagyachandra. This plaque of honour is still being preserved at Govindabari in Jiyaganj, Murshidabad district.

The following words are inscribed on the plaque: '*Shri Shri Krishna Chaitanya Mahaprabhu Goura, Shri Ganga Narayan Chakravorty Thakur Manipur Maharaja Shri Bhagyachandra Singh Dikshya graham Khunti pradan, Raas Purnima Sakabda 1682*'. Till today, an annual ritual of worshiping the Khunti plaque as symbolic of the reverence to Rajarshi Bhagyachandra is observed as part of the Kheturi Sammelan (now referred as Kheturi Utsav).

When kings of neighbouring states, the hill-chiefs or his subjects came to meet him, they would often be shocked to see him in ascetic plain clothes, sitting on a seat spread on the floor with a rosary in his hand. He had completely surrendered his throne to his beloved Shri Govindaji and was merely acting as a servitor to his lord. In a nineteenth-century Manipuri manuscript, *Awa Ngamba*, there is an elaborate description of how Bhagyachandra dedicated his kingdom to his deity and the historical necessities for this as responses to the contemporary challenges he faced.[10]

Like his multiple aliases, Bhagyachandra played distinctive roles, thereby projecting different images of his own to deal with the pluralistic socio-political situations and unrest of his times. In his attempts to unite the hill people and the Meiteis into a kingdom and also herald a religious renaissance, many have drawn parallels with Emperor Asoka.

As scholar L. Bishwanath Sharma opines:

> Of the first image, Bhagyachandra can be seen as a great warrior who could unify the various ethnic groups in the process of making a strong nation. The other Bhagyachandra is an ideologue who could profess a religious ideology for the establishment of a synthesized cultural matrix. The political, social and economic environments of Bhagyachandra's time demand the existence of two seemingly antagonistic roles. It is true that man is made of culture. The becoming of a man is one of the by-products of a cultural process. At the same time, the making of culture is also the process of finding his presence in what is manifested as culture. Thus, Bhagyachandra is also the

product of his own political circumstances and the then existing social and cultural milieu, to the extent he becomes part of a great presence in Manipuri culture.[11]

The Last Years

In 1798 CE, a Brahmin in his kingdom was put to death by the state officials on criminal charges.[12] When Bhagyachandra heard of this, he was discomfited that his state apparatus had put a Brahmin to death. To atone for this sin, he decided to renounce his kingdom and retire to Nabadwip to spend the rest of his life in spiritual pursuits. Accordingly, he abdicated the throne in favour of his son Labanyachandra (Rabino Chandra) and proceeded to Nabadwip. He visited several places of pilgrimage in Tripura, Dacca Dakshin and Nabadwip, accompanied by a fairly large group of queens, children and his nobles, and notably his daughter Bimbavati who travelled with her deity Anuprabhu. During his visit to Tripura, he married off one of his daughters to the Raja there, Radan Manik. After staying for a while in Nabadwip, he expressed a desire to proceed by boat to visit Vrindavan, the mystical place of Lord Krishna's growing up years. But unfortunately, on his way, he met his end at Bhagabangola in Murshidabad district. Bimbavati stayed back in Nabadwip where she spent the rest of her days singing and meditating on Lord Krishna. Bhagyachandra had permanently changed the political, cultural, social and religious legacy of Manipur and its people. Not only did he strive constantly for a strong and unified Manipur, but also the material and spiritual regeneration of his people.

Summarizing the amazing legacy of this valorous and saintly king, Bishwanath Sharma states:

> Bhagyachandra becomes a great saint 'Rajarshi' after the completion of his political journey. The journey of his life begins with 'sword' and ends with 'lotus'. The celebration of *Mera Haochongba*, composition of Raslila, and Dhumen and initiation of Gaudiya Vaisnavism are

symbolically the spiritual experiments with firm political underpinnings. These are the necessary means for him to end war and bring peace and tranquility in his land by washing our bloodstained hands. To him, there is no contradiction between the sword and lotus; and war and peace. There is no contradiction in his life. He uses religion and other creative works based on a religious theme not in the ordinary sense but with a far-sighted political vision.[13]

A legendary address to his subjects, attributed to Rajarshi Bhagyachandra Jai Singh demonstrates the quiet confidence that he reposed in his people and his belief in democratic traditions of soliciting their support, especially in times of strife and external aggression:

> My ancestral gods and goddesses, your land and people are in peril. Your homes are now occupied by aggressors. As a king, I have a duty to you and your other sons and daughters. Being now in the grip of chaos, the ancient land which is sacred because of your constant presence appears to have lost her strength. Yet my great deities, the ancient land cannot be defeated. It cannot be under alien rule. I was taught in my youth that man cannot succeed in anything unless he receives the blessings of his forefathers and spiritual preceptors. A great ordeal awaits me. I am not afraid of death. Yet, this ordeal is a challenge to my faith in you and the truth of my mission. Bless me from a distance. Let me be able to prove myself as your worthy child. If I fail because of my own individual follies and shortcomings, the blame is mine. Crush me if I involve your great names. If, however, I have been faithful to you and if I have so long fought for the establishment of your truth, stand by me in this hour of crisis. I crave your indulgence and forgiveness. Your hands are long and powerful. I seem to see you all near me. Enable me to defeat the enemy by overcoming all obstacles. Your powers are unlimited. May your blessings be with me ever afterwards.[14]

Notes

1 Jyotirmoy Roy, *History of Manipur* (Calcutta: East Light Book House, 1958), p. 31.
2 Ibid.
3 Ibid., p. 35.
4 Ibid., pp. 38–42, for more details on the spread of Vaishnavism in Manipur.

5   This event is supposed to have occurred in c. 1763 CE and is recorded in detail in a Bengali book titled *Gouranga Sundar*, as well as in *Shri Govinda Nirupan,* by Rajkumar Sanahal Singh, Jai Singh's son. Also see, Ch. Mainhar Singh, *A History of Manipuri Literature* (New Delhi: Sahitya Akademi, 1996), p. 157.

6   Roy, *History of Manipur*, p. 46. Also see R.K. Jhalajit Singh, *A Short History of Manipur* (Imphal: n.p., 1992), pp. 176–78, for wars with Burma.

7   For more details about the temples, see Laishram Hemantakumari Devi, 'Maharaas: Sri Sri Govindaji Temple and Other Local Temples of Manipur' in *International Journal of Research* -Granthaalayah, 9 (2), 2021, pp. 299–308.

8   Aheibam Koireng Singh et al., eds., *Rajarshi Bhagyachandra and the Bhakti Movement in Eastern Indian Literature* (Gurgaon: Shubhi Publications, 2000), p. 2. Also see, Soyam Lokendrajit, 'An Artist's Response to Contemporary Reality: A Case of Two Directors' in *Seagull Theatre Quarterly*, 14.5 (June/September 1999), p. 6.

9   Haobam Ibochaoba, *The Pre-World War II: Form of Ras Leela* (Imphal: Haobam Ongbi Shantibala Devi, 2009), p. 8.

10 L. Bishwanath Sharma, 'Rajarshi Bhagyachandra: The Harbinger of Manipuri Renaissance' in Aheibam Koireng Singh et al., eds., *Rajarshi Bhagyachandra*, p. 44.

11 Ibid., p. 42.

12 Roy, *History of Manipur*, p. 53.

13 Sharma, 'Rajarshi Bhagyachandra', p. 42.

14 N. Tombi Singh, *Manipur and the Mainstream* (Imphal: Chitrebirentombich and Khorjeirup, 1975), p. 6.

Velu Nachiyar
of Sivaganga

It was the festival that culminated the nine-days of celebration of the Divine Feminine. On the tenth day of Vijayadashami, the victory of good over evil was celebrated all over the country with pomp and gaiety. The Goddess Rajarajeshwari Temple located within the palace compound of Sivaganga was bedecked for the occasion. Fragrant flower garlands, auspicious plantain and mango leaves, festoons and drapes made the occasion more festive. As per the local tradition, since it was an occasion to celebrate the goddess, the temple had allowed exclusive access only to women devotees on that day. Thousands of women, decked in their finest garments, vermilion and turmeric, and jewellery thronged the temple in long, serpentine queues. Little did anyone know that among these seemingly innocent devotees were a large group of female military commandos, masquerading as common women. Even as the prayers and chants inside the temple sanctorum were gaining in crescendo, a huge, earth-shattering explosion was heard from within the palace. As if on cue, the women in the group pulled out their hidden weapons from within their garments with loud war cries of '*Vetrivel, Veeravel!*' (Victorious *Vel*! Courageous *Vel*!) The *vel* was the divine spear used by the God Murugan or Karthikeya and an exhortation to this victorious and courageous spear seemed appropriate on this occasion. Along with this cry, the women brigade hailed their leader who had inspired them on this path, the courageous Queen of Sivaganga 'Veeramangai' Velu Nachiyar—the Joan of Arc of India and the first queen to raise a revolt against the British.

The Sivaganga Principality

Sivaganga, located about 48 km from Madurai, was part of the principality of Ramanathapuram (or Ramnad). In 1725 CE, the principality of Ramnad was divided into two parts following several feuds. The smaller portion was given to Sasivarna Thevar, a former feudatory and son-in-law of the Ramnad chieftain Vijaya Raghunatha Sethupathy. Sasivarna had helped the chieftain recover his territories from a contender and was thus rewarded with the grant of two-fifths of the kingdom. This new principality—about 4,500 sq km in size and paying an annual tribute of 1,75,000 rupees to Ramnad—that was carved out came to be known as Sivagangai Samsthanam or Sivaganga. Cordial relations were maintained between the bigger Ramnad and the newly carved Sivaganga principality. These were further bolstered through matrimonial alliances between them. All these principalities formed part of the Poligar or Palayakkarar system that existed in south India even during the Kakatiyas and later consolidated during the Vijayanagara times, crystallizing later under the Nayakas of Madurai in the sixteenth century. It was a decentralized system of administration and military control. Madurai's Vishwanatha Nayaka (1530–1564 CE) had recognized about seventy-two Poligar/Palayakkarar feudatories who were granted suzerainty on the condition that they pay regular tributes and render military service at call when the ruler was in distress[1]. By the time the British began usurping land in south India, the Poligars had become disunited, engaged in several intrigues against one another and suffering from mutual insecurities and petty jealousies.

Early Years

It was in the Ramnad royal house that a girl, named Velu Nachiyar, was born on 3 January 1730 to its chieftain Chellamuthu Vijayaraghunatha Sethupathy and Sakandhi Muthathal Nachiyar. She was the only child of her parents and in the absence of a male heir, Chellamuthu brought up his daughter like a prince. She was taught the art of warfare, horse riding, sword fencing and archery, as also martial arts such as the *Valari* (a kind of boomerang) and *Silambam*, which involved fighting with bamboo sticks. The Thevar (Tamil for God) community that she belonged to was a warrior class and specialized in numerous such combative skills.[2] The Thevars claimed descent from a line of 'Sethupathis' tasked with protecting Lord Rama's *sethu* or bridge to Lanka. The chieftains of Sivaganga and Ramnad were Maravars (within the Thevar community), and they were served by other Thevar clans like the Agamudaiyars, who, along with the Maravars and the Kallars, form the larger community of Mukkulathor. But Chellamuthu also ensured that his daughter Velu was given the best of education and the little girl was fluent in several languages including Urdu, English and French—a rare feat for a woman of her times.

When Velu turned sixteen, she was married to Prince Muthu Vaduganatha Periya Oodaya Thevar, the son of Sasivarna, the chieftain of Sivaganga. After Sasivarna's death in 1740 CE, Muthu Vaduganatha became the king of Sivaganga and Velu Nachiyar, its queen. The couple had a daughter, Vellachi, born after several decades of marriage.

Tumultuous Deccan

Muthu Vaduganatha's ascent to the throne coincided with the most tumultuous era in Deccan history. The conflicts between the English and the French manifested itself in the two-decade long Carnatic wars that drew within its ambit several local players and kingdoms—the Nawab of Arcot, the kingdom of Mysore, the Nizam of Hyderabad, the Marathas and the rajas of the Malabar coast. Claims and counterclaims of succession among the various feuding kingdoms and protagonists were amply exploited by the Europeans to their advantage as witnessed during the Carnatic Wars in the Deccan.

Shortly around the time of the conclusion of the Carnatic wars, by 1761 CE, the kingdom of Mysore was rocked by a huge usurpation. Haidar Ali, a hitherto adherent of the Wodeyar Maharaja, appropriated the throne as the supreme dictator in the wake of weak and ineffective rulers. Haidar Ali came head-on against the English who had charted a series of successes in the Carnatic wars, as also in distant Bengal—in the Battle of Plassey (1757 CE). The East India Company was able to enforce the cultivation of opium in sufficient quantities in India and procure enough tea for the British market, reaping in significant profits. Mysore, under Haidar Ali, was emerging as the biggest menace for the expanding power of the English, leading to a series of four long-drawn wars between the two—called the Anglo–Mysore Wars—that lasted for nearly eighteen years. By 1769 CE, Haidar was literally at the gates of Madras, the stronghold of the English, forcing them into a submissive treaty. This first Anglo–Mysore war crushed the myth of British infallibility and made Haidar a hero for all anti-English forces.

The fallout of the defeat of the English in this war was felt on those principalities that were dependent on them. Given their increasing insecurity, they tried hard to consolidate their positions and punish any errant vassals. With Mohammad Ali Khan Wallajah (1717–1795)—the Nawab of Arcot—and the Tondaiman ruler of Pudukkottai allying with the British, many of the seventy-two poligars sought to retain their autonomy by rebelling against oppressive taxation. Haidar Ali became their beacon of hope against English hegemony. Sivaganga was one such proud inheritor of the nayaka heritage that refused to kow-tow to the arbitrary taxes that Arcot and their overlords, the British, had imposed on them. The nawab complained to the British headquarters, the Madras Council, about this dereliction, and added that his feudatory, the ruler of Sivaganga, had illegitimately ascended the throne and had evaded paying him taxes to the tune of one lakh rupees. Not willing to take any more lapses in the Deccan, the English forces were swift to subjugate any deviants. A British invasion of Sivaganga occurred on 25 June 1772 under Colonel Joseph Smith and Major Abraham Bonjour. This was a surprise attack that took Muthu Vaduganatha by complete shock. Though they had anticipated an attack and the wise minister Thandavaraya Pillai had instructed Muthu Vaduganatha to retreat to the densely forested Kaliyarkovil, they did not expect the British to trace them down in this cocooned village.

Velu Nachiyar's Exile[3]

Muthu Vaduganatha was offering prayers at the Kalaiyarkovil Temple with his second wife Gowri Nachiyar when the combined forces of the English and Arcot raided the temple as they came looking for him. In a valiant counterattack, Muthu Vaduganatha and his wife were martyred, and the temple was completely ransacked, its treasures worth 50,000 pagodas[4] appropriated by the British. Kalaiyarkovil became a scene of lamentable slaughter, as the British records were to note. Sivaganga was occupied by the Nawab of Arcot who made his son the king and renamed the place as Hussainnagar. The forty-two-year-old widowed queen Velu Nachiyar was heartbroken, but she swore to avenge this cowardly attack against her husband and her kingdom. She and her daughter were hurriedly packed off from Sivaganga by Thandavaraya Pillai to safer pastures. They were to be protected by two brave men, the Marudhu brothers—Vellai or Periya (elder) and Chinna (younger) Marudhu—who were to become potent symbols of British resistance in south India.

The Marudhu brothers were the sons of General Udayar Servai in the Ramnad state military and belonged to the Agamudaiyar clan. As young men they had worked as aides to the chieftain—as betel bearer and dog keeper respectively—and soon grew in importance within the military. They are popularly represented in folklore as tall, muscular, turbaned men, with gigantic moustaches, fiery eyes and brandishing swords. They jumped into the fray when the principality was plunged into chaos after the martyrdom of Muthu Vaduganatha and volunteered to save Velu Nachiyar and her daughter from the enemy's clutches. It is said that as the royal entourage was making its way to neighbouring Mysore kingdom for refuge, they were hotly pursued by the forces of Arcot and the English through the densely forested border areas. They caught hold of a poor shepherd girl Udaiyal who was grazing her cattle, to confess the whereabouts of the queen whom she had clearly seen in her transit. But such was Udaiyal's patriotic fervour that she refused to divulge any details to the combined forces, who then, in frustration, tortured and killed her. Udaiyal's sacrifice deeply moved Velu Nachiyar when the news of her sad death reached her. Overcoming all these odds, Velu Nachiyar managed to reach Virupakshi, a border fort in Dindigul within the Mysore kingdom, and sought shelter there under its hereditary poligar Gopala Nayakar.

Thandavaraya Pillai, who accompanied them, sent emissaries to Haidar Ali seeking his military support to help Velu Nachiyar win back her kingdom. Quite propitiously, Haidar was to visit Dindigul sometime soon and it was decided that he meet the queen of Sivaganga and promise her the help she sought for. It is said that when Haidar Ali entered the meeting hall, he found only men there and upon enquiring where the queen was, one of them stood up, pulled off her turban and revealed herself as Velu Nachiyar. She then conversed with him in fluent Urdu, presenting her case clearly and succinctly to him, impressing Haidar Ali further. He immediately made an allowance of 400 gold coins to the displaced queen, promised his support and also permitted her to stay on in Dindigul as a political refugee till the time she regained her principality. He released 5,000 infantry and 5,000 cavalry from the Mysore troops to aid the queen in her conquest to regain her lost territories.

Unfortunately for Velu Nachiyar, her elderly mentor Thandavaraya Pillai died shortly thereafter. But she had the strong support of the Marudhu brothers who stood by her like a rock. They began creating spy networks in Sivaganga that gathered information and also created local combatants to plan for the opportune moment to strike back. Velu Nachiyar began training an army of women corps and quite poignantly this was named by her as 'Udaiyal Padai' in memory of the brave shepherd girl who had sacrificed her life for her queen. Velu's *dalavai* or military commander was a Dalit woman, Kuyili, who was unmatched in her courage and determination. Thus, it was this group of underdogs that was actively working to strike at the might and power of the East India Company and the Nawab of Arcot, who had illegitimately occupied their principality.

Regaining Sivaganga

After the Treaty of Madras (1769 CE) that concluded the first Anglo–Mysore War, the relationship between Haidar Ali and the British worsened. Internationally, the situation was getting tough for the British. The American War of Independence broke out in 1775 CE, and soon France, Spain and the Netherlands were all up in arms against Britain. The British forces had recovered from a shameful debacle in the Maratha war. The strain of the American war reduced the possibility of reinforcements in India; British sea power was severely constrained, and it gave the French a chance of recovery. The French declared their war against the British in 1778 CE, and Haidar Ali, who had remained a trusted ally of the French, threw in his lot to fight what came to be known as the Second Anglo–Mysore War. Mysore, allied with the French, also convinced the Nizam and the Marathas to jointly invade the Carnatic in July 1780, descending on the territories of the British dependent—the Nawab of Arcot—on the east coast with about 80,000 soldiers. The outbreak of the Second Anglo–Mysore War came as a golden opportunity for Velu Nachiyar and her army, who had now spent eight long years in exile and military preparation, to strike at her enemy when they were already preoccupied in a bigger combat.

The opportunity presented itself during the most auspicious occasion—the festival of Vijayadashami. Velu Nachiyar along with her army of women warriors and the Marudhu brothers reached the outskirts of Sivaganga just on the eve of the festival. They noticed that the town was so well-guarded and fortified that it would have been difficult to breach it. On the day of the festival, it was a common practice for women to gather in large numbers at the local temple of Goddess Rajarajeshwari that was close to the palace. Velu and her women corps concealed their weapons and disguising themselves as common devotees who had gone to offer worship on the festive occasion thronged the temple. Even as they were busy infiltrating the temple, Kuyili managed to slip through into the palace complex and noticed the huge ammunition store of the British that would invariably be used against her queen and her adherents. She came up with the most brave and ingenuous method to counter this. Dousing herself with oil from the burning lamps in the palace, she set herself on fire and charged inside the ammunition store, blowing it all up in a huge explosion. The entire palace complex caught fire and was gutted. Kuyili went down in history as probably the first human bomb who caused such destruction. Almost simultaneously, the women army in the temple pulled out their hidden swords and pounced on the soldiers, with the Tamil battle cry of 'Vetrivel, Veeravel'. The temple bells were all rung vigorously to marshal the troops to take control of the fortress and the burning palace and the flag of the dynasty with the insignia of Hanuman went up atop the ramparts. Sivaganga had been recaptured in the most dramatic manner.

After regaining her principality, Velu Nachiyar honoured the memory of Udaiyal who had given up her life for the queen by enshrining her in a temple at Ariyakuruchi village that was about 13 km from Sivaganga, representing her as Goddess Kali. She donated her *mangalsutra* (her sacred matrimonial chain) to the temple.[5]

Meanwhile in the midst of the Second Anglo–Mysore War, Haidar Ali died in 1782 CE, and his son Tipu Sultan continued the war that eventually ended with the Treaty of Mangalore two years later. It is an important document in the history of India, perhaps the last occasion when an Indian power dictated terms to the English, who were the humble supplicants for peace. Warren Hastings, the British Governor General, called it a humiliating pacification and appealed to the monarch and the British Parliament to suitably punish the Madras Government for violating the British nation's faith and honour.[6] This shameful submission demoralized not only the British but also their subordinate, the Nawab of Arcot. Taking advantage of her enemy's weakness, Velu Nachiyar managed to extract a negotiation with the Nawab to allow her to retain Sivaganga on the payment of an annual tribute. He agreed as his focus was completely diverted towards the Mysore forces. Velu Nachiyar began to rule Sivaganga on behalf of her daughter Vellachi Nachiyar. She made Periya Marudhu the commander of the army and Chinna Marudhu, her chief minister. The Marudhus also extended their support to another legendary heroic character Veerapandiya Kattabomman (r. 1760–1799 CE), a poligar of Panjalamkurichi, who raised the bugle of revolt against the British.

Uneasy Calm

Despite being in power, Velu Nachiyar had to constantly face incursions from neighbouring states like Pudukottai and also her own relatives in Ramnad, in addition to occasional trouble that the Arcot forces kept giving her principality. Matters came to a pass for Velu Nachiyar when the relationship began to sour between her and her trusted commanders, the Marudhu brothers. The reason for this parting of ways was rather innocuous—the question of who would wed the princess Vellachi. The chieftain of Ramnad was keen on marrying Vellachi and thereby uniting the two principalities. But Vellachi was adamant against this, and an angered chieftain kept raiding the borders of Sivaganga and instigating hostilities. Velu wanted her daughter to wed a relative of her late husband, Gowri Vallabha Thevar and install him as her successor to the throne of Sivaganga. The Marudhu brothers, who should have ideally kept away from the personal decision of the royal family, insisted that the princess wed one Vengam Periya Udaya Thevar. They imprisoned Gowri Vallabha in the Kalaiyarkovil temple, though he managed to escape from there with the help of Karuppayee, a devadasi (a temple courtesan), and took refuge under the Pudukottai chieftain, Vijaya Raghunatha Tondaiman. Vellachi was eventually married off to the choice of the Marudhus, Vengam Periya Udaya Thevar. This caused much heartburn between them and Velu Nachiyar.

Things came to such a head by 1789 CE that Velu was constrained to even seek the support and intervention of her archrivals the Nawab of Arcot and the British to tame the Marudhus. On 29 April 1789, troops under British Colonel James Stuart, along with forces from Pudukottai, Madura, Tanjore and Tiruchirapalli, confronted the Marudhus, who initially lost a few battles. The French general of the Marudhus, Du Pre, abandoned them and moved over to Tipu Sultan and that caused further defeats to the already battered brothers. Beyond a point, the British did not want to precipitate the war and let Tipu Sultan enter the fray or establish his control over Sivaganga. So, they quickly sued for peace with Vengam Periya Udaya Thevar, who decided to suspend hostilities and announced Vellachi as the official ruler of Sivaganga in 1790 CE. Velu was thus abandoned midway, and she realized that she had lost control over the affairs of state.

Even as she was nearing sixty, all the travails of exile and war had taken a toll on her health, and she had developed a cardiac problem. She decided to relinquish her kingdom to her daughter, and in 1791 CE, she set sail to France for medical treatment. France was at that time in the peak of the revolution that brought about radical political and societal changes in the country. One wonders what soaking in into all those experiences of cataclysmic changes that she was witnessing around her meant for Velu Nachiyar while she was in France and whether she managed to meet any of the revolutionaries, given her fiery spirit. After two years, she returned to Sivaganga, only to realize that her beloved daughter Vellachi had died in childbirth and her husband had now wedded one of the daughters of the Marudhu brothers, who now seemed completely in control of the polity. Realizing that she had hardly any role to play and being disillusioned with everything, Velu Nachiyar retired once again to the fort of Virupakshi where she had hidden once. It was here that she died on 25 December 1796 under somewhat mysterious circumstances.

After Velu Nachiyar

The spirit of resistance against the British that Velu Nachiyar had instigated outlived her in the region she ruled over. Angered by the British disregard for public welfare during times of famine and drought, the Marudhus wrote several letters of complaint to the

Madras Council. When this yielded nothing, they began organizing a league of patriots from Sivaganga, Ramnad, Madura and Tirunelveli with the message and objective of unleashing a rebellion. The rebels looted firearms and foodgrains when the British were busy in the Third and Fourth Anglo–Mysore Wars and tried to foil the colonial powers' plans for south India. The anti-British campaign in south India, however, was dealt a huge blow, when in May 1799, the British managed to storm into Tipu's fort in Srirangapatna in the final Anglo–Mysore War and killed him in battle. But the poligars decided to group themselves and raise a banner of revolt against the British. The resultant Poligar Wars (1799–1801), as they are known in history, can be considered as the first true people's rebellion against British rule, more than half a century before the First War of Indian Independence in 1857. The first rebellion, also called the First Poligar War broke out in September 1799 in Tirunelveli district. This was led by Kattabomman. The Second Poligar War was also known as South Indian Rebellion due to its scale and reach. This large South Indian Confederacy against the British consisted of Marudhu Pandian of Sivaganga, Dheeran Chinnamalai of Kongu Nadu, Gopala Nayak of Dindigul, Krishnappa Nayak and Dhondoji Wagh of Mysore and Pazassi Raja Kerala Varma of Malabar. It took the British more than a year to suppress the rebellion that ended in the Carnatic Treaty of 1801, which ended Poligar rule permanently.

It has however been a forgotten chapter in the country's annals. Protesting against British exactions of tax revenues, the poligars revolted immediately after the capture of Mysore in 1799 CE. The Marudhu brothers were at the centre of these revolts and the palace of Sivaganga became the theatre of heavy intrigues. It sheltered some of the fiercest rebels from different parts of Tamil Nadu. The rebels, surviving on large stores of grain and firearms in the jungles of the Sivaganga principality, stormed British strongholds and tried to reclaim several forts, including Melur and Natham near Madurai, and Palamaneri and Thiruchuzhi in Ramnad, and established total control over the coast, forcing the Company to redirect supplies to Ceylon.

On 16 June 1801, the Marudhus issued their famous rebel proclamation that was found plastered at several places including the nawab's palace in the Tiruchirapalli Fort and one was addressed to the temple town of Srirangam. It is a unique and inspiring document that is unparalleled in the history of the freedom struggle in India. Calling himself an 'implacable enemy of the European low wretches', Marudhu censured the nawab for allowing the British to trample over the country's sovereignty and exhorted people to unite against them and overthrow the British from all of India:

> . . . in the island of Jamboo in the peninsula of Jamboo Dweepa this notice is given . . . the Europeans violating their faith have deceitfully made the kingdom their own and considering the inhabitants as dogs, accordingly exercise authority over them . . . in these countries now governed by these low wretches, the inhabitants have become poor . . . there existing no unity and friendship amongst you the above castes . . . therefore you Brahmins, Kshatriyas, Vysyas, Sudras and Musselmen, all who wear whiskers, whether civil or military, serving in the field or elsewhere, and you subedars, jamedars, havildars, nayaks and sepoys in the service of the low wretches and all capable of bearing arms, let them in the first place display their bravery as follows. Wherever you find any of the low wretches destroy them and continue to do so until they are extirpated.[7]

It took the British a long time to subjugate the rebellions of the Poligars, but eventually their military might prevailed. Kattabomman was hanged on 16 October 1799, the Marudhu brothers were publicly executed on 24 October 1801 along with their sons and grandsons. A raging Chinna Marudhu was apparently carried chained in a cage, to his hanging.

The spark of these heroisms that Tamil Nadu witnessed in one of the earliest anti-colonial struggles was lit by the indomitable Velu Nachiyar. In recognition of her valour, a commemorative stamp was issued in December 2008, and in 2014 the government of Tamil Nadu inaugurated the Velu Nachiyar Memorial at Sivaganga. The same year, a memorial commemorating Kuyili's bravery was also constructed at Sivaganga by the Tamil Nadu government. Due to her indomitable courage and bravery, the queen is fondly referred to as '*Veeramangai*' or the 'brave woman'.

While bravehearts like Velu Nachiyar or the Marudhu brothers may have been eclipsed in our historiography, their heroism lives on in ballads, folk songs and folk memory, even as they are immortalized and worshipped as gods in temples built for them by villagers. Where popular historiography failed them, folk memory redeemed this lapse and kept them alive till date.

Notes

1 For more details on the Palayakarar system, see S. Rajagopal, 'Formation of Palayakarar System by Visvanatha Nayaka (1530–1564): A Study' in *Pramana Research Journal*, 9.6 (2019), pp. 269–81.

2 The Thevars are native to central and southern Tamil Nadu and comprise the Agamudaiyar, Kallar and Maravar communities. They practice a Tamil martial art known variously as Adi Murai, Chinna Adi and Varna Ati.

3 For details on Velu Nachiyar's exile and the support given by Haidar Ali, see S. Vanajakumari and P. Vimala, 'Arc-Veera Mangai Velunachiyar in Antiquity India (1772–1780)' in *Shanlax International Journal of Arts, Science & Humanities,* 3.4 (April 2016), pp. 23– 30; A. Jekila & P. Barathi, 'Queen Velu Nachiyar: First Woman against British', *Infokara Research*, 9.3 (2020), pp. 891–97.

4 Pagoda was a measure of currency of the Vijayanagara Empire and equalled Rs 3 ½ in value.

5 Archana Garodia Gupta, *The Women Who Ruled India: Leaders, Warriors, Icons*, (Gurugram: Hachette India, 2019, p. 215.

6 Vikram Sampath, *Splendours of Royal Mysore: The Untold Story of the Wodeyars* (New Delhi: Rupa & Co, 2008), p. 229.

7 Gupta, *The Women Who Ruled India*, p. 218–19.

Begum Hazrat Mahal
of Awadh

With the tumultuous events of the Great Uprising of 1857 being quelled mercilessly by the English East India Company, India came directly under the British Crown through a proclamation issued by Empress Victoria on 1 November 1858. It was simultaneously translated into all Indian languages and circulated among the princely states. A copy of one such translation[1] reached Begum Hazrat Mahal, Regent of the minor prince Birjis Qadr, at the palace in Awadh. She was quite miffed by its contents, which she believed reeked of gross hypocrisy and blatant lies. Despite being in the thick of conflict while on exile, with the British in hot pursuit of her, she decided to issue a counter-proclamation to that of the Empress of England, which was termed as the 'Begum's Proclamation' and was widely circulated across Awadh and in the capital city Lucknow. It provided a point-by-point rebuttal of all of Queen Victoria's promises held out in her proclamation. Among other things it said:

> The proclamation of the 1st November 1858, which has come before us, is perfectly clear; and as some foolish people, not understanding the real object of the proclamation, have been carried away, there we, the ever-abiding government, parents of the people of Oude, with great consideration, put forth the present proclamation, in order that the real object of the chief points may be exposed, and our subjects placed on their guard . . . The Company had seized on the whole of Hindoostan, and, if this arrangement be accepted, what is there new in it . . . If our people were discontented with our royal predecessor, Wajid Ali Shah, how comes it they are content with us? And no ruler ever experienced such loyalty and devotion of life and goods as we have done. What then, is wanting that they do not restore our country? . . . there is a

well-known proverb—'A dying man is desperate' (*Murta kya na kurta*). It is impossible that a thousand should attach a million, and the thousand escape . . . In the proclamation it is written that the Christian religion is true, but that no other creed will suffer oppression, and that the laws will be observed towards all. What has the administration of justice to do with the truth or falsehood of religion? . . . the rebellion began with religion, and for it, millions of men have been killed. Let not our subjects be deceived; thousands were deprived of their religion in the North-West, and thousands were hanged rather than abandon their religion . . . we are deeply concerned for the condition of our people on reading this proclamation, which palpably teems with enmity. We now issue a distinct order, and one that may be trusted that all subjects who may have foolishly presented themselves as heads of villages to the English, shall, before the 1ˢᵗ of January next, present themselves, in our camp. Without doubt their faults shall be forgiven then, and they shall be treated according to their merits. To believe in this proclamation, it is only necessary to remember that Hindoostanee rulers are altogether kind and merciful. Thousands have seen this; millions have heard it. No one has ever seen in a dream that the English forgave an offence.[2]

The Early Life of Hazrat Mahal

The queen who was the central protagonist of Awadh's uprising against British rule hailed from extremely humble origins. Scattered details are all that are extant about her early life. She was born as Muhammadi Khanum to an African slave in Faizabad who was the bonded labourer of one Ghulam Ali Khan. A significant number of African slaves, largely from East Africa, had been traditionally imported into India by Arab slave traders for several centuries. Over time, they became an integral part of Indian society, and the nawabs of Awadh even had a *Hubshiyan Pulton* or Black Platoon comprising African soldiers.[3] The platoon even consisted of sturdy African women, whom the British writers describe as 'amazons'. Muhammadi was possibly born in one such family of mixed African–Indian lineage. At a very young age she was sold into the royal harem as a *khawasin* or attendant. This stint gave her an opportunity to acquaint herself with the ways and etiquette of royalty. Given her striking good looks, intellect and creativity, young Muhammadi soon naturally found her way to the royal *Pari Khana* or House of Fairies that Nawab of Awadh Wajid Ali Shah (1822–1887) had established. This was an institution that was intended to teach young and beautiful girls the arts of music, dance and theatre, so that they could entertain the nawab as professional courtesans later and also participate in his numerous experiments in art forms. All girls who found a place in the Pari Khana had their names suffixed with 'pari' or fairy and hence it was that Muhammadi too became Mehek Pari. Quite quickly she caught the eyes of the nawab who began to fancy her beauty and talent. As per the Shia form of Islamic marriages, he entered into a *mutah* or contractual wedding with her, with the grand title of '*Iftakar-un-Nissa*' (Pride of all Women).[4] The nawab had numerous such *mutah* wives or concubines, and whichever one of them gave him a son was soon elevated to the status of a 'begum' or official wife and granted a separate mahal or palace in their honour. In 1845 CE, Muhammadi gave birth to Wajid Ali Shah's son, who was named Birjis Qadr. As destiny's favoured child, she had made her way from being the daughter of a bonded slave to a courtesan to the nawab's concubine to finally an 'official' wife of the ruler of Awadh. She was rechristened as 'Begum Hazrat Mahal'. She became the apple of the eye of the already smitten nawab.

The nawab's increasing attention that she began to command caused great consternation in the royal household and bitter envy among the nawab's numerous other wives and concubines. Among her principal haters was the nawab's mother, Janab-i-Aliyyah, who despised this woman of lowly descent occupying the portals of royalty. Hazrat Mahal's fortunes were short-lived as by 1850 CE, under increasing pressure of his mother, the nawab gave *talaq* (divorce) to six such temporary wives that included her.[5] She was possibly stripped off her grand title and her estates, though she continued to live on in Lucknow. Little did she or her haters know that through a strange quirk of fate, she was going to be propelled back, right in the midst of a huge political storm and a rebellion that would etch her name forever in the annals of Indian history.

Political Situation in Awadh

The kingdom of Awadh was established in the early decades of the eighteenth century. Its rulers who claimed descent from Iran's Khorasan province were initially subservient to the Mughal Emperor in Delhi. Faizabad was their seat of power and they titled themselves as nawabs. With the death of Aurangzeb and the subsequent disarray that the Mughal Empire spiraled into, Delhi's position of pre-eminence gradually weakened, and several subordinate principalities began declaring their autonomy. Nawab Asaf-ud-Daula (r. 1775–1797), the fourth nawab wazir of Awadh, shifted the power centre from Faizabad to Lucknow and the city soon began to grow in strategic importance in north India. The substantial agricultural surplus produced by the fertile Doab region that was so generously watered by the northern rivers was no longer sent to Delhi but to Lucknow. All these developments created a new class of government officials, revenue collectors and merchants who emerged as the new aristocracy. This economic prosperity also attracted a host of courtesans, artists, musicians and dancers who made Lucknow a seat of the arts and poetry and a veritable last word in matters of genteel sophistication.

The prosperous province was obviously coveted by the English East India Company, which by then had slowly started emerging as not merely a trading outfit but as a military and political front with strong colonial ambitions. The early brush that Awadh had with the Company was in the Battle of Buxar in 1764 CE when Nawab Shuja-ud-Daula had formed a tripartite alliance against the British with Mughal Emperor Shah Alam and Nawab of Bengal Mir Qasim. But a crushing defeat smashed all hopes of Awadh's autonomy. They were forced to sign humiliating treaties with the British, including the Subsidiary Alliance that mandated the stationing of a permanent British force in Lucknow as a Residency on the payment of a subsidy, ostensibly to protect it against its foes but in reality to keep the nawab under their strict check. Exclusive trading rights, too, began to get granted. The British encroachment drained Awadh of all its economic resources. There was a steady ceding of territory and authority over time. In 1775 CE, the Banaras region was ceded to the Company as also the revenues of Ghazipur. In 1797 CE, Allahabad and its surrounding regions were subsumed by the Company and by 1801 CE the Lower Doab, Gorakhpur and Rohilkhand, too, were formally handed over by the nawab. While the powers of the nawab of Awadh shrunk this way, those of the British Resident in Lucknow grew exponentially. Most nawabs after this had virtually become figureheads and puppets in the hands of the British and had given up all attempts to govern. They retired to the harem and immersed themselves in hedonistic pleasures or in the pursuit of the arts.

Wajid Ali Shah, who became nawab in 1847 CE, was no different. He was known spending all his time in composing poems and songs, and in the company of beautiful women and artists. He enacted his own version of Krishna's Raas Leela[6] that came to be known as 'Rahas'. The nawab played the role of Krishna, and all the *paris* of the Pari Khana became his *gopis*. In his book titled *Bani*, more than thirty-six types of Rahas (all set in Kathak style) composed and choreographed by Wajid Ali are listed, with charming names like *Mor-Chhatri, Salami, Ghunghat, Mujra* and *Mor-Pankhi*.[7] Distinctive schools of the dance form Kathak and musical genres like the thumri began to flower in Lucknow under the nawab's patronage. The theatrical roles that he regularly donned and popularized heralded the Hindustani theatre scene in coming years.

While Wajid Ali Shah's reign was a golden period for the arts, this was not the expectation of a nawab to renege the last vestiges of his political control to the already powerful British. While he assumed that the British would let him live with his hedonism, he was in for a rude shock when Lord Dalhousie, the Governor-General of India, used his infamous Doctrine of Lapse to depose him on charges of misgovernance and maladministration, and annexed Awadh on 7 February 1856. Instead of keeping Wajid Ali Shah in Lucknow, the British decided to exile him to Calcutta, a month later on 13 March 1856. The nawab whined and whimpered but realized that the British had made up their minds. The shabby treatment meted out to their favourite nawab also caused a lot of heartburn among the people of Awadh. When his entourage was leaving Lucknow for the last time, several people voluntarily followed him all the way to Kanpur, singing melancholic songs. The nawab himself composed two timeless thumris that are still popular on the Hindustani music concert stage—*Babul Mora Naihar Chhooto Hi Jaaye* and *Jab Chhod Chale Lucknow*—both dealing with the intense pain of displacement from his favourite city of Lucknow.

Stepping on the gangway of the steamer *McLeod*, as it moored at Bichali ghat in Calcutta's Matia Buruj, little did Wajid Ali Shah know that Lucknow was lost to him for good. He and the royal family had immense hopes in the supposed sense of fair play and justice of the British and saw this only as a temporary measure. About three or four miles south of Calcutta, on the banks of River Hooghly, was a quiet quarter known as Garden Reach. The region's topography with its raised plateau structure made the locals call it Matia Buruj. There were also some fine houses, the grounds of which stretched for two to three miles along the riverbank. The deposed nawab was given three houses, two for himself (Sultan Khana and Asad Manzil) and one for his chief consort (Murassa Manzil). A large expanse of land, too, was granted to him for his personal use.

Refusing to accept the allowances allotted to him, the Nawab kept alive his hopes of reclaiming the crown that he believed had been unjustly snatched from him. The Queen Mother Janab-i-Aliyyah, along with Wajid Ali Shah's brother and son, even made it to England to meet Queen Victoria and plead their case in her presence to seek relief. But it was a futile exercise as the queen refused to grant them an audience. Wajid Ali Shah's mother died on their way back, in Paris.[8] With all hopes of reclamation of the throne having been dashed, Wajid Ali Shah soon began to accept the harsh reality. Calcutta was to become his new home and the entire courtly and artistic glory that Lucknow had been all these decades, now shifted scene to his new city of residence. The Hooghly reminded him of his dear Gomti River back in Lucknow. He recreated all the pomp and splendour of his zenana, as it was, back in Lucknow. The influence of Awadhi culture was soon to be felt in the Bengali aristocracy too.

One of the fallouts of his exile was that Wajid Ali Shah could not take along with him to Calcutta his vast harem of numerous wives and concubines, more so the ones that he had discarded by divorce. Consequently, Hazrat Mahal and her son were left behind to fend for themselves in Lucknow as the nawab's entourage moved away to Matia Buruj.

Popular Discontent in Awadh and Its Fallout

One of the main victims of the Summary Settlement of 1856[9] (imposed by the British) were the *taluqdars*, who held sway over forts, armies and the rural hinterland of Awadh. Through the settlement, the British destroyed several of these fortifications and dispossessed the *taluqdars* of their traditional fiefdoms. The land revenues that were settled were much higher and more oppressive than during the days of the nawabs. As per an estimate, the *taluqdars* lost 9,900 villages out of 23,500 villages, or approximately over 43 per cent of their total possessions held in 1856 CE.[10] Yet, the Summary Settlements were incomplete and there was a chance of more loss, making most of the *taluqdars* insecure and forcing them to the rebel side. The British, too, were alarmed by the large number of *taluqdars* who made common cause with the rebels, attributing their act to the fact that they had been reduced 'to a level with the meanest before the law . . . because it compelled them to disband their armies, pay their revenue regularly, and not oppress their ryots'.[11]

There was growing discontent and anger among sepoys that the new assault rifles that had been commissioned in the army had bullet casings laced with grease made of animal fat. Since they had to be bitten off by the sepoy before use, the idea of consuming cow or pig fat was anathema to the religious sentiments of both Hindus and Muslims. This, along with numerous attempts by the British and the missionaries to look down upon native traditions and faiths to convert them to Christianity, added to the angst. In Awadh, the ill-treatment meted out to Nawab Wajid Ali Shah was another spark that was waiting to set the scene ablaze as there was popular public discontent against British excesses from almost all sections of society—rich and poor, Hindus and Muslims, royalty and peasants alike. The Doctrine of Lapse through which Dalhousie had annexed several princely states had caused widespread anger among the other royals too, be it Jhansi or the peshwa in exile in Kanpur. The hanging for treason of a popular sepoy Mangal Pandey in Barrackpore on 8 April 1857 acted as the final trigger, and what started as a mutiny in the army platoons soon spread like wild forest fire across vast swathes of the country.

It was just a matter of time before the battalion in Lucknow, too, raised the flag of revolt. Once this happened the fire spread to several cantonments across Awadh in quick succession—Sitapur, Faizabad, Gonda–Bharaich, Sultanpur and Salon. The rebels needed a leader to represent and guide them. As the last remnants of the nawabi household that also had a male heir, the mantle providentially fell on Hazrat Mahal. Her twelve-year-old son was provisionally proclaimed king and she, the regent queen and the principal power behind the throne. Having been consigned to oblivion and desertion after the divorce and the nawab's exile, fortune had yet again smiled on its favourite child. Under the leadership of Hazrat Mahal, the rebels took charge of Lucknow by 30 May 1857. Unlike the mass slaughter of Europeans—men, women and children that had happened in Kanpur at the behest of the rebels—in Lucknow the farsightedness of Sir Henry Lawrence, the newly appointed chief commissioner of Awadh saved many lives. He shifted his troops and all Europeans to seek refuge in the Residency at Alambagh Palace and fortified it. The begum and her troops kept attacking the Residency, even as Lawrence awaited reinforcements and assistance from other areas. The begum's troops not only confined them to the Residency for a long time, but also took measures to defend the city from the British.

The Battle of Chinhat and Afterwards

A clash between the rebels and the British occurred on 30 June 1857 in Chinhat when the latter made a surprise attack in the morning.

Columns were quickly organized to counter this from the Lucknow side. A rebel army of close to 7,000 to 8,000 was waiting to strike back. However, two factions began to emerge during this conflict. The rebels who owed their allegiance to Begum Hazrat Mahal and her minor son and another one led by a holy man named Maulvi Ahmadullah Shah.[12] Not much is known about his origins, except that he was in Gwalior where he lived and preached, and later even moved to the North Western Provinces, all the while declaring a *jihad* (holy war) against the infidel British. After the annexation of Awadh and the deposing of Wajid Ali Shah, he came to Faizabad and began to gather men with the war cry against the British and also to avenge the death of another fellow maulvi Amir Ali who was martyred at Hanumangarhi fighting the enemy forces. For this, Maulvi Ahmadullah was also arrested and put in the Faizabad jail and was freed later by the rebels. He joined them in the Chinhat battle where he and his contingent overpowered the British in hand-to-hand fights. The lack of unity and coordination between the two factions led to the British getting away with a defeat that was not significant enough to cause a complete rout and allowed them room for consolidation.

The British defeat, however caused great jubilation in the rebel army. Sweets were distributed in the streets of Lucknow as the end of British hegemony was considered a given now. Sir Henry Lawrence lost his life to a grievous injury on 4 July 1857 and is buried within the Residency. Most of the Indian soldiers in the British army defected to the rebel side, enabling the latter to hold the Residency by siege for a long time. The messages of these successes from Lucknow were being dutifully sent under the royal seal of the begum to Mughal Emperor Bahadur Shah Zafar in Delhi, who had been declared as the king and leader of all the rebels, nationwide.

Maulvi Ahmadullah was also injured in the foot during the Chinhat ambush and later retreated to Tara Kothi that was his headquarters. With the British rule effectively relegated to the confines of the Residency where they were held hostage, the rebels formally placed Birjis Qadr on the ancestral throne in Baradari at Kaiserbagh Palace (built by his father) on 5 July 1857, and his mother was officially declared the regent of Awadh. Her army commander was a Hindu Raja Jai Lal Singh, a former nizam of Azamgarh; her confidante Mammu Khan was superintendent-in-charge; the women's units were led by Uda Devi, a Dalit woman. The begum issued several proclamations, all in the name of her son Birjis Qadr, urging people to join this war, to donate generously for this righteous cause and also motivated the rebels and the sepoys to continue their brave acts. One such proclamation makes common cause of the consternation that faced both Hindus and Muslims under the British rule: 'All the Hindus and Muslims know that four things are extremely dear to every human being i.e. (a) *deen* and *dharam*, (b) honour and respect; (c) Life of his own and the family members; (d) Property and other belongings.'[13]

The Maulvi however was virulently opposed to the queen and her son and constantly defied their authority. Quite contrary to the begum's proclamations, issued in the name of Prince Birjis Qadr, that urged for a syncretic Hindu and Muslim unity, the maulvi saw the uprising as solely a Muslim religious war. Academic Saiyid Zaheer Husain Jafri notes some of the reasons for their estrangement:

> As a result of the military victory against the British, the sepoys as well as the army commanders had become very arrogant, causing much hardships to the inhabitants of the city, and even the people of means were being plundered indiscriminately. This lawlessness on the part of the sepoys was objected to by the *mujahideens* who brought the matter before the Shah. Thereupon it was decided that a leader should be chosen to check the indiscipline and disorderly conduct of the sepoys. Quite contrary to his expectations, the army leaders decided in favour of prince Birjis Qadr. The Shah sharply reacted to this. His plea was that since *jehad* could be conducted only under the leadership of an *imam*, it was necessary that the creed of the *imam* should be the same as that of *mujahideens*; moreover, jehad is not obligatory for the *shias*, therefore by declaring Birjis Qadr as the leader, the most important ingredient of jehad was missing. Therefore, the fight against the British could no more remain a battle for religion. Hence, the *mujahideens* could fight only for self-defence. Further, since the *mujahideens* had offered the stiffest resistance to the British, they had an inflated sense of importance. Also, the Shah had arrived to fight at the behest of his *pir*,

and the leadership should have been conferred upon him. However, this seems to be only a theoretical position taken by Shah, but practically he did lend full support in attacking the Residency.[14]

The maulvi made tall claims of invincibility and magical powers; he began to issue proclamations assuming the airs and ceremonials of royalty and even called upon the begum and her son to accept him as their king and become his disciples. An enraged begum organized a force to cut his clout and he was forced to flee Lucknow to take shelter at a garden house in the suburbs. But the two joined hands later, relinquishing their differences, though the association was seemingly fraught with intense mutual suspicion. Saiyid Zaheer Husain Jafri states that 'after reaching Bari, prince Birjis Qadr had the honour of offering *bay'at* (spiritual allegiance) to Shah. The arrangement put the entire management in the Shah's hands; he forced the officers of the begum to part with their wealth. This would have certainly caused resentment. Therefore, when the Shah decided to make a surprise attack on the Gorkha army of Nepal returning after much plunder, his new allies ditched him. As a result, the *mujahideens* were left alone in the assault.'[15]

Purging British Rule in Awadh

The rebels now focused their attention entirely towards the Residency where the harried Europeans were held hostage. It was constantly bombarded and surrounded by more than 35,000 sepoys and other retainers of the *taluqdars*, under the orders of Queen Hazrat Mahal and her court. About twenty to twenty-five superior-quality guns were stationed, directing their fire at the Residency. The begum's court quickly slipped into the process of governance and administration. One part of the court oversaw administration, payments and other details, while given the fluid situation, another one focused entirely on military preparations. Even as the British were making desperate attempts to send out relief to those holed inside, common villagers, too, joined in to put a spirited resistance to the columns headed to Lucknow from Kanpur under Henry Havelock and James Outram.

The begum directed attacks against Lt General James Outram nine times and even contemptuously rejected his offer of a peace treaty with Queen Victoria and the promise of a pension of one lakh rupees.

The rebels had created a strong fortification of men and material around the Residency to prevent any relief from coming through. However, by 25 September 1857, the 'First Relief of Lucknow' managed to hoodwink the rebels and reach the Residency, only to get trapped inside with their co-nationalists. But by October 1857, even as the uprising in Delhi and other neighbouring areas were being quelled successfully, the British attention shifted to rescue Lucknow that had still managed to hold its fort strong against them for this long.

Through the next couple of months, the begum's army managed to hold the siege that had begun on 30 May and lasted till 27 November 1857. More than 50,000 fighting men were there to resist any British attempts to breach the siege.[16] British forces under Colin Campbell were rushing towards Lucknow to liberate their compatriots. Campbell first attacked Sikandar Bagh, a pleasure garden that had been built by Wajid Ali Shah and was now occupied by three sepoy regiments. In a brutal pushback, the British managed to assert their strength and almost all including another 2,000 rebels were killed on 16 November 1857 as retribution for the Kanpur massacre.

Notably, when Campbell attacked Sikandar Bagh, he was faced with several Dalit women who were part of the women's regiment of Begum Hazrat Mahal. Chief among these was the commander Uda Devi, who was a heroic Dalit warrior of the Pasi community and confidante of the queen. Known also as Jagrani, Uda Devi is supposed to have been born in Lucknow's Ujriaon village and was married to Makka Pasi. Her husband had been martyred in the battle of Chinhat and Uda Devi was burning with the rage of avenging his death. W. Gordon Alexander's account of the storming of Sikandar Bagh mentions how several 'black women'—possibly the African women soldiers—led a successful defence:

> In addition . . . there were . . . even a few amazon-negresses, amongst the slain. These amazons having no religious prejudices against the use

of greased cartridges, whether of pigs or other animal fat, although doubtless professed Muhammadans, were armed with rifles, while the Hindu and Muhammadan East Indian rebels were all armed with musket; they fought like wild cats, and it was not till after they were killed that their sex was suspected.[17]

Uda Devi, their commander, climbed over a pipal tree and shot dead some thirty-two to thirty-six British soldiers. Someone on the enemy side spotted a silhouette in the tree and shot at it. The person fell down dead and only then did the troops realize that she was a woman. Seeing her brave feat, even British officers like Campbell supposedly bowed their heads reverentially over her corpse.[18]

Campbell managed to completely evacuate the British residents who were holed in for so many months as hostages. But given the strong resistance from the begum's army they fled Lucknow. Though he had managed to kill so many rebel sepoys, Campbell's actions were seen in Lucknow as one of British fright that made them flee. Buoyed by this, the rebel strength kept swelling and by January 1858 had become a 100,000-strong force.

Towards a Perilous Fall

Anticipating a fierce retaliation and also to prevent British re-entry, the begum ordered massive fortifications around the city, with more than 15,000 workmen deployed for the task. Water from the Gomti was diverted to a new moat that was constructed around the Kaiserbagh to protect it. Streets, lanes and houses, too, were all barricaded or loopholed. These decisions were emanating from the court of the begum and as historian Rudrangshu Mukherjee states: 'All the decisions may not have emanated directly from Hazrat Mahal, but they certainly came from a court of which she was not only an integral part, but also likely the one who asked for it to be set up.'[19] But despite this, the small force of the British of about 4,000 men under British Commander Outram that were left behind by Campbell was still active in Alambagh and the rebels failed to either throw them out or even consider it important. The sweet smell of success, even as fellow rebels in other parts of the country were being ruthlessly crushed, perhaps got to their heads and made them complacent. Delhi and Kanpur had been won back by the British and the net was slowly closing in on Lucknow too. The begum possibly realized this and hence in her characteristic fashion gave a stirring speech to the rebels, laced with sarcasm and also threats of her making peace with the British:

> Great things were promised from the all-powerful Delhie, and my heart used to be gladdened by the communication I used to receive from that city but now the King has been dispossessed and his army scattered, the English have bought over the Seikhs and Rajahs, and have established their Government West, East, and South, and communications are cut off; the Nana has been vanquished; and Lucknow is endangered; what is to be done? The whole army is in Lucknow, but is without courage. Why does it not attack Alumbagh? Is it waiting for the English to be reinforced, and Lucknow to be surrounded? How much longer am I to pay the sepoys for doing nothing? Answer now, and if fight you won't, I shall negotiate with the English to spare my life.[20]

The speech produced the desired impact and stirred the rebels to continue their fight. However, by March 1858, the tide slowly began to turn in favour of the British, even as Campbell prepared to attack Lucknow. He was met with fierce opposition all through the route to Lucknow and in the city, too, with constant bombardments on the invaders. Eventually, about 3,000 rebels were killed and some eighty guns seized from their side. The rest of the rebel army dispersed away into hinterland Awadh, as the British failed to prevent a free pass. Lucknow, that had held on for the longest and strongest time, had finally fallen to the British, but it was by no means an easy accession for them. As Rudrangshu Mukherjee rightly notes: 'The British had annexed Awadh in 1856 without a shot being fired; in 1858 they had to conquer it through a show of arms.'[21] Lord Canning's Proclamation, popularly known as the Awadh Proclamation of March 1858, announced that just six *taluqdars* were to be considered as the sole hereditary proprietors of land that was in their possession during the annexation of Awadh in 1856. These were the loyalists who had sided with the British and hence got their rewards. This caused further consternation among the other *taluqdars* who were already suffering dispossession under the clauses of the Summary Settlements.

The begum meanwhile escaped to a fort across the Gogra with her army and attendants. Maulvi Ahmadullah Shah declared himself as an independent ruler on 15 March 1858 and continued his military campaigns against the British in Rohilkhand before his eventual treacherous assassination by the Raja of Pawayan, who was on the payroll of the British. The raja even received a cash reward of 50,000 rupees for his treachery from the British, who were relieved that the maulvi was finally killed. [22]

Hazrat Mahal was still active in the trans-Gogra region and was conducting her courts and issuing proclamations as though nothing had changed. She received support from the rajas of Gonda and Bahraich and this entire belt remained out of British reach till late 1858 CE. Hazrat Mahal also found support in Shrimant Nana Saheb Peshwa (1824–1859), who was a close associate of another braveheart woman ruler of the times, Rani Laxmibai of Jhansi. Nana Saheb's father was an official in the court of Peshwa Baji Rao II in Pune. The childless peshwa had been living on British pension in Bithoor after the Third Anglo–Maratha War. He adopted Nana as his successor before he died. However, invoking the Doctrine of Lapse, the British refused to recognize the adoption and stopped the pension to Nana Saheb, the legal heir of the peshwa. In retaliation, in June 1857, Nana Saheb decided to launch a massive anti-British battle. Nana also created a group of sadhus to light the fire of revolution. He confabulated with Mughal Emperor Bahadur Shah Zafar in Delhi on how to organize this war that broke out on 10 May 1857 in Meerut. Nana declared the uprising on 4 June 1857 and revolts picked up in Meerut, Bundelkhand and other places. British rule was extinguished in Kanpur by Nana and his soldiers in June 1857, and the British were mercilessly hacked. In July 1857, the British under General Havelock were successful in recapturing Kanpur by defeating Nana's forces. Nana escaped to Bithoor where his associates Tatya Tope, Rani Laxmibai and Azimullah Khan proclaimed him as the new peshwa. His support to Begum Hazrat Mahal added strength to her efforts, though it was short-lived. By late September 1858, this group tried to make elaborate plans for coordinated actions of the rebels across Awadh and northern and eastern Rohilkhand and block Campbell. However, Campbell and Lord Clyde managed to circle the rebel forces from all over and pushed several of them into the Terai region of Nepal. With the British in hot pursuit, Nana Saheb, too, crossed over to Nepal in disguise and nothing was known about what happened to him thereafter. Rani Laxmibai died fighting in battle at Kotah-ki-Serai near Gwalior on 18 June 1858, dressed as a soldier even in her martyrdom. Nana's associate Tatya Tope was deceitfully arrested by the British and was eventually executed at the gallows in Shivpuri on 18 April 1859. One by one, all the protagonists of the First War of Indian Independence were liquidated, and the revolution was unravelled.

The Swan Song

Refusing to surrender, Begum Hazrat Mahal decided to cross the Gandak River and move to Nepal with an army comprising 40,000 infantry and 10,000 cavalry accompanied by eighteen guns. Her forces suffered from hunger and disease. She initially sought political asylum from Nepal's King Jung Bahadur, who under British coercion refused to grant it to her unless she laid down her arms. Having carried some of her wealth and jewellery with her, the begum managed to negotiate terms with Jung Bahadur and purchase her political asylum and a life of dignity in that kingdom. The British made several appeals to her to return to India, with a promise to pardon her and to allot a pension to her. But she haughtily refused all the overtures and decided to live on her own terms. Begum Hazrat Mahal died in exile in 1879 CE in Nepal and was buried in an unmarked grave near the Jama Masjid in Kathmandu. Ironically, she had helped build that mosque and had named it Hindustani Masjid—named in honour of the country that she so dearly loved and sacrificed her everything for.

Decades later, writing about her in his magnum opus on the First War of Indian Independence in 1857, revolutionary and freedom fighter Vinayak Damodar Savarkar was to say:

This Begum of Oudh, though not quite another Lakshmi Bai, was undoubtedly a great organizer, full of love of liberty and the spirit of daring. She had perfect confidence in an *Omrah* (nobleman) of the court, called Mahbub Khan. She appointed various officers to the judicial, revenue, police and military departments. These officers selected were such as were loved and honoured by the representatives of the Sepoys, by Mahbub Khan and other leading Sirdars, and also by the large numbers of the people who hurried from all parts of Oudh to Lucknow to join in the great war of Independence. Every day, a Durbar was held to discuss political affairs, and there, the Begum Sahiba exercised authority in the name of the Nabob. The news that Oudh was free and that not a trace of English rule remained there was sent to the Emperor of Delhi, under the Begum's seal, along with valuable presents. Letters were sent to all the neighbouring Zemindars and vassal Rajas to come to Lucknow with armed followers. From the appointment of the various civil officers, from the good order in all the departments of Government, from the daily Durbars and other signs, it was apparent that the revolt had ended and constructive government had begun. But unfortunately, the revolutionaries did not show as much zeal in obeying the officers appointed as they showed in participating in their appointment.[23]

Notes

1. On the 1 November 1858, Charles Canning, then Governor-General of India, announced Queen Victoria's proclamation to 'the Princes, Chiefs and Peoples of India'.

2. Rudrangshu Mukherjee, *A Begum and a Rani: Hazrat Mahal and Lakshmibai in 1857* (New Delhi: Penguin Random House India, 2021), pp. 147–51.

3. For more details, see the seminal work of historian Rosie Llewellyn-Jones, ed., *The Uprising of 1857* (Ahmedabad: Alkazi Collection of Photography and Mapin, 2017).

4. https://www.livehistoryindia.com/story/people/begum-hazrat-mahal-a-revolutionary-queen

5. Mukherjee, *A Begum and a Rani*, p. 14.

6   This is well-documented. In fact, legendary filmmaker Satyajit Ray opened a window to the life of Nawab Wajid Ali Shah in *Shatranj Ke Khilari* in a unique way. Please refer to 'The making of a Queer Figure: Satyajit Ray's interpretation of Nawab Wajid Ali Shah in *Shatranj Ke Khilari*' by Madhuja Mukherjee in https://frontline.thehindu.com/cover-story/the-making-of-a-queer-figure-satyajit-ray-interpretation-of-nawab-wajid-ali-shah-in-shatranj-ke-khilari/article37090441.ece (accessed on 27 May 2022). Also, Rosie Llewellyn-Jones's work *The Last King in India: Wajid Ali Shah* (New Delhi: Penguin Random House India, 2014) offers a fascinating account of the life, times and works of Wajid Ali Shah.

7   For more on Wajid Ali Shah's contribution to music and dance, see Tahir Hussain Ansari, 'The Cultural and Literary Contribution of Nawab Wajid Ali Shah', *International Journal of English Language, Literature and Humanities*, 3.3 (2014), pp. 181–89.

8   https://www.livehistoryindia.com/story/people/begum-hazrat-mahal-a-revolutionary-queen

9   After the annexation of Awadh, the first revenue settlement system that the British imposed was known as the Summary Settlement of 1856. This further undermined the position and importance of the *taluqdars*. It proceeded on the assumption that the *taluqdars* were interlopers with no permanent claims on the land and that they had established their control over the land fraudulently and through coercive means, and they lost their land holdings en masse.

10 Iqbal Hussain, 'Awadh Rebel Proclamations during 1857–58' in *Proceedings of the Indian History Congress*, 58 (1997), p. 487.

11 Ibid.

12 For his early life and antecedents, see Saiyid Zaheer Husain Jafri, 'The Profile of a Saintly Rebel: Maulavi Ahmadullah Shah' *Social Scientist* 26.1 (Jan–April 1998), pp. 39–52.

13 Hussain, 'Awadh Rebel Proclamations During 1857–58', p. 482.

14 Jafri, 'The Profile of a Saintly Rebel', p. 44.

15 Ibid., p. 46.

16 Rudrangshu Mukherjee, *Awadh in Revolt, 1857–58: A Study of Popular Resistance* (New Delhi: Oxford University Press, 1984), pp. 93–94.

17 W. Gordon-Alexander, *Recollections of a Highland Subaltern: During the Campaigns of the 93rd Highlanders in India, under Colin Campbell, Lord Clyde in 1857, 1858 and 1859* (London: Edward Arnold, 1898), p. 104.

18 Raj Kumar Pasi, *Pasi Samaj ka Swatantrata Sangram Mein Yogdan* (Lucknow: Pasi Shodh Evam Sanskritik Sansthan, 1998), pp. 7–20.

19 Mukherjee, *A Begum and a Rani*, p. 35.

20 Ibid., p. 38.

21 Ibid., p. 40.

22 Jafri, 'The Profile of a Saintly Rebel' p. 47.

23 Vinayak Damodar Savarkar, *The Indian War of Independence, 1857* (London, 1909), p. 260.

Acknowledgements

Several people and institutions generously supported the research and the writing of this book. I am grateful to the National Archives of India, New Delhi; India Office of the British Library, London; the Arquivo Histórico Ultramarino, Lisbon; the Tulu Sahitya Akademi, Mangaluru and the Department of Historical and Antiquarian Studies, Guwahati, and their staff for all the assistance in research and procuring of archival documents. Mr T.V. Mohandas Pai has always been a generous source of support in all my endeavours, and I am thankful to him for this. My grateful thanks to Smt. Asha Jadeja Motwani and the Motwani Jadeja Foundation for reposing faith in my work and supporting the research for this project. Dr Chinnappa Gowda has been so magnanimous in his support and to him, I owe my immense gratitude. I am indebted to several other people who have contributed in various capacities to this project—Dr Prabhakara Joshi, Mr Kuldeep Chowta, Mr Ashwin Kumar, Dr Ishwar Oza, Mr Chirayu Pandit, Mr Sriram Sharma and Mr Yeshwant Holkar. I am extremely thankful to my friends and well-wishers—Dr Rajendra Pratap Singh and Mr Rakesh Naithani for being encouraging supporters of all my endeavours. I am indebted to the following scholars who took the trouble of going through the manuscript, suggested changes and also endorsed it for me—Dr Bibek Debroy, Dr Meenakshi Jain and Mr Sanjeev Sanyal, to whom in particular I owe my thanks for germinating the idea of this book in the first place. Mr Sundeep Bhutoria, my friend and well-wisher, and the Prabha Khaitan Foundation (especially Smt. Anindita Chatterjee) have always supported my literary endeavours, and I am very grateful to them for this. I am grateful to my family and friends for standing by me through thick and thin and for putting up with my vagaries in the course of the research—my father Mr Sampath Srinivasan for being so nurturing and supportive, my aunt Roopa Madhusudan, Ranak Singh Mann, Pratibha Chopra, and to Sandeep Singh Chauhan for always being there for me through my tribulations. My respectful obeisances to my spiritual mentor Sadhguru Sakshi Ram Kripal ji for his love, guidance and blessings. This book would not have seen light of day but for my publisher Penguin Random House India, Premanka Goswami, my dear friend and editor, Binita Roy, who leads the copy editorial team, Shaoni Mukherjee, Priti Anand, and Gunjan Ahlawat, who leads the design team—my heartfelt thanks to all of them for enriching this work with their inputs and toil. Last but not the least, my obeisance unto the Divine, without whose inspiration and grace, not a word could have been written.

Bibliography

Published Sources

A Gazetteer of the Province of Sindh. Sindh: G. Bells & Sons, 1874.

'A Report on South Indian Epigraphy 1968–69 Ap. A. No. 7'. *Annual Report of Indian Epigraphy* (ARIE). New Delhi: Director General of Archaeological Survey of India, Government of India, 1968-69.

Abraham, M. *Two Medieval Merchant Guilds of South India*. New Delhi: Manohar, 1988.

Abu-Lughod, J. *Before European Hegemony: The World System A.D. 1250–1350*. New York: Oxford University Press, 1989.

Aiya, V. Nagam. *The Travancore State Manual*, Vol. 1. Trivandrum: Travancore Government Press, 1906.

Aiyer, K.V. Subrahmanya. *South Indian Inscriptions*, Vol. LII. Madras: Government Press, 1937.

Allan, J., Sir T. Wolseley Haig and H.H. Dodwell eds. *The Cambridge Shorter History of India*. Cambridge: Cambridge University Press, 1934.

Ansari, Tahir Hussain. 'The Cultural and Literary Contribution of Nawab Wajid Ali Shah.' *International Journal of English Language, Literature and Humanities*, 3.3 (2014).

Apte, B.K. *A History of the Maratha Navy and Merchant Ships*. Bombay: State Board for Literature and Culture, 1973.

Arunachalam, B. *Chola Navigation Package*. Mumbai: Maritime History Society, 2004.

Bamzai, P.N.K. *Cultural and Political History of Kashmir*, Vol. 1. Srinagar: Gulshan Books, 1994.

Bayley, Sir Edward Clive. *The Local Muhammadan Dynasties of Gujarat*. London: W.H. Allen & Co., 1886), p. 148.

Beal, Samuel. *Si-Yu-Ki: Buddhist Records of the Western World*. This is a translated version of the original by Hsuan-Tsang. London: Trubner & Co., 1884.

Besant, Annie. *Children of the Motherland*. Banaras: Central Hindu College, 1906.

Bhuyan, S.K. *Lachit Barphukan and His Times: A History of the Assam–Mogul Conflicts of the Period 1667 to 1671 A.D.* Guwahati: The Department of Historical and Antiquarian Studies, Government of Assam, 1947.

Briggs, John. *History of the Rise of the Mahomedan Power in India, till the year A.D. 1612.* Translated from the original Persian of Mahomed Kasim Ferishta. Calcutta: R. Cambray & Co., 1910.

Browne, James. *India Tract,* Vol. 2, *The History of the Origin and Progress of the Sikhs.* London: Zogographic Press, 1788.

Burway, Muntazim Bahadur Mukund Wamanrao. *Life of Subhedar Malhar Rao Holkar, Founder of the Indore State (1693–1766 A.D.).* Indore: Holkar State Printing Press, 1930.

Chandler, Tertius. *Four Thousand Years of Urban Growth: An Historical Census.* New York: St. David's University Press, 1987.

Clark, Francis Murgotten. *The Origins of the Islamic State*, pt. 2, translated from the *Kitab Futah al-Buldan* by al Baladhuri. New York: Columbia University, 1924.

Commissariat, M.S. *A History of Gujarat*, Vol.1. Bombay: Longman, Green & Co., 1938.

Corpus Inscriptionum Indicarum, Vol. 1.

Couto, Diogo do. *Decada Da Asia IV*. Lisboa: Na Regia Officina Typografica, 1790, MDCCLXXXX.

Cowley, Captain Cecil. *Tales of Ahmednagar*. Bombay: Thacker & Company Ltd., 1919.

Dalal, C.D. (ed.). *Sukrita Kirti Kallolini* of Udayaprabha Suri. Baroda, 1920.

De, B. *Tabaqat-i-Akbari*. Translation into English of the original by Nizam-ud-Din Ahmad, Vol. 1, Pt. I (Calcutta: The Royal Asiatic Society of Bengal, 1913).

Devi, Laishram Hemantakumari. 'Maharaas: Sri Sri Govindaji Temple and Other Local Temples of Manipur'. *International Journal of Research -Granthaalayah*, 9 (2), 2021.

Dow, Alexander. *The History of Hindostan from the Earliest Account of Time to the Death of Akbar*. This is a translation of the original *Tarik-i-Firishta* by 'Mahomed Kasim Ferishta, Vol. 1, 2. London: T. Becket & P.A. De Hondt.

Downing, Clement. *A History of the Indian Wars*. London: Oxford University Press, 1924.

Elliot, H.M. and John Dowson. *The History of India as Told by Its Own Historians: The Muhammadan Period*, Vol.1, 2, 3, 4. London: Trubner and Co., 1867.

Fredunbeg, Mirza Kalichbeg. *The Chachanamah: An Ancient History of Sind*. This is a translated version of the Persian original *Tarikh al-Hind wa al-Sind*. Karachi: Commissioners Press, 1900.

Goel, Sita Ram. *Heroic Hindu Resistance to Muslim Invaders*. New Delhi: Voice of India, 1984.

Goitein, S.D. 'From the Mediterranean to India: Documents on the Trade to India, South Arabia and East Africa from the Eleventh and Twelfth Centuries.' *Speculum* 29 (1954).

Goetz, Hermann. *Studies in the History and Art of Kashmir and the Indian Himalaya*. Wiesbaden: Otto Harrassowitz, 1969.

Gordon-Alexander, W. *Recollections of a Highland Subaltern: During the Campaigns of the 93rd Highlanders in India, under Colin Campbell, Lord Clyde in 1857, 1858 and 1859*. London: Edward Arnold, 1898.

Grey, Edward. *The Travels of Pietro Della Valle in India*, Vol. 2. London, Hakluyt Society.

Grousset, René. *The Rise and Splendour of the Chinese Empire*. Berkeley: University of California Press, 1962.

Gupta, Archana Garodia. *The Women Who Ruled India: Leaders, Warriors, Icons*. Gurugram: Hachette Book Publishing India Pvt. Ltd., 2019.

Hall, Kenneth R. 'International Trade and Foreign Diplomacy in Early Medieval South India'. *Journal of the Economic and Social History of the Orient* 21.1, January 1978, pp. 75–98.

Hasan, Mohibbul. *Kashmir under the Sultans*. New Delhi: Aakar books, 1959.

Hultzsch, E. ed. *Epigraphia Indica*, Vol. 8. Calcutta: Office of the Superintendent of Government Printing, India, 1905–06.

Hussain, Iqbal. 'Awadh Rebel Proclamations during 1857–58'. *Proceedings of the Indian History Congress*, 58. 1997.

Ibochaoba, Haobam. *The Pre-World War II: Form of Ras Leela*. Imphal: Haobam Ongbi Shantibala Devi, 2009.

Irvine, William. Ed. Jadunath Sarkar. *Later Mughals*, Vol 1, *1707–1720*. Calcutta: M.C. Sarkar & Sons.

Jafri, Saiyid Zaheer Husain. 'The Profile of a Saintly Rebel: Maulavi Ahmadullah Shah.' *Social Scientist* 26.1 (Jan–April 1998).

Jain, Meenakshi. *Flight of Deities and Rebirth of Temples: Episodes from Indian History*. New Delhi: Aryan Books International, 2019.

Jekila, A., and P. Barathi. 'Queen Velu Nachiyar: First Woman against British'. *Infokara Research*, 9.3 (2020)

Johar, Surinder. *The Sikh Sword to Power*. The University of Michigan: Arsee Publishers, 2002.

Kapur, M.L. *Kingdom of Kashmir*. Srinagar: Gulshan Books, 2005.

Karashima, N. 'Relations between South India and China in Chola Times.' *Professor K.A. Nilakanta Sastri Felicitation Volume*. Madras: Prof. K.A. Nilakanta Sastri Felicitation Committee, 1971.

Keay, John. *India: A History*. New York: Grove Press, 2000.

Konow, Sten ed. *Epigraphica Indica*, Vol. XXII. Bombay: British India Press, 1913–14.

Kulkarni, Uday S. *The Maratha Century: Vignettes and Anecdotes of the Maratha Empire*. Pune: Mula Mutha Publications, 2021.

Kulke, Hermann, K. Kesavapany and Vijay Sakhuja eds. *Nagapattinam to Suvarnadwipa: Reflections on the Chola Naval Expeditions to Southeast Asia*. Singapore: ISEAS Publishing, 2009.

Litvinsky, B.A., et al. (ed.). *History of Civilizations of Central Asia*, Vol. 3. Paris: UNESCO Publishing, 1996.

Llewellyn-Jones, Rosie ed. *The Uprising of 1857.* Ahmedabad: Alkazi Collection of Photography and Mapin, 2017.

Majumdar, R.C. 'The Overseas Expeditions of King Rajendra Cola.' *Artibus Asiae.* 24 (3/4), pp. 338–42.

Malcolm, Major General Sir John. *A Memoir of Central India including Malwa and Adjoining Provinces: With the History, and Copious Illustrations of the Past and Present Condition of That Country,* Vol.1. London: Kingsbury, Parbury & Allen, 1824.

Malgonkar, Manohar. *Kanhoji Angey, Maratha Admiral: An Account of his Life and His Battles with the English.* Bombay: Asia Publishing House, 1959.

Mazumdar, Asoke Kumar. *Chaulukyas of Gujarat.* Bombay: Bharatiya Vidya Bhawan, 1956.

Menon, P. Shungoonny. *A History of Travancore from the Earliest Times.* New Delhi: Gyan Publishing House, 2020.

Mishra, Shyam Manohar. *Yas'ovarman of Kanauj: A Study of Political, Social and Cultural Life of Northern India during the Reign of Yas'ovarman.* New Delhi: Abhinav Publication, 1977.

Misra, Ram Gopal. *Indian Resistance to Early Muslim Invaders up to 1206 A.D.* Bengaluru: Sahitya Sindhu Prakashana, 2020.

Mookerji, Radha Kumud. *Indian Shipping: A History of the Sea-Borne Trade and Maritime Activity of the Indians from the Earliest Times.* Bombay: Longmans, Green & Co., 1912.

Moraes, G.M. *The Kadamba Kula: A History of Ancient and Mediaeval Karnataka.* Bombay: B.X. Furtado and Sons, 1931.

Mukherjee, Rudrangshu. *A Begum and a Rani: Hazrat Mahal and Lakshmibai in 1857.* New Delhi: Penguin Random House India, 2021.

Muni, Chaturvijaya, ed. *Sukrita Sankirtana* by Arisimha. Bhavnagar: Sri Jaina Atmanandasabha, 1917.

Nagrale, N.N. 'Ahilyabai and Her Benevolent Administration.' *Proceedings of the Indian History Congress,* 40. 1979.

Nambiar, O.K. *Our Seafaring in the Indian Oceani.* Bangalore: Jeevan Publications, 1975.

Nazim, Muhammad. *The Life and Times of Sultan Mahmud of Ghazna.* Cambridge: Cambridge University Press, 1931.

Panikkar, K.M. *Malabar and the Dutch: Being the History of the Fall of the Nayar Power in Malabar*. Bombay: D.B. Taraporevala Sons & Co., 1931.

Pasi, Raj Kumar. *Pasi Samaj ka Swatantrata Sangram Mein Yogdan*. Lucknow: Pasi Shodh Evam Sanskritik Sansthan, 1998.

Punjala, Alekhya. *Rani Rudrama Devi*. New Delhi: National Book Trust, 2016.

Rajagopal, S. 'Formation of Palayakarar System by Visvanatha Nayaka (1530–1564): A Study.' *Pramana Research Journal*, 9.6 (2019).

Rajamanikkam, M. *Tamilmoli Ilakkiya Varalaru*. Madras, 1963.

Ramaiya, J. *The South Indian Inscriptions, Vol. X: Telugu Inscriptions from the Madras Presidency*. Archaeological Survey of India, 1948.

Ranking, G.S. (Lt Col). *Muntakhwab-ut-Tawarikh* Vol. 1. Translation of the original into English by Abdul Qadir al-Badauni. Calcutta: The Asiatic Society, 1913.

Raverty, Major H.G. *Tabaqat-i-Nasiri*. Translation of the original by Minhaj ud-Din bin Siraj ud-Din. Calcutta: Asiatic Society of Bengal, 1880.

Ricci, Aldo. *The Travels of Marco Polo: Translated into English from the Text of L.F. Benedetto*. New Delhi: Asian Educational Services, 2001.

Rice, Benjamin Lewis. *Mysore Gazetteer*. Vol. 2, Pt. 2. Government Press, 1930.

Roy, Jyotirmoy. *History of Manipur*. Calcutta: East Light Book House, 1958.

Sampath, Vikram. *Splendours of Royal Mysore: The Untold Story of the Wodeyars*. New Delhi: Rupa & Co, 2008.

Sarda, Har Bilas. *Rana Kumbha: Sovereign, Soldier*. Ajmer: Scottish Mission Institutions Company Limited, 1917.

Sarma, R. *Zayn ul Akhbar*, Vol. IX. This is a translation into English of the original by Al Gardizi.

Sastri, K.A. Nilakanta. *The Colas*. Madras: University of Madras, 1955.

Sastry, R. Shama ed. *South Indian Inscriptions*, Vol. 9, Pt. 1, No. 77. Madras: Manager of Publications, 1939.

Savarkar, Vinayak Damodar. *The Indian War of Independence, 1857*. London, 1909.

Sen, Sailendra Nath. *Ancient Indian History and Civilization*. New Delhi: New Age International Publishers, 1999.

Sen, Surendra Nath. *The Military System of the Marathas*. Calcutta: Orient Longman Private Ltd., 1928.

Sen, Tansen. 'Kashmir, Tang Dynasty, and Muktapida Lalitaditya's Ascendancy over the Southern Hindukush Region.' *Journal of South Asian History*, Vol. 38, no. 2 (2004).

_____. 'Maritime Contacts between China and the Cola Kingdom of South India: 850–1279.' *Mariners, Merchants and Oceans: Studies in Maritime History*, ed. K.S. Mathew, pp. 25–42. New Delhi: Manohar, 1995.

Sewell, Robert. *A Forgotten Empire (Vijayanagar): A Contribution to the History of India*. London: Swan Sonnenschein & Co. Ltd., 1900.

Singh, Aheibam Koireng et al., eds. *Rajarshi Bhagyachandra and the Bhakti Movement in Eastern Indian Literature*. Gurgaon: Shubhi Publications, 2000.

Singh, Ch. Mainhar. *A History of Manipuri Literature*. New Delhi: Sahitya Akademi, 1996.

Singh, Ganda. *Life of Banda Singh Bahadur: Based on Contemporary and Original Records*. Amritsar: The Sikh History Research Department, Khalsa College, 1935.

Singh, Gurbaksh. *The Khalsa Generals*. Vancouver: Canadian Sikh Study & Teaching Society, 1927.

Singh, N. Tombi. *Manipur and the Mainstream*. Imphal: Chitrebirentombich and Khorjeirup, 1975.

Singh, R.K. Jhalajit. *A Short History of Manipur*. Imphal, 1992.

Slaje, Walter ed. *Kingship in Kashmir (A.D. 1148–1459): From the Pen of Jonaraja, Court Pandit to Sultan Zayn al-'Abidin*. Germany: Studia Indologica Universitatis Halensis, 2014.

Someshwar, Amritha, ed. *Abbakka Sankathana*. Mangalore: Veerarani Abbakka Uthsava Samithi, 2011.

Sonawani, Sanjay. *Emperor of Kashmir: Lalitaditya the Great*. Pune: Chinar Publishers India, 2019.

Stein, Marc Aurel. *Kalhana's Rajatarangini: A Chronicle of the Kings of Kashmir*, Bk 3. This is a translation of the original by Kalhana. London: Archibald Constable & Co. Ltd., 1900.

Talbot, Cynthia. *Precolonial India in Practice: Society, Religion, and Identity in Medieval Andhra*. New York: Oxford University Press, 2001.

Tawney, C.H. *Prabhanda Chintamani*. Ed. Jinavijaya Muni, trans. into English from original by Merutunga. Calcutta: The Asiatic Society, 1901.

Tod, James (Lt Col). *Annals & Antiquities of Rajasthan or, the Central & Western Rajpoot States of India*, Vol. 2. London: Routledge & Kegan Paul Ltd., 1832.

_____. *Travels in Western India*. London: W.H. Allen & Co., 1839.

Tripathi, Rama Shankar. *History of Kanauj: To the Moslem Conquest*. Motilal Banarsidass, 1989.

Vaidya, Chintaman Vinayak. *History of Mediaeval Hindu India: Being a History of India from 600 to 1200 A.D*. Poona: The Oriental Book-Supplying Agency, 1921.

Vanajakumari S., and P. Vimala. 'Arc-Veera Mangai Velunachiyar in Antiquity India (1772–1780).' *Shanlax International Journal of Arts, Science & Humanities*, 3.4 (2016).

Vasantha Madhava, K.G. *Abbakka Deviyaru*. Mangalore: Karnataka Tulu Sahitya Akademi, 1998.

Wink, Andre. *Al-Hind, The Making of the Indo-Islamic World: Early Medieval India and the Expansion of Islam, 7th–11th Centuries*. Brill, 2002.

Wolters, O.W. *Early Indonesian Commerce: A Study of the Origins of Srivijaya*. Ithaca and London: Cornell University Press, 1967.

Younghusband, Sir Francis. *Kashmir*. London: Adam & Charles Black, 1911.

Manuscripts

Assam Buranji, DHAS, Guwahati.

Biker. J.F. Judice. 'Biker Manuscripts.' Arquivo Histórico Ultramarino, Lisbon.

Bombay Public Consultations, India Office, British Library, London.

Bombay Public Proceedings, India Office, British Library, London.

Factory Records, Bombay, India Office, British Library, London.